W9-AOE-941

FRIENDS, COLLEAGUES, AND NEIGHBORS

FRIENDS, COLLEAGUES, AND NEIGHBORS

Jewish Contributions to American History

DAVID A. RAUSCH

PROCLAIM LIBERTY THROUGHOUT ALL THE LAND UNTO ALL THE INHABITANTS THEREOF. LEV XXV, 10 ✡ PROCLAIM LIBERTY THROUGHOUT ALL THE LAND UNTO ALL THE INHABITANTS THEREOF. LEV XXV, 10 ✡ PROCLAIM LIBERTY THROUGHOUT ALL THE LAND UNTO ALL THE INHABITANTS THEREOF. LEV XXV, 10 ✡ PROCLAIM LIBERTY THROUGHOUT ALL THE LAND UNTO ALL THE INHABITANTS THEREOF. LEV XXV, 10 ✡

Baker Books

A Division of Baker Book House Co
Grand Rapids, Michigan 49516

AMERICAN INTERFAITH INSTITUTE

To Lynne

©1996 by David A. Rausch

Published by Baker Books
a division of Baker Book House Company
P.O. Box 6287, Grand Rapids, MI 49516-6287

Printed in the United States of America

Library of Congress Cataloging-in-Publication Data
Rausch, David A.
Friend, colleagues, and neighbors: Jewish contributions to American history/ David Rausch.
     p. cm.
Includes index
ISBN 0-8010-1119-1
    1. Jews—United States—Civilization. 2. United States—Civilization—Jewish influences. 3. Jews—United States—Biography. 4. Jews—United States—Public opinion. 5. Puplic opinion—United States. 6. Gentiles—United States—Attitudes.
    I. Title.
E184.J5R38 1996   95-51824
973'.04924—dc20   CIP

CONTENTS

INTRODUCTION

FRIENDS, COLLEAGUES, AND NEIGHBORS IS ON THE ONE hand a tribute to American Jewish contributions in the history of the United States and, on the other hand, a reflection of a historian's personal journey along the path of knowledge and understanding. As a professor of history and current chairman of the history and political science department at Ashland University in Ashland, Ohio, I have a difficult time imagining that twenty years ago I would have been incapable of writing such a work. Although a Christian who was at the top of my graduating class in history, I had little knowledge of Jewish people and no knowledge of the Holocaust. Encouraged to take a graduate research course on the Holocaust, the murder of six million Jewish men, women, and children by the Nazi regime and their collaborators, I found that my life was turned upside down as I dug deeper and deeper into the primary historical materials of that gruesome era. The case study of the Holocaust pierced the depths of my soul and steadily taught me the ramifications of religious and racial prejudice. I have since been privileged as a professor to see the same study change the lives of hundreds of my students and to receive grateful letters from thousands of those who have read my books and articles on the subject.

As I continued my studies in history, in which I finally amassed eight fields of history and postdoctoral work in philosophy and geography, I began encountering Jewish women and men who had made significant contributions to world history. And, as I taught American history courses, these contributions sparkled like diamonds as I uncovered them one by one. My students wanted to know more about American Jews, and fellow professors asked numerous questions about the role of Jews in the history of the United States. The more I looked, the more I uncovered. The more I traveled, the more Jewish acquaintances and friends I made. I found that contributions were being made in the smallest of towns and villages as well as in the major cities of the land. Often unheralded, these women and men were joining others in a symphony of charitable efforts, scientific achievement, cultural endeavors, and business enterprises. For the most part, the fact that they were from Jewish backgrounds went unnoticed in an age where peoplehoods are acknowledged and thanked for specific contributions.

The purpose of *Friends, Colleagues, and Neighbors* is neither to glorify American Jews nor to have them appear smarter than other peoples. Rather, I as a Gentile Christian have endeavored to take a professional historical look at the significant contributions they have made (and are currently making) in the history of our great nation. This history includes famous men and women who many Americans may not be aware are from Jewish backgrounds, as well as those whose contributions are integral to everyday life but who are not known to the general public. In addition, I have examined throughout these pages men and women who have made or are making an impact on the community in which they live—an impact that is significant to their neighbors and colleagues, but is virtually unknown to the general public. The process is one of adding layer upon layer of knowledge—a process that I as a historian had to undergo myself.

For instance, I will never forget the day that I stumbled across the compassionate words of social reformer Lillian D. Wald. As an American Jew, Miss Wald turned a chance visit to a squalid New York tenement flat in 1893 into a life's work to alleviate the suffering and sickness among poor families and to befriend the downtrodden. She moved into the poverty-stricken neighborhood, bringing a combination of medical skill, passionate optimism, and undeterred determination. I would catch glimpses of her now and then in the primary historical documents of the latter nineteenth and early twentieth centuries, and I marveled as her "Nurses Settlement" turned into the famed Henry Street Settlement. By 1905, even *The New York Times* realized the significance of Lillian Wald's successful work. In a feature story complete with large drawings on the first page of its April 23, 1905 Sunday social section captioned "A Pioneer Among Settlement Workers Is Miss Wald," the editors emphasized that the work "presided over by Miss Lillian D. Wald, who, under the modest title of headworker has brought the resources of abundant human sympathy, practical knowledge and experience, and a remarkable executive faculty to the undertaking." Servant-leadership at its best.

Relating my newfound knowledge concerning this social reformer to my American history classes had a profound effect. That a cultured Jewish woman, Lillian Wald, had given up a life of privilege to help others challenged both the men and women in my American history classes. In addition, several young women in my classes were majoring in social work. Miss Lillian Wald became an important role model in shaping the course of their lives. They would come back to me in ecstatic glee with bits and pieces of additional information on how this remarkable woman functioned and stories of her encounters. A young woman who no one imagined would make a significant contribution actually turned a community (and, later, through legislation a nation) upside down as she quietly worked in a seemingly impossible niche. Several generations later, her life had a meaningful effect on numbers of young students who had never heard her name. Chapter 1 of *Friends, Colleagues, and Neighbors* (entitled "Helping Hands") briefly discusses Lillian Wald among many other Jewish contributors, from heroes of the American Revolution to unheralded philanthropists.

Chapter 2 relates contributions in areas of "Government Service," while chapter 3 involves the fascinating world of "Medicine and Health." I find that the American public is sorely lacking in knowledge with regard to these findings. In addition, Jewish contributions to journalism and literature never cease to amaze my young protégés. During the two decades of my teaching career, I do not believe a year has gone by that scores of students have not "discovered" that one of their favorite authors, newspaper writers, editorialists, or television news personalities is Jewish. Old and young alike seem to be oblivious to the contributions of a Joseph Pulitzer (who begins and ends chapter 4, "Journalism and Literature"), and his involvement with others in saving the Statue of Liberty as it languished in a warehouse. Regardless of age, Americans seem to want to identify, learn from, and sometimes emulate the *best* in the lives of prominent creative personalities, whether it be a Joseph Pulitzer, a Barbara Tuchman, an Isaac Asimov, a Lillian Hellman, an Arthur Miller, or an Art Buchwald.

This fascination is also clearly evident in the world of "Sports and Entertainment." Of the multitude of historic Jewish sports personalities noted in this book, none has had the effect of Hank Greenberg. Practically all of my younger students had never heard of him when we spent a bit of time on him in the general survey course, and my older students had foggy recollections. Nevertheless, the tenor of his life and the strength of his character made Hank Greenberg somewhat of a role model for my students. Several university athletes have made a point to tell me how learning about Hank Greenberg and other Jewish athletes helped to mold their philosophy of athletics. The coaches (such as Marv Levy) and athletes that appear in chapter 5 will give the reader an inkling of the significant and diversified contributions that have been made in this arena. In addition, the Jewish actors and actresses that grace the pages of the "Sports and Entertainment" chapter only scratch the surface of a phenomenal contribution by Jews.

In the realm of "Ideas and Inventions," which is the content of chapter 6, I have to chuckle at my first experience of trying to explain to students the experimentation process that the brilliant scientist Albert Abraham Michelson pursued with regard to the velocity of light. My crude drawing on the chalkboard of the interferometer that he developed left much to be desired, but the point was absorbed by both the budding scientists and nonscientists in the class of the important work that preceded another Jewish scientist and theorist, Albert Einstein. As might be expected, however, my students were just as impressed with the story of Levi Strauss and his "idea" and subsequent development of *Levis* in the nineteenth century.

Chapter 7 ("Business and Design") has some names that are generally recognized as "important figures," but for the most part many of the contributions of the individuals in this chapter have eluded the historical consciousness. Only a small percentage of the population would know that these contributors are Jewish. In fact, each of the subject areas covered in the first seven chapters has had a profound effect on the United States and on the world as the twenty-first century unfolds. It is important in these cases not only to illustrate what has been done in the past, but also to relate what currently is being discovered, created, and molded toward a better future.

My summary chapter, "A Dynamic Peoplehood" (chapter 8), puts into perspective the lessons from this study and the historical statistics, as well as tying together the loose ends of additional areas that need to be mentioned and individuals who must not be neglected. Throughout, I have sought to present an interesting and manageable manuscript that might reach a large variety of readers and be used as supplemental reading for a spectrum of courses. I am fortunate that through my students and my colleagues, as well as my interaction with the general public, I have been privileged to view on numerous occasions the value of such a study. Nothing can take away the joy of discovery I have witnessed or the stereotypes and caricatures that have dissipated right before my eyes. I am sure that this fact alone would surprise many of *my* Jewish friends, colleagues, and neighbors.

Nevertheless, the concepts related in *Friends, Colleagues, and Neighbors* are not without historical foundation. While reading some years ago through the voluminous papers of Woodrow Wilson, who became a noted historian before he became president of the United States, I was struck by an address he gave to a large audience in Carnegie Hall in December 1911, protesting Czarist Russian discrimination toward the passports of American Jews. With great fervor, Woodrow Wilson spoke of the moral principles, freedom, and human rights that undergirded the quest for life in the United States. Emphasizing that these concepts were not incompatible with the material prosperity engendered by trade with Russia, Wilson declared nonetheless that Americans should not be willing to have prosperity "if our fellow citizens must suffer contempt for it, lose the rights that belong to every American in order that we may enjoy it. The price is too great!"

Then, in thoughtful words, the historian in Woodrow Wilson spoke clearly about American Jews. Woodrow Wilson recounted:

Here is a great body of our Jewish fellow citizens, from whom have sprung men of genius in every walk of our varied life, men who have become part of the very stuff of America, who have conceived its ideals with singular clearness and led its enterprise with spirit and sagacity. They are playing a particularly conspicuous part in building up of the very prosperity of which our Government has so great a stake in its dealings with the Russian Government with regard to the rights of men. They are not Jews in America; they are American citizens. In this great matter with which we deal to-night, we speak for them as for representatives and champions of principles which underlie the very structure of our Government. They have suddenly become representatives of us all. By our action for them shall be tested our sincerity, our genuineness, the reality of principle among us.

"There is here a greater stake than any other upon which we could set our hearts," Woodrow Wilson asserted near the end of this speech, and then summarized in conclusion: "We are not here to express our sympathy with our Jewish fellow citizens, but to make evident our sense of identity with them. This is not their cause; it is America's. It is the cause of all who love justice and do right."

In like manner, it is my hope that my encounter as an American Christian and historian with contributions made by Jewish men and women in America will at least in part become your encounter. May it enhance your life and principles, even as it continues to enlighten me and my students.

DAVID A. RAUSCH
Ashland University
Ashland, Ohio
Fall 1995

Helping Hands

Isaac Gilman (1865–1944), a devout Jewish immigrant, touched tens of thousands of lives and helped thousands of Americans in the twentieth century. His life had a deep impact on those around him, and his concern for others as well as his devotion to his adopted American homeland left an impression on the age in which he lived. And yet Isaac Gilman has been all but lost in the annals of American history, including American Jewish history. When the all-encompassing *Encyclopedia Judaica* appeared in print in 1972, Isaac Gilman was not mentioned (not even in the article on the Jewish community in "Vermont"). Two decades later the highly acclaimed five-volume *The Jewish People in America* (1992) omitted him as well.

In some ways, the life of Isaac Gilman symbolizes the hundreds of thousands of Jews who were (and are) "helping hands" to their local communities and nearby neighbors. Although in his latter years he and his wife Blanche stayed in the Beekman Hotel in New York City and were active members of Manhattan's Temple Emanu-El, Isaac Gilman fittingly died at his home in a small Gentile community—a Gentile community that came to love him so much that decades before they had changed the name of their Vermont village to "Gilman."

Born in Russia, young Isaac immigrated to the United States and began peddling papers in the 1880s. In 1911 he entered the paper industry with a mill in Fitzdale, Vermont. Although Fitzdale consisted of four farmhouses, Isaac Gilman built his enterprise into the Gilman

Paper Company, a company that at the time of his death employed 3,000 people in the Vermont town and had corporate offices on New York's Fifth Avenue. On the eve of the First World War, Isaac Gilman's gracious manner and entrepreneurial skill soon led a grateful townsfolk to change the name of their hamlet in 1914 from "Fitzdale" to "Gilman." By the Second World War, the Gilman Paper Company included the affiliates of Millett Corporation (manufacturer of newsprint), Kraft Bag Corporation (manufacturer of paper bags), Gilman Electric and Power Company, Northern Kraft Corporation (woodpulp mill in Howland, Maine), and St. Mary's Kraft Corporation (pulp and paper mill in St. Mary's, Georgia).

In Gilman, Vermont, Isaac was known as an owner faithful to his employees. He knew each one and called them by their first names. He treated them as his extended family, showing concern about their personal problems and even paying hospital and doctor bills when an employee's family was in trouble. Owner Gilman made sure that wages were high and that his mills continued to run even during the Great Depression. Consequently, Isaac had no labor problems. His workers maintained a high morale, sustained a firm devotion to their owner, and produced a quality product.

As he and his wife raised two sons and four daughters, Isaac Gilman became concerned that Gilman, Vermont, had no churches. He spent $28,000 toward the building of a Methodist church and $15,000 to build St. Theresa's Roman Catholic Church in the town. St. Theresa's became self-sustaining, while the Methodist church required several hundred dollars a year in Gilman contributions. When Isaac opened his pulp and paper mill in St. Mary's, Georgia, he refurbished an old unused railroad that for years had been in disrepair and turned it into the St. Mary's Railroad, a local railroad that traveled the ten miles between St. Mary's and Kingsland, Georgia.

Highly respected in a number of communities by the time of his death, Isaac Gilman was president and director of the International Folding Paper Box Company and a director of the Pennsylvania Exchange Bank. His four daughters (Pauline, Celia, Leah, and Sadie) were married and living in New York. His older son, Frederick, remained with the company in St. Mary's, Georgia, while his younger son, Charles, remained with the company in Gilman, Vermont. His wife, Blanche, was president of the Federation of Jewish Women's Organizations, and three months after his death addressed three hundred members of its Manhattan Borough chapter, pleading that segregation and sectarianism in women's groups be ended and urging that the terms "Catholic women," "Jewish women," and "Protestant women" be dropped from all organizations. She favored the more generic term "women's division" to guide philanthropic and social enterprises in a unified female force for good. Isaac Gilman would have applauded his wife's efforts as his whole life was devoted to his "neighbor," regardless of race, religion, or creed. Upon hearing that Isaac Gilman's body was finally laid to rest from Manhattan's Temple Emanu-El, Father William H. Cassidy, priest at St. Theresa's in Gilman, Vermont, declared: "HE WAS A GOOD MAN."

Help in the American Revolution

By the time of the Revolutionary War, the Jewish community was as firmly entrenched in colonial life as any other community. Outside of the Native Americans (the American "indians") who had inhabited the eastern seaboard for thousands of years, all other peoples were immigrants to this "New World." A small but vibrant Jewish peoplehood was evident from the very beginnings of a permanent European bulwark. In fact, three years before George Washington's great-grandfather immigrated to Virginia, the first Jewish community was established in the Dutch settlement of New Amsterdam (in 1654). A century later (in 1664), the Dutch surrendered New Amsterdam to the British, and the name changed to New York.

Jews settled in other urban centers during the 1740s, such as Philadelphia, Pennsylvania, and Charleston, South Carolina. Small Jewish communities that did not survive in earlier decades in Newport, Rhode Island, and Savannah, Georgia, would be reestablished by the time of the American Revolution. A few Jews moved west during the Colonial Period, but most lived near the East Coast. Approximately 250 Jews lived in the colonies before 1700 (out of a total colonial population of 250,000 in 1700); by the American Revolution the

15

number had expanded to between two and three thousand. Never more than one-tenth of one percent of the American colonial population, Jews were heavily involved as merchant shippers and were an important factor in the candle industry (an indispensable commodity before electricity). The majority of the Jewish breadwinners were lower-middle-class shopkeepers and craftsmen.

It was during the Colonial Period that the American Jewish community established patterns that are detectable in the Modern Period. For instance, they concentrated in urban areas and yet were not adverse to the pioneering spirit. They faced legal restrictions and anti-Semitism but tenaciously struggled for freedom, dignity, and equality. They established social services through the synagogue to take care of their own (and other unfortunates) and to bury their dead (a cemetery was the first acquisition of the Jewish settlers). Education was a priority, both religious and secular, and the Jewish community even subsidized teachers for poverty-stricken colonial families.

The colonial Jews held fervently to their peoplehood, and yet they became community figures, intensely involved in the emerging American culture. They attempted to unload their Old World prejudices, while contending with Christians and their children who immigrated from Europe with millstones of hatred and bigotry hanging around their psyches. For example, early in the 1700s, New York Jews generously contributed to the building of an Anglican church.

As with many colonial Americans, the quest for religious freedom and individual conscience permeated the souls of Jewish colonists. They firmly believed that they had found more acceptance in their new land than could be found in any other part of the world. Along with other American protesters, eleven colonial Jewish merchants signed the Non-Importation Articles which sought to repeal the Townsend Revenue Acts in which Britain had imposed duties on items such as tea, glass, paper, and paints. One of the signers was Jonas Phillips of Philadelphia, who would later urge the Constitutional Convention of the fledgling nation not to deprive an American citizen of civil rights because of religion. New York signatoree, Hayman Levy (1721–1789), an immigrant from Hanover, Germany, and partner in Levy, Lyons and Company, the largest fur trading firm in the colonies, would soon link the new nation's interior to the much larger world of Atlantic commerce. His eleven children became important members of New York society.

During the Revolutionary War (1775–1783), Jews helped the warring colonies break blockades and obtain supplies. Polish immigrant and merchant Haym Salomon (1740–1785) was captured twice by the British, yet managed to pass strategic information to the American army. While operating a business in British-occupied New York, he helped a number of war prisoners escape back to the revolutionary forces. Haym Salomon has become almost a legendary figure in American history, because of his help in raising $600,000 to keep the American war effort alive and because of his later generous contributions toward the poverty-stricken Continental Congress. Although a once-wealthy entrepreneur, Haym Salomon's property was confiscated by the British. He died in poverty, and his widow was left destitute. The personal risks he took and his deep patriotism are representative of many other Jewish patriots during the war.

A considerable number of Jews volunteered for colonial army duty, and many were found in local militias. A French Jewish military officer, Major Benjamin Nones (d. 1826), served under both Marquis de Lafayette and George Washington. Other Jewish servicemen during the War of Independence attained historical distinction. Philadelphia-born Solomon Bush (1753–1795) was seriously wounded and taken prisoner by the British but returned to fight after being released. He obtained the rank of lieutenant-colonel in the Continental Army in 1779, the highest rank held by a Jewish officer during the Revolutionary War. He later joined an abolitionist society to try to end the evil of black enslavement.

David Salisbury Franks (c. 1743–1793) likewise was promoted to the rank of lieutenant-colonel in 1780. As an American merchant in Montreal, he aided the colonial attack on Quebec. Returning to Pennsylvania, Franks served as a major in the Continental Army, later becoming a courier to John Jay in Madrid and Benjamin Franklin in Paris. He also served John Adams and Thomas Jefferson and in 1790 became assistant cashier to the newly created Bank of the United States.

The American Revolution brought more colonists in touch with the Jewish community, and many gained a deep respect for a people they found to be much like themselves. Further-

17

more, the promise of the Declaration of Independence that "all men are created equal" and are endowed with "certain unalienable Rights" was interpreted by the Jewish community in the most positive manner. The Early National Period was an exciting time for Jewish people, and they felt quite comfortable in American society. They loved their new nation, and they strove diligently to be a part of its culture. Most did not suffer the misfortune of patriot Haym Salomon. For example, Isaac Moses also helped finance the War of Independence. He later became one of the founders of the Bank of New York.

When newly elected President George Washington visited Newport, Rhode Island, in 1790, Moses Sexias, warden of the Hebrew Congregation, was authorized to write: "Permit the children of the stock of Abraham to approach you with the most cordial affection and esteem for your person and merits and to join with our fellow-citizens in welcoming you to New Port." Moses Sexias compared "the God of Israel's" deliverance of George Washington and the revolutionary forces to that of divine deliverance of David, and "the same Spirit" that rested on Daniel to that which rested on Washington. Quite pleased with his welcome in Newport, President Washington responded with his own allusions to the Bible, underscoring that "the government of the United States, which gives to bigotry no sanction, to persecution no assistance, requires only that they who live under its protection should demean themselves as good citizens, in giving it on all occasions their effectual support . . . every one shall sit in safety under his own vine and fig tree."

Receiving similar support from Jewish congregations in New York, Philadelphia, Charleston, and Richmond, President George Washington wrote: "The affection of such a people [the Jews] is a treasure beyond the reach of calculation." Later, the second president of the United States, John Adams, would write to the greatest Jewish leader during his presidency, Mordecai Manuel Noah (1785–1851), that although the United States "has done much" he wished "it may do more; and annul every narrow idea in religion, government and commerce." When England and the United States clashed once again in a "Second War of American Independence," the War of 1812 (1812–1815), sons of the revolutionary Jewish generation, such as Myer Moses (1779–1833) of Charleston and Aaron Levy (1771–1852) of New

York, bravely served their country. Aaron Levy was the son of Hayman Levy and the son-in-law of Isaac Moses. He served as a captain of artillery during the War of 1812, becoming a lieutenant-colonel of artillery in 1816. He finally relinquished his military commission in 1819, becoming active in the Lake George area of New York State.

By the 1820s, most Jews were second-generation or third-generation Americans who spoke fluent English. They shared in the prosperity of the nation and wanted to immerse themselves in its culture. As a community, they had done their share to lend their country a helping hand in its infancy and would continue fervently to support the United States of America in its subsequent years of growth and transition.

Help in Charitable Endeavors

Nineteenth-century America gave birth to a multitude of voluntary and charitable societies that historians have dubbed the "Benevolent Empire." The rapid rise of the Industrial Revolution in the United States encouraged massive immigration to fill the ever-increasing slots for cheap labor. Poverty and despair increased as industrialization, immigration, and urbanization presented social and economic dilemmas that demanded response, yet seemingly defied solution.

Between 1848 and 1860, the Jewish community of New York City supported nearly one hundred incorporated charitable associations and many other unincorporated philanthropic endeavors. This was approximately one-half of all of the charitable organizations New York City had (although the total Jewish population was under 5 percent of the city's total population). The "Jews' Hospital in New York" was incorporated in 1852 in an effort "to relieve a vast amount of human misery and suffering." In 1866 it became the famed Mt. Sinai Hospital and admitted more free patients than any other private institution in New York City. During the 1880s the number of patients treated without charge at Mt. Sinai Hospital approached a phenomenal 90 percent.

In Philadelphia, Rebecca Gratz (1781–1869) spent much of her life in community service and philanthropic endeavors. Some scholars believe that she was the inspiration for the character Rebecca in Walter Scott's novel *Ivanhoe*. The Gratz family of merchants had supported politically the American Revolution and had supplied goods to the Continental Army. During the Early National Period, they remained important community leaders in Philadelphia and provided a helping hand to charitable causes. For example, as early as 1819, Rebecca Gratz worked diligently with other members of the Jewish community to found the Female Hebrew Benevolent Society and helped to support foster homes and orphanages throughout the city. In fact, indefatigable efforts such as these were so successful that by 1854 Jewish charitable associations had become so numerous in Philadelphia that the Hebrew Charitable Fund was organized to coordinate the diverse efforts for social welfare in the city. The next year a children's orphanage was established in Philadelphia and in 1856, Rebecca's brother, Hyman Gratz (1776–1857), donated more than $150,000 to found Gratz College, the first Jewish-sponsored teacher-training institution in the United States.

In the Midwest, Chicago's Jewish community had raised funds for a hospital as early as the 1840s. Within two decades it was necessary to form the United Hebrew Relief Association to manage the scores of Chicago Jewish philanthropic organizations and in 1868 this relief association built its own "Jewish Hospital" (which served both the Jewish and Gentile communities). The Cincinnati Jewish community in southern Ohio had begun its own benevolent society in 1838 and in 1850 opened Jewish Hospital. In 1883 the community funded a home for the aged. By the 1890s the number of Jewish charitable associations had grown to such an extent that they had to be federated in 1896 into the United Jewish Charities. In northern Ohio, several prominent Jewish leaders (including a rabbi) dedicated long hours of service on Cleveland's board of trustees of the Society for Organized Charities (founded in 1881). Many other men and women from Cleveland's Jewish community worked in relief societies, settlement houses, houses for the aged, orphanages, and schools in the latter decades of the nineteenth century. Jewish leaders established a Federation of Jewish Charities in 1903 and founded Mt. Sinai Hospital in Cleveland the same year.

Across the United States, Jewish charitable endeavors attempted to meet local challenges and to alleviate American social distress. Almost every local Jewish community had a relief or benevolent society. Jewish leaders, such as Nathan Straus and Jacob H. Schiff, devoted their talents and funds to such endeavors. Nathan Straus (1848–1931), who had worked his way to co-owner of Macy's Department Store with his brother Isidor, served as the park commissioner and later health commissioner of New York City. Nathan was instrumental in establishing a milk pasteurization laboratory in New York, milk distribution centers for the needy, inexpensive boarding houses for the poor, and emergency relief centers to distribute coal and food. The entire Straus family was deeply involved in philanthropic endeavors. Sadly, Isidor Straus (1845–1912) died in the sinking of the *Titanic*. Nathan Straus continued his philanthropic efforts. During the severe winter of 1914 to 1915, he served one-cent meals in the milk stations he had established in New York City. In following years he would give away a large part of his fortune to charitable causes and in service of humanity.

Jacob H. Schiff (1847–1920), who had immigrated from Germany to America at the age of eighteen, joined the banking firm of Kuhn, Loeb, and Company in 1875. He was named head of the firm a decade later. Generous and compassionate, Jacob Schiff personally participated in many of the numerous philanthropies he supported. For example, he not only provided the major funding for Montefiore Hospital in New York City (of which he assumed the presidency for thirty-five years), but also visited there on a weekly basis. In some cases, Schiff required matching funds for his charitable contributions, initiating a form of accountability that would ultimately lead to national campaigns and national federations that emphasized efficient administration.

As the twentieth century dawned, the American Jewish community was so entrenched in community service and philanthropic endeavor that the National Conference of Jewish Charities in the United States was established "to discuss the problems of charities and to promote reforms in their administration." By 1909 there were more than two thousand *incorporated* Jewish charities in the United States. In fact, a professional journal, *Jewish Charities*, was first published in 1910, and creative ideas flowed from an involved Jewish peoplehood. For instance, in "The Public School as the Neighborhood Center"

(June 1915), Jennie F. Purvin, president of Chicago's Women's Aid, suggested that the public schools be opened nationally in the evenings and weekends for supervised recreational and educational use by the local communities. In this "social center" movement, young people would have an inexpensive option to commercial recreation, while adults could organize for both sporting events and lectures. Jennie Purvin wrote that there was a "great need for this clubhouse of the people, where, with intelligent guidance, young and old may again create their own recreation." Although the native Chicagoan Jennie Franklin Purvin went on to become a business executive, the cause of social welfare continued to be close to her heart.

The early twentieth century witnessed the rise of Jewish social activists who alerted Americans to deteriorating societal conditions. Between 1881 and 1914, two million Jewish immigrants had come to the United States, and the Jewish community was well aware of the social problems that faced the nation and the need for solutions. Preventing conditions that gave rise to social distress and providing family rehabilitation became as important as relief efforts. For example, Lee Frankel (1867–1931), who taught chemistry at the University of Pennsylvania in the 1890s, became so involved in charitable endeavors that he dedicated his life to social work. He emphasized the importance of using professional standards in Jewish social work and the importance of adequate funding that promoted rehabilitation. Frankel supported a pension program for widowed mothers and championed public health nursing services. To accomplish these goals, Lee Frankel went to work for Metropolitan Life Insurance Company in 1909 to expand their program of social insurance and health care, eventually becoming a vice president in the company.

In like manner, Russian-born Isaac Max Rubinow (1875–1936) gave up his medical practice to concentrate on social work and to theorize on the necessary development of a national social insurance program that would cover old age, unemployment, work-related accidents, and health care. In the early decades of the twentieth century, I. M. Rubinow emphasized that American society should help those in need without damaging the recipient's ego and self-respect. His early theories became essential in the midst of the Great Depression. Rubinow was asked to prepare the report of the Ohio Social Security Commission in 1933 and, at the bidding of President Franklin Delano Roosevelt, went on to help develop the national Social Security Act of 1935. In the midst of such social activism, local Jewish community experimentation and creativity increased as national planning expanded. The Graduate School for Jewish Social Work in New York City trained professional social workers from 1927 to 1936.

By 1940, the American Jewish population hovered around 4.8 million, over 3.6 percent of the total population of the United States. This was the largest percentage of the total population that the American Jewish community would ever reach. The Jewish peoplehood had not only increased its giving each year, but continued to give systematically far beyond what its community numbers seemed to allow. After the Second World War, philanthropy emerged as one of the organizing arms to bind together Jewish communities across the nation. Jewish community councils and federations banded together in the postwar years in a single yearly campaign for local, national, and overseas needs. Nevertheless, hundreds of thousands of Jewish women and men worked fervently for local and national causes outside the perimeters of the yearly campaigns. To the historian, the American Jewish community's "helping hands" have provided one of the most inspiring examples in the annals of charitable endeavors and philanthropic enterprise.

The vast majority of these Jewish charitable workers go unheralded, while they faithfully dedicate time and money to a nation in need. Once in a while, however, the gift is so vast that it makes national and even world news. Such was the gift of Jewish philanthropist Walter Annenberg on December 17, 1993. Walter Annenberg donated $500 million to U.S. education, the largest grant ever made to public education. "I am deeply troubled by the violence in some grade schools and high schools," Mr. Annenberg warned, "and if this continues, it will not only erode the educational system, but will destroy our way of life in the United States." A grateful President Clinton declared that the money could not have come at a better time, on the eve of Congress considering major education legislation and the key educational issues to be discussed in 1994. "This is a very, very important day," President Clinton emphasized about the half-billion-dollar grant.

Walter Annenberg (b. 1908), founder of a publishing empire that includes *TV Guide,* asked that his contribution be matched by individuals, corporations, and foundations. "We have to reverse what is going on in our country," he asserted. When an incredulous reporter asked why he would give so much to public education, Annenberg responded emphatically, "I've had the best out of this country. I owe it a great deal . . . don't you see . . . ?"

Help in Reform Movements

The connection between the Jewish community's involvement in philanthropic endeavors and the Jewish community's involvement in reform movements is readily seen. Jews have a tradition of diagnosing societal needs and working to better society. While a score of the American reform movements that have received considerable Jewish support could be catalogued, a historian readily can turn to reform movements in education, labor, and civil rights to underscore Jewish contributions. Let us briefly consider these areas and the "helping hand" extended by the Jewish peoplehood.

Education

It is perhaps most fitting, historically, that the major portion of Walter Annenberg's half-billion-dollar contribution to American education in December 1993 was slated for educational reform programs, because one of the most creative educators in the twentieth century was Abraham Flexner (1866–1959), a Jewish man who became one of the most influential forces for change in American education. Born in Louisville, Kentucky, Abraham Flexner studied classics at Johns Hopkins University. After graduating in 1886, he returned to Louisville High School and taught Latin and Greek for fourteen years. In 1900 he opened a revolutionary college preparatory school in Louisville which eliminated examinations, records, reports, and rules. With this successful endeavor, Abraham Flexner was well on his way to promoting educational reform.

Realizing the need for more education himself and curious as to innovative practice around the world, Flexner traveled to Harvard University and other institutions, leaving the daily operation of his school to others. At Harvard he studied educational psychology and educational philosophy as well as some science (ever relating it to his educational goals). Traveling to New York, he spent time at the Rockefeller Institute for Medical Research, concentrating on the anatomy of the brain. From 1906 to 1907 he traveled overseas to the University of Berlin. In Berlin he studied psychology and philosophy, becoming intrigued with the theories of Friedrich Paulsen. In 1908 Abraham Flexner published *The American College*, his review of higher education in the United States.

Flexner's study impressed Henry S. Pritchett, president of the Carnegie Foundation for the Advancement of Teaching. Pritchett commissioned Flexner to review medical schools in America, and Abraham Flexner surveyed 154 of them, including seven Canadian medical schools. Published in 1910 as *Medical Education in the United States and Canada*, Flexner's critical analysis brought about significant reform in the teaching methods and curriculum in medical schools across the United States. In the midst of such sweeping changes, Flexner turned his attention to European medical schools from 1910 to 1911, research which culminated in his book *Medical Education in Europe* (1912).

Appointed staff member and secretary of the General Education Board in 1912, Abraham Flexner was able to complete numerous studies and books on many facets of education and on particular school systems in the United States. The General Education Board provided financial aid to U.S. education. Among his many works, Flexner's *A Modern College* (1923) contained important suggestions and broad ideas for reforming secondary and higher education. Seven years later, his *Universities: American, English, German* (1930) criticized functionalism in American higher education.

The same year that *Universities* was published, Abraham Flexner became the first director of the Institute for Advanced Study at Princeton, New Jersey, an institution founded to give young men and women an opportunity to do advanced research. Funded and founded in 1930 with a $5 million gift by philanthropist Louis Bamberger (see chapter 7) and his sister Mrs. Felix Fuld, both of Newark, the Institute for Advanced Study was divided into a School of Mathematics and a School of Historical Research. On the cutting edge of research methods, the institute had no set program, no examinations, and no degrees. Both faculty and students were given offices, books, and the time to pursue individual research projects. The Fuld House provided quarters for the institute, a building which was also funded by Bamberger and Mrs. Fuld. Flexner directed the institute until 1939, when he retired at the age of seventy-five. Nevertheless, he continued to speak and to publish. He completed his last book, *Funds and Foundations,* in 1952.

Abraham Flexner's life is indicative of the immense influence of the American Jewish community on education and educational reform. Jewish psychologists and psychiatrists entered the field of educational psychology during the twentieth century, contributing to basic American educational theory and initiating reforms that affected the world. A number of these individuals immigrated to the United States from Germany under the worst of circumstances. For example, Kurt Zadek Lewin (1890–1947) was a professor of psychology at the University of Berlin. He emigrated in 1932 in the midst of the rise of Adolf Hitler and the Nazi regime. Immediately making his mark on the U.S. educational system, he taught at Stanford University, Cornell University, and the University of Iowa, pioneering the concept of group dynamics and introducing field theory.

Kurt Lewin was one of the first psychologists to use mathematical models, and he presented field theory in the language of topology and vector analysis. Lewin's field theory maintained that an individual's behavior is determined by his or her "contemporary life space." Nevertheless, Professor Lewin asserted that the "life space" was not the actual environment, but rather the way an individual *perceives* his or her surroundings. From 1945 until his death in 1947, Professor Lewin organized and directed the research center for group dynamics at the Massachusetts Institute of Technology. He was fond of saying that "there is nothing so practical as a good theory."

Another emigrant from the Nazi terror, Bruno Bettelheim (b. 1903), pioneered techniques of diagnosis and therapy in the treatment of emotionally disturbed children. A licensed psychologist, Bettelheim miraculously had escaped Nazi persecution in 1939, after suffering in the concentration camps of Dachau and Buchenwald. Immigrating to the United States, he worked with the Progressive Education Association and later was appointed a professor of educational psychology at the University of Chicago. His published studies also gave American educators a better understanding of the dynamics of prejudice in the educational process.

New Yorker Irving Lorge (1905–1961) pioneered new avenues in measuring mental capacity and the ability of the human being at various ages to learn. The Jewish educator significantly contributed to understanding the gifted child, and yet he also made important contributions in understanding and measuring the intellectual prowess of the elderly. He even studied the effects of retirement on industrial workers. Irving Lorge is also credited with formulating indexes of readability in textbooks and other educational materials. Working closely with the Institute of Educational Research in the Teachers College at Columbia University in his earlier years, Lorge went on to head the Institute of Psychological Research in 1946. He and Professor Edward L. Thorndike of Columbia University developed *The Lorge–Thorndike Intelligence Tests* in 1954.

Another New Yorker, Brooklyn-born David P. Ausubel (b. 1918), a practicing physician and psychiatrist, became head of the Bureau of Educational Research at the University of Illinois in 1950 and pursued a study of cross-cultural research. By the 1960s his studies advocated that cultural deprivation could cause educational malfunctioning and that culture could be used successfully as a variable in psychological research. He published *The Psychology of Meaningful Verbal Learning* in 1963.

University of Chicago professor Benjamin Samuel Bloom, who was born in 1913, pioneered educational measurement and evaluation techniques in the 1950s and 1960s. The U.S. Office of Education appointed this professor of education to help set guidelines for federally appointed research efforts, and Benjamin Bloom's studies contributed to further research in analyzing stability and change in human behavior as well as analyzing educational objectives.

In the realm of educational philosophy, the work of Jewish educators has been legion. Isaac B. Berkson's *Theories of Americanization* (1920), *Preface to an Educational Philosophy* (1940), *Education Faces the Future* (1943), *The Ideal and the Community* (1958), and *Ethics, Politics and Education* (1968) charted new ground in the synthesis of Jewish values with progressive educational theory. Harry S. Broudy's *Building a Philosophy of Education* (1954), *Democracy and Excellence in American Secondary Education* (1964), and *Exemplars of Teaching Method* (1965) influenced a lasting concern on the role of education in molding intellectual discipline

27

and moral character. Professor Broudy insisted that our national survival depended on the implementation of a proper educational philosophy. Harvard Professor Israel Scheffler's *Philosophy and Education* (1958), *The Language of Education* (1960), *The Anatomy of Inquiry* (1963), *Conditions of Knowledge* (1965), and *Science and Subjectivity* (1967) applied philosophical methods to educational ideas, stressing that clarity and validity of methods should overrule general synthesis.

The list of Jews involved in educational reform in the United States is seemingly endless, but the individuals mentioned give the reader a glimpse of the untold riches a historian finds when uncovering Jewish contributions to the betterment of American education. Countless Jewish individuals also used their divergent fields of expertise to protect and enlarge the scope of American education. For instance, famed lawyer and civil rights advocate Louis Marshall (1856–1929), the son of German-Jewish immigrants in Syracuse, New York, argued on behalf of the rights of private schools, influencing the U.S. Supreme Court's Oregon decision in 1925 that upheld the constitutionality of parochial schools. The Supreme Court's decision actually stated that no state can require all children to attend public schools. In another area of reform, Louis's son, George Marshall, who was born in 1904, devoted his life to the American conservationist movement. George was managing editor of *The Living Wilderness* (1957–1961) and a director of the Sierra Club.

In the life of famed social worker Lillian Wald (1867–1940), one also notes social reform and educational reform merging. Born in Cincinnati, Ohio, to an affluent German-Jewish immigrant family and raised in Rochester, New York, Lillian decided to take a nursing course from a New York City hospital. Here she came into close contact with the poverty and misery of New York's Lower East Side and determined to make changes. Lillian Wald believed that charity could not solve social problems because it left the individual and the environment unchanged. She resolved to make a difference, establishing the Nurses Settlement in 1895 (which later would become the well-known Henry Street Settlement). This pioneering social agency provided a broad range of services and, through its efforts, an educational breakthrough. Through her programs of educating nurses and providing nursing services to the poor, Lillian Wald founded the first nonsectarian visiting nurse program in the United States. In addition, she pioneered public school nurses training in New York City. A new avenue of education had begun and continues to this day.

Labor

Lillian Wald was also upset by the social effects of America's Industrial Revolution. She described the "whir of machines" that continued day and night and the "unpleasant conditions" in which goods were manufactured in tenement flats, each member of the family forced into a new form of slave labor. Wald wrote that the living conditions of the poor families she and her colleagues nursed "disquieted us more than the disease we were trying to combat." She would support the fledgling trade union movement and would campaign against child labor. Jewish women and men, in fact, played a leading role in labor reform in America between the 1880s and the 1930s—a role that would never completely end.

Perhaps no individual played a more formative and stabilizing role in the American labor movement than Samuel Gompers (1850–1924). Born into a London Jewish family, he was apprenticed in the English cigar-making trade while in primary school. During the Civil War, his family immigrated to the United States, renting on the Lower East Side of New York City. Though barely a teenager, Samuel became the first registered member of the Cigar-Makers' National Union. He had found his niche, and union activities consumed his life from that day forward. Within a decade, he was a leader in the union, and in 1879 directly participated in its reorganization. He increased sickness and death benefits while strengthening the national organization.

In 1886, Samuel Gompers helped to establish the American Federation of Labor (AFL), and he became its first president. His name would be linked to the AFL and to American labor history long after his death. Ironically, it was this fame that Gompers had to rely upon during his lifetime to gain any strides for trade unionists, because the American labor movement was weak, divided, and indecisive at the turn of the twentieth century. Samuel Gompers had to be a national spokesman for a group of decentralized union organizations, even when he disagreed at times with the general policies they had negotiated with one another to uphold.

Realizing that the unions had little political support and that the worker could not expect much help from the American middle class, Gompers worked to strengthen trade unions and to exert economic pressure on the factories. Through collective bargaining agreements, he believed workers progressively could change their poor working environment, limit their long hours, and gain a decent wage. He fought vigorously against labor injunctions issued by courts to curb strikes. Although he believed that unions should avoid ties with political parties and government, he worked diligently for measures in the Progressive movement to break up monopolies and business trusts. By the time of his death in 1924, Samuel Gompers had seen substantial changes in labor organization and collective bargaining, but for the majority of his lifetime he viewed millions of workers that he could not help out of the depths of their misery. The plight of tens of millions of new immigrants haunted him.

Eighty percent of the 27 million new immigrants to the United States between 1880 and 1930 settled in the northeastern section of the United States, mainly in the cities, where they provided the labor for America's Industrial Revolution. Few of these men, women, and children went to the South. The northern factories at the turn of the century were dangerous and enslaving. The average immigrant worked ten- to twelve-hour shifts, six days a week. In some areas, as Lillian Wald recalled, whole families (including small children) sewed clothes in their crowded ghetto apartments for a pittance. At times garment workers earned a mere ten cents an hour. Sometimes they were locked in a room so that they would be at their machines for the duration of their shift.

A highly publicized fire at the Triangle Shirtwaist [blouse] Company in New York City in 1911 brought to the fore the plight of the immigrant laborer. Locked in their upper story room, 146 young women died, scores leaping to their deaths to escape the flames. "They hit the pavement just like hail," one fireman explained. "We could hear the thuds faster than we could see the bodies fall." And yet, those factories were not the worst. In 1913, nearly eighty percent of the clothing firms averaged only five employees. Those were the notorious "sweatshops," where employees during rush periods might work sixteen hours a day in hot, unventilated cells.

Jewish involvement in labor unions was active, committed, and self-sacrificing. Clothing workers in New York and Chicago went out on strike in 1910 and after a long struggle won the right to collective bargaining. Unions such as the ILGWU (International Ladies Garment Workers' Union) and the ACWA (Amalgamated Clothing Workers of America) fought for shorter hours, higher pay, and safety codes. In 1924, Jewish women and men constituted sixty-four percent of the ILGWU membership, the large majority of Eastern European origin. These men and women brought a well-defined and socially progressive labor movement from Europe. They were deeply committed to trade unions and were highly literate and articulate. Furthermore, their leadership emerged from deplorable working conditions and understood the plight and needs of the worker.

The health of the workers was a major concern of the emerging leadership. Joseph Breslaw (1887–1957), who was born into a Jewish family in Odessa in southern Ukraine, immigrated to the United States in 1907. He worked long hours as a cloak presser in the New York garment industry. By 1922 he had been elected vice president of the ILGWU and took as one of his chief activities to establish a ILGWU health center. Soon a small portion of union dues was being set aside for health and welfare, as well as other philanthropic causes. In like manner, union leaders Pauline Newman and Fannia Cohn worked tirelessly to improve the health and education of female union members. Newman had spent years working for the Triangle Shirtwaist Company and well understood the plight of working women. She had begun working in the Triangle factory at the age of eleven, toiling not only in the poor labor conditions, but also under the "fines" taken out of the meagre wages of working girls—fines randomly applied for being late, talking, laughing, making mistakes on material, and losing parts of machines. Russian immigrant Fannia Cohn insisted that it was the Triangle Shirtwaist Company fire that determined the dedication of her life to the union movement. She refused money from well-to-do American relatives and worked hard while gaining further education. Fannia Cohn became the director of the ILGWU's education department, inspiring working women to loftier goals and fulfillment.

Polish-born Rose Schneiderman (1882–1972), who had immigrated to the United States in 1890, also worked in a factory in New York City. She had wanted to be a teacher, but her father died shortly after they arrived in the city. Although her mother disliked her factory work, Rose found it less embarrassing than other jobs available. She ended up "teaching" through her union work. At the age of twenty-one, she helped to organize the United Cloth, Hat, Cap and Millinery Workers Union, becoming a member of its national executive board. Her organizational skills established and her devotion to the trade union movement proven, she was called upon to organize other unions, and by 1914 was a general organizer for the ILGWU.

From 1918 until her retirement in 1949, Rose Schneiderman was president of the Women's Trade Union League. From this position, she began to influence government policy. In 1918 she was a delegate to the first National Working Women's Congress in Washington, D.C. She was even a delegate to international conferences and visited other countries to evaluate their labor situation. In 1933 newly elected President Franklin D. Roosevelt gave her the duty of drawing up guidelines to govern industrial working conditions for women. In 1935 Congress passed the National Labor Relations Act (Wagner Act) to protect union rights. A National Labor Relations Board was finally established.

For Jewish women deeply involved in labor reform, sacrifice became synonymous with their lives. Most wrote of the loneliness and weariness, traveling from city to city by train as they attempted to organize, befriend, and instruct; living out of a suitcase in a cheap hotel, while spending long hours on the picket lines in dismal weather. Forced to forgo friendships and family considerations for total commitment to labor reform, they embarked on a seemingly endless, complicated task. The labor movement emerged as a strong force after World War II, but it was not until 1963 that Congress passed the Federal Equal Pay Act, requiring employers to pay men and women equal wages if they perform the same duties.

A second generation of union leaders emerged after the Second World War, and a number of Jewish men made their mark on the labor movement at the higher echelons. Born during the First World War, Sol "Chick" Chaikin, the son of Russian immigrants who were lifelong members of the ILGWU, rose through the ranks to assume the presidency of the union in 1975. Although he earned a Bachelor of Laws degree in 1940, he was drawn to the labor movement because he wanted to have a central role "to make life better for those whose lives were difficult." By the 1980s, many of the members of the ILGWU were African Americans and Hispanics, eighty percent of them women. Many of these women were single heads of households, encountering dilemmas that reminded President Chaikin of the struggles that faced early immigrant communities.

Jewish union leader Murray Howard Finley was born in 1922 and after World War II rose through the ranks to president of the Amalgamated Clothing and Textile Workers Union of America (in 1976). He often described the union as his "whole life," and for decades he fought for better working conditions and higher wages for his constituents. He also labored for union day care centers, educational funds, housing projects, and retirement centers. An advocate of civil rights, Finley served on the board of directors of the African American Labor Center.

Brooklyn-born Marvin Miller was born during the First World War in a Jewish family who strongly supported unionization. Finishing his bachelor's degree in economics, Miller worked a number of jobs before receiving his first union post at the age of thirty. Known as an effective negotiator, he was appointed by President John F. Kennedy to a national labor-management panel in 1963 and became executive director of the Major League Baseball Players Association in 1966. He is credited with creating a legitimate labor movement among athletes. In like manner, Albert Shanker, who was born in 1928 to Jewish working-class parents on the Lower East Side of New York, led the movement in the 1960s to unionize teachers. In 1972, he became president of the American Federation of Teachers.

Throughout the twentieth century, Jewish men and women have been involved as labor mediators, negotiating terms and agreements between employers and employees. In the early twentieth century, Rabbi Stephen S. Wise supported the 1913 strikes in the shirtwaist, dress, and other garment industries. He played a crucial role in mediation efforts. In 1929, his daughter, Attorney Justine Wise Polier (b. 1903), became the first female referee in the Workmen's Compensation Division of the New York State Department of Labor. This second generation among Jewish labor mediators was exemplified by another world war baby, Theodore Woodrow Kheel (b. 1914), who completed his law degree in 1937 and entered private practice. Throughout his legal career, Kheel had been called upon by prominent political figures, from mayors to presidents, to serve as an impartial mediator in labor disputes. For example, his skills were required to end the 114-day New York newspaper strike (1962–1963) during the John F. Kennedy administration, and President Lyndon Johnson asked him to join the mediation team to settle the railroad industry's work rules dispute. Like so many other Jewish leaders in this time period, Theodore Kheel devoted much time to the cause of civil rights.

As some unions became large corporations themselves, Jewish critics of big unions also enhanced the second- and third-generation labor movement. Jewish journalist Abraham Henry Raskin (b. 1911) tenaciously tracked the inner workings of the labor movement, publicizing the seedier side of corruption and infighting that accompanied the growth of some unions. His exposés covered the feelings and conditions of the lowest laborer to the highest echelons of union management. While he was known as a supporter of labor, he was disliked by some leaders for probing into their affairs. For instance, it was said that Teamsters president Jimmy Hoffa hated A. H. Raskin. On the other side of the coin, Gus Tyler (also born in 1911), a Jewish union leader and a writer of articles and books, underscored the need and importance of labor unions in works such as *The Labor Revolution: Trade Unionism in a New America* (1967) and *Scarcity: A Critique of the American Economy* (1976). Tyler emphasized that unionism is as much a part of American history as the corporation (and needed to be taught as such), and that some greedy corporations and conglomerates were continuing to create artificial scarcities and to circumvent government regulations.

As has been seen in the lives of many of the second-generation labor leaders above, Jewish efforts at labor reform in the 1950s and 1960s coincided with civil rights reform. Hyman "Harry" Bookbinder, who was also born during the First World War, is a case in point. The son of Polish Jewish immigrants, he completed his college education and then went to work for the Amalgamated Clothing Workers of America. After serving in World War II, he became the economist and research director for the union. From 1950 to 1964 he held positions with the AFL-CIO, until he was chosen to be executive officer of President Lyndon B. Johnson's Task Force on Poverty and to serve as assistant director of the Office of Economic Opportunity at its inception in 1964. He combined the economic and legislative skills that he honed during his union positions with a keen interest in social justice and civil rights. These concerns of Hyman Bookbinder were the ultimate concerns of a cadre of Jewish men and women during the twentieth century who were determined to support and work for civil rights reform in the United States.

Civil Rights

With the growth of the Jewish community in the United States at the turn of the twentieth century, there was renewed Jewish involvement in reform movements to protect all American citizens. These efforts not only combated anti-Semitism, but also fought for civil rights for African Americans. Jewish leaders were actively involved in the founding of the National Association for the Advancement of Colored People (NAACP) in New York City in 1909, the oldest and largest civil rights organization in the United States. The aim of the NAACP was the elimination of all barriers to political, educational, social, and economic equality for blacks and other minorities. Jewish philanthropists played a crucial role in the funding of these endeavors.

For example, Julius Rosenwald (1862–1932), the president of Sears, Roebuck and Company, was one of the key Jewish leaders involved in the founding of the NAACP in 1909. While he gave great sums to a variety of charities and philanthropic endeavors throughout his lifetime (even becoming president of the Associated Jewish Charities of Chicago in 1907), the plight of African Americans captured his heart. In his concern for social justice and civil rights, Rosenwald heavily financed the building of black YMCAs in twenty-five cities across the United States. A year after he helped found the NAACP, he began donating millions of dollars to establish more than 4,500 rural schools for African Americans in fifteen southern states. He also donated nearly three million dollars for the construction of model housing for African Americans in Chicago. From

1912 to his death, Julius Rosenwald served as a trustee at Tuskegee Institute, the famed Alabama trade school brought to prominence by Booker T. Washington.

From the beginning, the NAACP emphasized legal action in areas such as employment, housing, voting, and education. Jewish leaders in the American Jewish Committee (founded in 1906) had been able by the outbreak of World War I to get the New York State Legislature to pass a law which made it a misdemeanor for any public accommodation to advertise a policy of excluding any person because of race, creed, or color. Famed lawyer Louis Marshall, president of the American Jewish Committee from 1912 to 1929, believed in civil rights for all minorities and, as an active Jewish member of the NAACP, fought major legal battles on behalf of the African American community. One of the battles he lost was to convince the state of New York to put an antilynching law on its books.

Rabbi Stephen S. Wise, who was also involved in the founding of the NAACP, helped to found the American Civil Liberties Union (ACLU) in 1920. Some Jewish legal scholars staffed both organizations. Milton Ridvas Konvitz, for instance, was on the legal staff of the ACLU while holding the position of assistant counsel of the NAACP. Versatile and eloquent, Konvitz had expertise as general counsel for the New Jersey housing authority, later teaching industrial and labor relations as well as law at Cornell University. Milton Konvitz authored numerous books and articles on a broad range of topics. Becoming one of the foremost American experts on constitutional law, Konvitz's *The Constitution and Civil Rights* (1947), *Civil Rights in Immigration* (1953), *Bill of Rights Reader: Leading Constitutional Cases* (1954), and *Expanding Liberties: Freedom's Gain in Postwar America* (1966) became standards in the field.

Along with Arthur Spingarn, Jack Greenberg, and others, Milton Konvitz founded the Legal Defense and Education Fund of the NAACP, harnessing legal talent for the cause of civil rights. This group of Jewish lawyers was the first to mount a legal challenge to segregation. The Spingarn family had a long history in defense of civil rights. Both Arthur B. Spingarn (1878–1971) and his brother Joel E. Spingarn (1875–1939) had devoted themselves to the cause of integration and to the successful growth of the NAACP. Joel was one of the Jewish founders of the NAACP and served as its chairman from 1913 to 1919. He was president of the organization at the time of his death in 1939. Arthur was named honorary president of the NAACP in the 1960s. Ever immersed in black culture, he donated his large collection of African American literature to Howard University.

In the field of entertainment, Jewish musicians (such as Benny Goodman) were the first Americans to interact with and record black musicians and black singers. Billie Holiday credited her breakthrough to such empathetic entertainers, and it may be stated that it was through such Jewish efforts that African American "rhythm and blues" entered into the mainstream of American culture.

In the labor movement, Jacob Potofsky and Joseph Schlossberg of the Amalgamated Clothing Workers Union (as well as other Jewish labor leaders) supported A. Philip Randolf, the African American leader of the Sleeping Car Porters Union in his important negotiations with President Franklin D. Roosevelt. This led to Roosevelt's famed "fair employment" executive order in 1941 that established the Fair Employment Practices Committee. This committee worked diligently throughout the Second World War against discrimination in employment. By 1944 two million African Americans were at work in the war industry. Many previous barriers to economic opportunities for African Americans were permanently cracked. Jacob Potofsky prided himself on his fervent support of both the American Jewish Committee and the Anti-Defamation League in their efforts for human rights.

After World War II, however, there was much work to be done in the civil rights arena. Jewish activism in the South can be illustrated in the life of Rabbi Jack M. Rothschild, who in 1946 became rabbi of the Hebrew Benevolent Congregation in Atlanta, Georgia (known as "The Temple"). Soon after arriving at The Temple, Rabbi Rothschild began to educate both his congregation and his community in the area of race relations. This took a great deal of courage in a state where the Ku Klux Klan wielded tyrannical power and where it was against the law to have an integrated dinner. Jack Rothschild condemned both blatant forms of racism and also genteel cultural segregation. "When our country tries to implement standards of equal opportunity set forth in the Constitution, the South considers it an infringement of its way of life," he preached in 1948. "When the government wants to insure the safety of its citizens, the South reacts as though such simple justice were an affront to its moral codes." To a PTA group in 1951, he declared, "Dignity is due all people, not just a chosen few." Those who knew him insisted that he stood firm for civil rights while maintaining compassion for those ignorant oppressors who had been victims of their culture.

Nevertheless, in 1958 The Temple was bombed. A powerful explosive had been placed against one of the doors of the building. Exploding inward, it demolished everything its path, ruining the upstairs as well as the downstairs area of the large, beautiful house of worship. While Rabbi Rothschild attempted to prevent hysteria, a police officer was assigned to protect him and round-the-clock police patrols monitored the home to safeguard the family. The bombing served as a wakeup call to a lethargic community, and Christian ministers as well as newspapers expressed their outrage. The incident made national and international news, and President Dwight D. Eisenhower assigned the FBI to investigate. In a Friday evening sermon, "And None Shall Make Them Afraid," Rabbi Jack Rothschild explained to a huge crowd that filled the sanctuary of The Temple that "blame" for the bombing belonged equally to those "good decent people who choose to remain silent" and that this violence had finally "freed their tongues and loosed their hands for the work of righteousness."

From that time forward, a cadre of citizens did speak out in the Atlanta community. Rabbi Jack Rothschild forged even stronger relations with the African American community and strong friendships in the burgeoning civil rights movement. Dr. Martin Luther King, Jr. was invited to dinner at the Rothschild's home and was later honored at The Temple. The wives, Coretta Scott King and Janice Rothschild, got to know one another. Realizing that the majority of the South's Jewish community firmly supported civil rights, Rabbi Rothschild wrote the article "No Place to Hide," published in the *Southern Israelite* (August 1963). The article was aimed directly at those who were still using illogical and inconsistent excuses for not becoming involved in the civil rights movement. "No white American can evade any longer his personal involvement in the Negro's struggle for full citizenship," he emphasized. "The law guarantees equality—so he is involved as an American citizen." Insisting that Judaism was a religion devoted to civil and human rights (and pointing out that Christianity had a similar devotion that many Christians were ignoring), Rabbi Jack Rothschild rhetorically questioned: "Does the Southern Jew really want to establish a dichotomy between his patriotism and his religion?" In an article for the *CCAR Journal,* Rabbi Jack M. Rothschild applauded the Jewish and Christian clergymen who joined the Selma March in "a long overdue statement of deep spiritual commitment." Indeed, in the civil rights march from Selma to Montgomery, Alabama, March 22–26, 1965, Abraham Joshua Heschel, leading philosopher and theologian from the Jewish Theological Seminary in New York, was in the front row with Dr. King, Ralphe Bunche, and Ralph Abernathy. Many Jewish leaders participated in the march, joining hands with Protestant and Catholic leaders. Rabbi Rothschild gently reminded his readers, however, that they should not revel "in the mistaken belief that the war is won."

It must be mentioned that in the 1960s Jewish college students and young adults were extremely active in the civil rights movement. Over half of the white freedom riders in the 1960s were Jewish and nearly two-thirds of the white volunteers involved in Freedom Summer in Mississippi in 1964 were Jewish, most of them young people. Two of them, Andrew Goodman and Michael Schwerner, were murdered by white racists. Furthermore, Jewish young people swelled the ranks of the Congress on Racial Equality (CORE), the Student Nonviolent Coordinating Committee (SNCC), and Dr. King's Southern Christian Leadership Conference (SCLC). A cadre of young lawyers complemented the ranks of their older brethren, and Jewish lawyers made up nearly half of the white civil rights attorneys in the South in the 1960s. To this day, organizations such as the Anti-Defamation League continue to monitor racist groups and to defend human rights in a tradition of Jewish commitment to legal equality. This tradition is much more appreciated and better understood by the historian today than it was during the conflagrations and civil rights battles during the twentieth century.

✡ ✡ ✡

Many of the examples in the following chapters underscore this theme of Jewish "helping hands" and overlap significant

Jewish contributions to American culture, American society, and the American way of life. Jewish people were important contributors in this growing nation, and they have linked their peoplehood into the very fabric of the United States. Perhaps the brief life of a young Jewish woman of the nineteenth century expressed it well. U.S poet and essayist Emma Lazarus (1849–1887) wrote about the evils of racism and the need for human rights, but she also believed firmly that the United States of America was a special nation that could be a leader in love and compassion as it breathed freedom and opportunity. As a "helping hand," Emma donated her time to working among the poor immigrants who landed at Ward's Island. In her sonnet "The New Colossus," composed in 1883, she expressed an intense pride in her country, a deep regard for its heritage, and a vision of hope for its future. Emma Lazarus died at the tender age of thirty-eight, more than a decade before the dawn of the twentieth century, but her sonnet was affixed to the Statue of Liberty in 1903. It read: "Give me your tired, your poor, your huddled masses yearning to breathe free. . . ."

GOVERNMENT SERVICE

DR. JUDITH RESNIK (1949–1986), JEWISH-BORN ENGINEER and astronaut, became the second American woman to make a flight into space (August 30, 1984). A former design engineer for Radio Corporation of America (RCA) and a biomedical engineer for the National Institute of Health, the Ohio native was selected for the National Aeronautics and Space Administration's flight training program in 1978 while she was working for Xerox Corporation in California. Judy's mission as a flight crew specialist on the *Discovery* space shuttle lasted seven days and made her the first Jewish person to orbit the earth. After a June 26, 1984 aborted takeoff 2.6 seconds after engine startup due to a fuel valve malfunction, Judy Resnik and her colleagues endured three more delays until the August flight. They successfully launched the SBS–4, Leasat–2, and Telstar–3 communications satellites on the rescheduled mission. "I'd like to stay around as long as NASA wants me," Dr. Judy Resnik told ABC correspondent Lynn Sherr a few months before her first flight. "This is the happiest I've been in my career." She expressed the wish that she might still be flying when the space station took on crew members.

Excited about the prospects of a second mission, Dr. Resnik was elated at her assignment to the seven-member flight crew that was scheduled to depart in January 1986. Bright and attractive, she drew the assignment of flight engineer on the *Challenger,* which meant that she had to know all of the orbiter systems. This twelfth Space Shuttle mission included a Gentile high school social studies teacher, Christa McAuliffe, who had won the honor in a nationwide contest to be the first private citizen to fly in space. One minute after the space shuttle *Challenger* was launched from Cape Canaveral on a cold January 28, with schoolchildren throughout the United States watching the educational event from their classrooms, Judy Resnik and her fellow crew members (including teacher Christa McAuliffe) perished in a blasting ball of fire. To the horror of all who watched, *Challenger* had exploded, a faulty O-ring seal between segments on one of the solid-fuel booster rockets later determined to be the culprit. A nation mourned the valiant men and women who were lost in the pursuit of knowledge and service to the United States of America.

Military Service

Throughout history, the supreme offering a human being could make for a nation was to put one's life on the line for the ideals and freedom of that nation. In American history, Jewish men and women have made that sacrifice since the foundations of the republic. From colonial militia service and the American armies of the War of Independence of the eighteenth century (see chapter 1) to the fighting forces of the wars of the twentieth century, Jewish men and women have served their country with dedication and distinction. Approximately 250,000 Jews served in the American forces during the First World War, and more than 15,000 of them lost their lives or were seriously wounded in the eighteen months of fighting. Ten thousand Jewish officers led the American forces in various capacities, including General Abel Davis (1878–1937), General Milton J. Foreman (1863–1935), and General Charles Laucheimer (1859–1920). Six Jewish veterans were awarded the Congressional Medal of Honor for their extraordinary bravery during World War I, and over two hundred Jewish soldiers were awarded the Distinguished Service Cross. It is estimated that over half of the 77th Division from the state of New York was Jewish. Even a veteran Jewish "soldier of fortune," Sam Dreben (1878–1925), known as the "fighting Jew" for his South American exploits, put his life on the line for the Allies in the 1918 battles in France. He too was awarded the Distinguished Service Cross, returning to the United States to do "battle" against the Ku Klux Klan in Texas during the 1920s.

During the Second World War, approximately 550,000 Jews served in the American forces and more than 50,000 of them were killed or wounded. For a particularly heroic action during the heat of battle against the Nazis, a Jewish lieutenant, Raymond Lussman, was awarded the Congressional Medal of Honor for single-handedly capturing thirty-two Nazi soldiers and killing seventeen others. Another Jewish hero, Rabbi Alexander Goode, gave his life jacket to a serviceman and held hands with fellow Protestant and Catholic chaplains as their military transport, the *S.S. Dorchester,* sank to the bottom of the ocean under enemy fire. Six other Jewish chaplains died in service during the Second World War. Jewish military service did not end with the world wars. One hundred and fifty thousand Jewish men and women served in the Korean War and 30,000 in the Vietnam War.

Some Jewish men, such as Herman Feldman, Melvin L. Krulewitch, Samuel T. Lawton, and Maurice Rose volunteered for both World War I and World War II. For his service in the area of field artillery in both wars, Herman Feldman was promoted to major-general. Melvin Krulewitch served in Europe during the First World War and, after practicing law for several years, returned to the U.S. military service, volunteering for Pacific duty at the beginning of the Second World War. Decorated for meritorious service for his bravery during the fighting at Iwo Jima, he retired in 1956 with the rank of major-general. Samuel Lawton served with distinction as a captain during World War I and commanded the 33rd division as a major-general during the early months of the U.S. entry into World War II. Maurice Rose, the Connecticut-born son of a rabbi, served with the American Expeditionary Force as a lieutenant in World War I and served as chief of staff of the 2nd Armored Division during the North African Campaign in World War II. In fact, Brigadier General Rose negotiated the unconditional surrender of the German forces in Tunisia. Promoted to major-general, Rose commanded the 3rd Armored Division in heavy fighting through France, Belgium, and Germany. Major-General Maurice Rose was killed in action during the latter days of the Second World War.

Other Jewish soldiers served in a variety of capacities. A 1904 West Point graduate, Irving Phillipson, fought in the Philippines in 1906–1907 and the devastating Meuse-Argonne battles of the First World War. Major General Phillipson was approaching seventy years of age when the Japanese bombed Pearl Harbor. Commanding the Second Corps area, Phillipson was sent months later to Washington, D.C., to plan and administer a program of aid to help the wives and dependents of American soldiers. His years of knowledge and able military service produced a number of needed reforms and helped tens of thousands of families. One of the founders of the Jewish War Veterans of the United States, Chicago-born Julius Klein (b. 1901) as a teenager served as a war correspondent during World War I and volunteered for duty in the South Pacific and the Philippines during World War II. After the Second World War, Klein was appointed special assistant to the Secretary of War, Robert P. Patterson. Klein retired in 1951 with the rank of major-general. Another journalist pressed into service, South Carolinian George Chaplin (b. 1914), entered the Army and was sent to the Hawaiian Islands shortly after Pearl Harbor. He founded and served as the first editor of the Mid-Pacific Edition of *The Stars & Stripes* (the newspaper of the American Armed Forces). The son of immigrants from Poland, George Chaplin was majoring in chemistry at Clemson when he began editing the *Clemson Tiger*. It was the beginning of a lengthy and productive journalistic career (city editor of the *Greenville Piedmont* and Nieman journalistic fellow at Harvard before the war; after the war managing editor of the *Camden Courier Post* of New Jersey, managing editor of the *San Diego Journal;* New Orlean's editor of *The Item*). Ironically, George Chaplin ended up back in Hawaii as the editor-in-chief of the *Honolulu Advertiser* for twenty-eight years (1958–1986). Today, vibrant and productive in his eighties, he continues to write and to jet across the nation. His son, Steve Chaplin (b. 1941), is a career diplomat with the U.S. Foreign Service.

Naval Service

In addition to the army veterans, Jewish volunteers and career officers have served with distinction in the American Navy as well. This naval tradition has a long and illustrious history. During the War of 1812, Captain John Ordraonaux (1778–1841) captured at least ten British ships. Uriah Phillips Levy (1792–1862) also volunteered for and fought in the War of 1812. His ship sunk twenty-one enemy merchant vessels before being captured. Uriah Levy spent over a year in a British prison.

Returning to freedom and to naval service, this Jewish officer rose through the ranks to command the U.S. fleet in 1859 as Commodore Uriah Levy. In the midst of a busy career, Uriah Phillips Levy found time to write *A Manual of Informal Rules and Regulations for Men of War* and to draw a number of useful navigation charts. He bravely lobbied Congress to put an end to the practice of flogging on naval vessels. He spent much of his earnings on refurbishing Thomas Jefferson's former estate at Monticello. In fact, Uriah's mother is buried along the walkway approaching the main house. Later, the refurbished Monticello would become a national monument.

German-born immigrant, Adolph Marix (1848–1919) was the first Jewish naval officer to attain the rank of rear admiral (in 1908). The son of a translator for the U.S. Treasury Department, Adolph graduated from the U.S. Naval Academy at Annapolis in 1872 and commanded a number of ships during the 1890s. One of them, the *U.S.S. Maine,* sunk in Havanna Bay shortly after Marix had transferred command of the vessel, and he was appointed to the board of inquiry into the mysterious sinking (fifteen Jewish sailors were among those who died on the *Maine*). The findings of this committee led to a declaration of war on Spain. At the dawn of the twentieth century, Adolph Marix presided over a naval committee that experimented with the use of submarines.

Other Jewish naval officers served commissions of distinction. Some attained the rank finally given to Adolph Marix, the first Jewish naval officer to become a "rear admiral." During World War I, Rear Admiral Joseph Strauss (1861–1948) commanded the battleship *Nevada.* This Jewish admiral was responsible for placing a barrage of mines across the English Channel. In contrast to laying mines, Commander Walter F. Jacobs commanded a flotilla of minesweepers to rid areas of enemy mines. Spanish-American War veteran Captain Joseph K. Taussig (1877–1947) escorted World War I convoys in a successful effort to protect them against German submarine attacks. The son of a career naval officer, Rear Admiral Edward David Taussig (1847–1921), Joseph went on to serve as assistant chief of naval operations during the Roosevelt administration (1933–1936) and to command the flagship *U.S.S. Idaho.* He retired in September of 1941 as a vice admiral, but was recalled to service in

1943 in the midst of World War II. Both Joseph and his father, Edward, later were honored by the United States government with warships named after them.

Connecticut-born Rear Admiral Edward Ellsberg turned his naval academy experience and his engineering background into an expertise in salvage and restoration of ships for the U.S. government. As a young ensign during the First World War, Ellsberg worked in a New York navy yard refitting captured German liners for American naval use. Intrigued by the potential of sunken vessels, he studied salvage techniques and soon became one of the foremost experts on the raising of sunken vessels. In fact, in his mid-thirties, Edward Ellsberg became the very first individual in a time of peace to be awarded the Distinguished Service Medal when he raised a sunken submarine in 1925. During the Second World War, he was appointed the chief salvage officer for the entire Mediterranean. In addition, Ellsberg was called upon for advice concerning the Artificial Harbors project to facilitate the Allied invasion of France in 1944. Retiring in 1951 with the rank of rear admiral, Edward Ellsberg received numerous awards and accolades. Books that he has written, such as *Hell on Ice* (1938), *Men Under the Sea* (1940), *Under the Red Sea Sun* (1946), *No Banners, No Bugles* (1949), and *The Far Shore* (1960), give an expert's firsthand glimpse of naval procedures and practices as well as challenges and adventure.

Admiral Claude Bloch (1878–1967), a Jewish native of Woodbury, Kentucky, entered the U.S. Naval Academy at the age of seventeen, and distinguished himself in the Spanish-American War for saving Spaniards from burning ships. A naval transport commander during World War I, Bloch was appointed assistant chief of the Bureau of Ordinance in 1918 and promoted to rear admiral in 1923. In 1927, Rear Admiral Bloch commanded the battleship *California* and, after serving as commandant of the Washington Navy Yard, the commander was promoted to full admiral. In 1938 Admiral Claude Bloch was appointed commander-in-chief of the United States Fleet and, although he was forced to retire at the age of sixty-five, continued as a valued administrative board member for the government through the rest of the Second World War (until 1946).

Admiral Ben Moreel became the first engineering officer in the Navy to reach the rank of full admiral. Born into a Jewish family in Salt Lake City, Utah, in 1892, Ben Moreel was an able engineer when he joined the Navy engineer corps during World War I. By 1937, he had risen in the ranks to chief of the bureau of naval yards. When the Second World War erupted, Moreel organized the naval construction battalions known as "Seabees." He became a vice admiral in 1944 and retired as a full admiral in 1958.

In the field of naval intelligence, Rear Admiral Samuel Benjamin Frankel (b. 1905) has had an illustrious career. Raised in Cincinnati, Ohio, the Jewish-born Frankel graduated from the U.S. Naval Academy in 1929 and served on a number of warships during the early 1930s. He was sent to Latvia to study Russian in 1936 and then was assigned to the U.S. embassy in Moscow. After the Second World War, Samuel Frankel was appointed a naval intelligence officer and a naval attaché to China. He bravely remained in China for a year after the Communist Revolution and, upon returning to the United States, became director of the naval intelligence school (1950–1953). Promotions to assistant supervisor of naval intelligence in the Pacific, senior intelligence officer for the Navy in Washington, D.C. (where he was promoted to rear admiral), deputy director of naval intelligence, and chief of staff of the Defense Intelligence Agency (1960–1964) followed. Rear Admiral Samuel Frankel retired in 1964.

Chicago-born Admiral Hyman G. Rickover (1900–1986) is honored by military historians as the father of the atomic-powered submarine. A graduate of the U.S. Naval Academy (1922), Rickover completed his early sea duty by returning to graduate school and studying electrical engineering. Serving aboard submarines during the 1930s, he returned to base to head the electrical section of the U.S. Navy's Bureau of Ships during the Second World War. His genius at organization won him commendations and decorations. With the explosion of the atomic bomb, Hyman Rickover became convinced that such destructive power could be channeled into more productive energy capabilities. Against considerable opposition, he boldly lobbied naval officials to design and construct a nuclear submarine. The Navy, in turn, knew that there was only one man capable of bringing such a complicated and technical program to fruition—Hyman Rickover. In 1947, Rickover was put in charge of the Navy's nuclear power program and was appointed head of the Atomic Energy

Commission's naval reactor branch. Under his tireless and able leadership, the Navy designed and constructed the first nuclear-powered submarine, the *U.S.S. Nautilus.*

The *Nautilus* was launched in January of 1954, and became fully operational in 1955. As Hyman Rickover had predicted, it was a great success. Its nuclear reactor produced an intense heat that generated the submarine's turbines without consuming oxygen or producing noxious gases. A single fuel charge could propel it tens of thousands of miles at a submerged cruising speed of twenty knots (twenty-three miles per hour). Carrying a crew of 105, the sleek 323-foot-long *Nautilus* demonstrated its prowess when it carried out a dramatic mission beneath the polar ice cap to the North Pole in August 1958. Two years later, the *Triton,* powered by twin nuclear-power plants, traveled around the world under water, covering 41,500 miles in eighty-four days. By this time, Admiral Hyman G. Rickover had become a legend as well as a prominent fixture in the U.S. Navy. The admiral lived to see one of his Navy protégés in nuclear engineering, Jimmy Carter, become president of the United States. President Carter presented him with the Medal of Freedom early in 1980. Admiral Hyman G. Rickover retired at the age of eighty-three in 1982.

Admiral Rickover had been a strong proponent of peaceful uses of atomic energy. The *Nautilus*'s reactor served as the prototype for the first commercial nuclear power plant built in Shippingport, Pennsylvania, in 1957. Hyman Rickover also criticized the nuclear armaments race between the United States and the Soviet Union during the decades of the Cold War. In these stands, he joined many of the Jewish scientists in earlier years who helped the United States to develop the atomic bomb, but warned the nation and its leaders of the consequences of focusing upon the destructive potential of nuclear energy.

The Atomic Bomb and Nuclear Energy

In the waning months on the European front during the Second World War, Nazis looked to Adolf Hitler for the "secret weapon" he proposed would win the war for the Third Reich. In retrospect, a historian realizes that Adolf Hitler could have had the atomic bomb if he had not denigrated, cast out, and massacred his German Jewish scientists and academicians.

Hitler, however, did not understand physics and thought the science to be "Jewish babble." Albert Einstein, Edward Teller, Lise Meitner, Otto Frisch, and others were forced to flee Nazi Germany to save their lives.

The subsequent Jewish involvement in harnessing nuclear energy and creating the atomic bomb for the United States is a contribution that is controversial, but noteworthy. There is little doubt that the development of the atomic bomb saved hundreds of thousands of American servicemen's lives even as it took the lives of hundreds of thousands of Japanese. Furthermore, the scientists' hopes for nuclear energy, even amid their warnings about its destructiveness, propelled the world into a new age that may only reach its positive technological horizons in the twenty-first century.

Ironically, it was the pacifist Jewish immigrant physicist, Albert Einstein (1879–1955), who was called upon by other physicists to convince President Franklin Roosevelt that the United States must develop a nuclear capability before the Nazis could develop the capability. Some Jewish scientists, such as Hungarian Leo Szilard, had kept their earlier calculations secret in the hope of preventing military use of nuclear fission; they had to change their tactics when some German scientists discovered nuclear fission in 1938 and announced their theory about uranium fission in 1939. After a series of letters between Einstein and the White House in 1939, as well as supportive notes and letters from other scientists, President Roosevelt took the bold step of authorizing the "Manhattan Engineer District" (the initial research on the atomic bomb occurred in New York). From these roots came the birth of the "Manhattan Project," the code name for the American effort during World War II to produce an atomic bomb.

In 1943, scientist Robert J. Oppenheimer (1904–1967) organized in Los Alamos, New Mexico, a cadre of men and women into one of the finest research blends of theoretical and applied physics. A child prodigy born in New York City, Robert Oppenheimer had studied under world famous scientists at Harvard, Cambridge, and Goettingen. Sought after by major universities upon his return to the United States, Dr. Oppenheimer held professorships simultaneously at the California Institute of Technology and at the University of California at Berkeley

(1929–1947). Appointed director of the Los Alamos weapons laboratories built on an isolated New Mexico mesa, he was placed in charge of the construction of an atomic bomb. Dr. Robert Oppenheimer oversaw the testing of the first atomic bomb at Alamogordo, New Mexico, on July 16, 1945. After an ultimatum to surrender was rejected by the Japanese government, President Truman decided to use the atomic bomb, rather than send troops into Japan. At 8:15 A.M. on August 6, 1945, the B–29 bomber *Enola Gay* dropped the first atomic bomb on Hiroshima, a Japanese city of 250,000 residents. The world had entered the Atomic Age. Instinctively, Dr. Oppenheimer recited the ancient Hindu text: "I am become Death, Destroyer of Worlds."

Albert Einstein had written a letter in 1945 to President Roosevelt which stated his opposition to the use of the atomic bomb, but Franklin Roosevelt died before reading it. Einstein became chairman of the Emergency Committee of Atomic Scientists, a group that advocated the outlawing of nuclear weapons (a number of other Jewish scientists were members as well). Dr. Robert Oppenheimer resigned as director at Los Alamos in October of 1945, but accepted an appointment as chairman of the General Advisory Committee of the Atomic Energy Commission, where he continued to have a voice on nuclear policy. Dr. Oppenheimer clearly stated his viewpoint that there must be international control and cooperation concerning such a lethal weapon. President Dwight Eisenhower, in fact, soon decided after his 1952 election victory to declassify much nuclear-related information in an effort to promote positive uses of nuclear energy. In an "Atoms for Peace" speech (December 1953), President Eisenhower told the assembled United Nations that the countries of the earth must search for peaceful applications for nuclear energy.

Jewish government service did not end with the scientific development and philosophical viewpoints concerning atomic weapons, but continued in diplomatic efforts concerning nuclear energy. For instance, the first chairman of the Atomic Energy Commission, David E. Lilienthal, was a Jewish attorney from Illinois appointed by President Harry Truman in 1946. As a former director and chairman of the Tennessee Valley Authority (1933–1946), David Lilienthal became known as a specialist in natural resources and an able administrator. During his five years as chairman of the Atomic Energy Commission, he proposed what became known as the "Lilienthal Plan," a call to end the nuclear arms race through international control of atomic weapons. David Lilienthal returned to private enterprise in the 1950s, devoting his Development and Resources Corporation to help developing nations in the Third World. Bernard Baruch (refer to the concluding section of chapter 7), among his many services to the nation, was appointed chairman of the American delegation to the first United Nations Atomic Energy Commission in 1946.

Truman also appointed a West Virginia-born Jewish naval officer, Lewis L. Strauss, to the Atomic Energy Commission in 1946. Lewis Strauss's life combines aspects of government service, business acumen, naval duty, innovative creativity, and nuclear concern. His family owned a wholesale shoe business and, as a young man, Lewis became a traveling shoe salesman. During the First World War he volunteered to help an able government administrator, Herbert Hoover, organize Belgian relief. When Hoover became the director of the Food Administration, he chose Lewis Strauss as his administrative assistant. In 1919 Lewis joined the Kuhn, Loeb & Company banking firm, and four years later fell in love with and married Alice Hanauer, a daughter of one of the partners in the firm. In addition to his work for Kuhn, Loeb & Company during the Roaring Twenties, Lewis Strauss joined the Navy Reserve, invested in the Kodachrome process, and funded the construction of a surge generator to produce experimental isotopes for cancer treatment (both of his parents died from cancer). Known as a young man of exceptional ability, thirty-three-year-old Lewis Strauss became a partner in Kuhn, Loeb & Company in 1929.

During the Second World War, Lewis Strauss was appointed an advisor to Navy Undersecretary James Forrestal (who would become Secretary of the Navy in 1944 and would become the first United States Secretary of Defense in 1947). Strauss made quite a name for himself in defense and administrative areas by directing the development of the radar proximity fuse and creating the Big "E" war production incentive program. President Truman promoted Lewis Strauss to the rank of rear admiral in 1945. Rear Admiral Strauss served as a member of the Atomic Energy Commission from 1946 to 1950 under Truman's administration. Searching for an appropriate and experienced chairman of the Atomic Energy Commission, President Eisenhower appointed Lewis Strauss to that position in 1953. Rear Admiral Strauss opened the first meeting he chaired with the prayer that "the fruits of our labor be peace and not war."

Skunk Works

One of the most prestigious positions in American aerospace for much of the Cold War was held by an aerospace executive with authority in Lockheed's secret Advanced Development Projects division. Nicknamed the "Skunk Works" soon after its inception in 1943 because of its first location's proximity to a smelly plastics factory, the modernized Lockheed branch in Burbank, California, became the preeminent research and development facility of military aircraft in the free world. A Jewish aerothermodynamicist, Ben R. Rich (1925–1995), joined the division in 1950, working closely with government and military officials. Fresh out of UCLA with his master's degree (M.S., 1950), the former teaching associate grew into a respected Lockheed Aircraft Corporation engineer and manager. Ben Rich helped to develop some of the most advanced military aircraft in the twentieth century and became one of the few Jewish executives in the top management echelons of the aerospace industry.

At Lockheed, Ben Rich was promoted to program manager of advanced development projects in 1965, to vice president in 1972, and, finally, to the top position of president of Lockheed Advanced Aerospace Company (1984–1990). Ever intent on being a more skilled manager as well as an engineer, Ben went back to school in his forties and graduated from Harvard University's Advanced Management Program in 1968. Until his death from cancer of the esophagus on January 5, 1995, Ben Rich was a senior consultant for Lockheed. Because of his groundwork and continued supervision, Lockheed defeated the Northrop Corporation in a 1991 fly-off competition for military contracts. Ben Rich's historic contributions range from the state-of-the-art U–2 spy plane developed in the 1950s (virtually a powered glider that carried an array of cameras and monitors to nearly 90,000 feet) to the F–117A Stealth fighter-bomber (one of the most significant aeronautical triumphs in the history of military aircraft). In 1988, Ben Rich was awarded *Aviation Week & Space Technology*'s Aero/Propulsion Laurel Award and, in 1989, he received the Silver Knight Award from the National Management Association. (The same year Rich and his team received the Collier Award from the National Aeronautic Association for developing the F–117A.) Throughout the Cold War, Soviet military analysts knew the importance of the Skunk Works and had a nuclear missile targeted on it at all times.

Only recently have the exploits of this division's "glory days" and Ben Rich's contributions been more fully appreciated as the veil of Cold War secrecy has been lifted in the last decade of the twentieth century. For example, while the Air Force was trying to promote its ill-fated commitment to Rockwell Corporation's B–1 bomber, President Jimmy Carter's National Security Council Executive Secretary, Dr. Zbigniew Brzezinski, flew out west secretly to meet with Rich and to learn more about stealth technology during the early months of Carter's presidency in 1977. Ben Rich allowed the National Security chief to look inside the prototype's cockpit and briefed him on the stealth program. As he was leaving, Brzezinski bluntly asked Rich, "If I were to accurately describe the significance of this stealth breakthrough to the president, what should I tell him?" "It changes the way that air wars will be fought from now on," Ben Rich explained, "and it cancels out all the tremendous investment the Russians have made in their defensive ground-to-air system. We can overfly them any time, at will."

When the Carter administration cancelled the B–1A bomber program a few weeks later, most Americans were baffled and the Air Force was livid with anger. Administration officials had to take the outcry without explanation—the Skunk Works' advancements were too secret to acknowledge. During the 1991 Gulf War, however, the F–117A Stealth bomber accounted for approximately 40 percent of all targets damaged in Iraq (while only flying 1 percent of the air missions).

In his forty years with the Skunk Works, Ben Rich helped to develop twenty-seven specialized aircraft, as diverse as the F–104 jet fighter and the C–130 transport plane. Perhaps the futuristic looking and performing SR–71 Blackbird exemplifies the life of the extraordinary Ben Rich. Capable of flying over 2,000 miles an hour at over 85,000 feet, the SR–71 became the premier operational surveillance aircraft of the 1960s, 1970s, and 1980s. Its two turbojet engines each had a thrust of 34,000 pounds which, with afterburning, could propel the Blackbird at a maximum speed three times the speed of sound (Mach 3). At such speeds, the standard aluminum air-frame was useless. Beta B–120, a titanium alloy, was developed specifically for this aircraft in a brilliant design and development strategy. Furthermore, Ben Rich convinced his mentor and boss, Clarence "Kelly" Johnson, to paint the outside skin black so that they could use a softer titanium and maintain strength at temperatures over 550 degrees. From his college days, Ben had remembered that such a process would radiate more heat than it would absorb through friction. It was this dark prototype that established the nickname "Blackbird."

Virtually a sleek, flying fuel tank that would heat its fuel to 350 degrees in supersonic flight, the Blackbird used a specially developed high-flashpoint fuel that was safe, stable, and efficient, while propelling the most powerful air-breathing engine ever devised. In 1972, Ben received the American Institute of Aeronautics and Astronautics Award for designing Blackbird's propulsion system. To this day, the SR–71 Blackbird holds the record for flights from Los Angeles to Washington, D.C. (64 minutes), and New York to London (1 hour and 55 minutes). "Had we built Blackbird in the year 2010," Ben Rich was fond of saying, "the world still would have been awed by such an achievement." In the winter of 1990, with Ben contemplating official retirement on January 1, 1991, the SR–71 Blackbird was "retired" as well. Satellite technology was thought to have replaced the Blackbird's piloted reconnaissance function. And yet, some military analysts acknowledged that with the ever-present cloud cover and satellite atmospheric difficulties, the SR–71 Blackbird may have been retired too soon.

In 1994, Ben Rich conveyed his exciting experiences in *Skunk Works: A Personal Memoir of My Years at Lockheed.* In his last chapter, "Drawing the Right Conclusions," one senses his passion to look toward the future while learning the lessons of the past. Ben Rich wrote: "The Skunk Works has always been perched at the cutting edge. More than half a dozen times over the past fifty years of cold war we have managed to create breakthroughs in military aircraft or weapons systems that tipped the strategic balance of power for a decade or longer, because our adversaries could not duplicate or counter what we had created. That must continue to be our role into the next century, if we are to preserve what we have accomplished and be prepared for the hazards as well as the opportunities for the uncharted, risky future."

Months before his death, Ben Rich was honored with the Pentagon's highest civilian award, the Distinguished Service Medal. President Clinton's Secretary of Defense, William Perry, made a point to present the award in person. "The Skunk Works enjoys a preeminence in aerospace development based largely on unbounded enthusiasm and a willingness to tackle just about anything," Perry would later write in the epilogue of *Skunk Works,* concluding with a statement that might well capsulize the aerospace executive Ben Rich's life: "They are the best around."

Beltway Bound

"Inside the Beltway" has served as a code phrase for government institutions in the heart of Washington, D.C., ever since the multilane bypasses that surround outskirts of the Capitol were built. Government is the business of Washington, and Congress governs the District of Columbia. For much of American history, the president of the United States has appointed leading city officials. As for Congress, the Capitol is built on an eighty-three-foot hill that boasts the name "Capitol Hill." In turn, Pennsylvania Avenue radiates northwest from the Capitol, soon traveling around the grounds of the White House. From the power centers inside the Beltway, government servants and offices radiate out to each of the fifty states and, indeed, to every nation of the world. Throughout the history of the United States, Jewish people have shared in the responsibilities of white-collar government service and have made considerable contributions. The historian has only to read through the personal correspondence and papers of American presidents to gain an understanding of the high esteem in which these Jewish governmental "servants" were held.

Judicial Service

The United States has fifty-one separate court systems, including each state court system and the court system maintained by the national government. Jewish men and women have served faithfully in these systems throughout American history, and Jewish legal experts dutifully work in such government service today. Most Jewish jurists have never made it to the highest echelon of judicial service but, as the famed Julian W. Mack (1866–1943), have labored faithfully in the bowels of the state and federal systems. The abilities of these thousands of Jewish men and women may be represented to some extent by those Jewish individuals who have attained appointments as justices to the highest court of the land—the Supreme Court of the United States of America.

Louis D. Brandeis (1856–1941), a Jewish native of Louisville, Kentucky, was so gifted a law student that Harvard Law School had to change its regulations so that he could graduate before the age of twenty-one. Becoming a successful Boston lawyer, Louis Brandeis was known as the "people's attorney," often working for important causes and reform without pay. The first Jewish person to be appointed a justice of the Supreme Court, Brandeis took up his judicial responsibilities in 1916 at the age of fifty-nine. A master at judicial craftsmanship and analytical argumentation, Louis Brandeis upheld important social reform legislation, fought for freedom of speech and thought, and advocated the diffusion and sharing of governmental power. He retired from the Supreme Court in 1939.

Benjamin N. Cardoza (1870–1938) was another Supreme Court Justice who was distinguished for adapting existing law to the changing needs of American society. Born into an American Jewish family that was noted for its legal scholars, jurists and academicians, Benjamin's relatives helped defend Charleston Harbor during the American Revolution. The son of Philadelphia-born Albert Jacob Cardoza (1828–1885), who rose to the position of judge on the New York State Supreme Court, Benjamin Cardoza graduated from Columbia Law School and was admitted to the New York State Bar in 1891, six years after his father's premature death. His father left him a magnificent law library, and Benjamin soon made a reputation as the "lawyer's lawyer." In 1913 Benjamin Cardoza was elected a New York State judge. Five years later he was appointed to the Court of Appeals for the state of New York, maintaining a distinguished career (1918–1932) and writing decisions that drew national attention. In 1927 Benjamin Cardoza became chief judge of this Court of Appeals and, in 1932, President Herbert Hoover appointed him to the U.S. Supreme Court. In a key case, Benjamin N. Cardoza wrote the majority opinion that upheld federal social security legislation.

With the death of Justice Cardoza in 1938, President Franklin D. Roosevelt appointed Felix Frankfurter (1882–1965) to the Supreme Court in 1939. The decision was a natural one, based on the intellect, fame, and philosophy of this preeminent public servant and law professor. Born in Vienna, Austria, Felix immigrated to the United States with his Jewish family in 1894 and graduated from Harvard Law School in 1906. Subsequently serving as Assistant U.S. Attorney in New York, personal assistant to the Secretary of War, and legal officer for the U.S. Bureau of Insular Affairs, Felix Frankfurter returned to Harvard in 1914 to teach law. While at Harvard (1914–1939), Professor Frankfurter lent his abilities to government service by advising presidents, serving as legal advisor during the First World War to Newton D. Baker (the Secretary of War and the chairman of the War Labor Policies Board), and aiding as a key advisor during the Versailles Peace Conference.

An advocate of judicial restraint (reluctance to interfere with decisions made by Congress or state legislatures), Justice Frankfurter often amazed reporters and onlookers by his scholarly expounding *from memory* of the majority opinion of a current Supreme Court decision (including citations of volume and page numbers of pertinent historic cases bearing on the Supreme Court's decision). When he suffered a stroke in 1962 at the age of seventy-nine, Justice Felix Frankfurter resigned from the Supreme Court. In 1963 he was awarded the Presidential Medal of Freedom by John F. Kennedy. The citation to Felix Frankfurter read: "Jurist, scholar, counselor, conversationalist, he has brought to all his roles a zest and a wisdom which has made him teacher to his time."

Since the appointment of Louis D. Brandeis in 1916, the Supreme Court often has had one or two Jewish justices, chosen on their merits rather than on religious affiliation. Justice Arthur J. Goldberg (1908–1990), a prominent Chicago labor lawyer and John F. Kennedy's Secretary of Labor, was appointed to the Supreme Court in 1962. Only reluctantly did Justice Goldberg resign three years later when President Lyndon B. Johnson begged him to become U.S. Ambassador to the United Nations. Johnson's presidential advisor and a prominent Washington,

D.C. attorney, Tennessee-born Abe Fortas (1910–1982) was appointed to the Supreme Court in 1965 and served until 1969.

Brooklyn-born and Harvard Law School graduate Ruth Bader Ginsburg (b. 1933), had an outstanding legal career as a professor in several prominent law schools (1963–1980) and a judge on the U.S. Circuit Court of Appeals for the District of Columbia (1980–1993) when she was appointed to the Supreme Court by President Clinton in 1993. Dr. Ruth Bader Ginsburg had become an expert on affirmative action and sex discrimination cases when she was first appointed to the Federal Appellate Court by President Jimmy Carter. Another recent appointee, San Francisco-born Stephen G. Breyer (b. 1938), a former law clerk to Justice Goldberg, had served in the U.S. Justice Department (1965–1967) before becoming a professor of law at Harvard University in 1967. He served the government in a variety of capacities from the 1960s to the early 1990s before he was selected as a Supreme Court Justice in May of 1994. Both Justice Ginsburg and Justice Breyer survived the cut from longer lists of candidates to a short list, as well as the subsequent congressional scrutiny that undid the nominations of others among their judicial colleagues. Today both of these competent justices serve with distinction.

Presidential Advisors and Appointees

Although Judge Julian Mack never attained appointment to the U.S. Supreme Court, his early experience as judge of Chicago's Juvenile Court (1904–1907) gave him a special interest in the welfare of children. He was appointed to an important White House conference on children in 1908, several years before he was appointed to the U.S. Commerce Court (1911–1913) and the U.S. Circuit Court of Appeals (1913–1941). This Jewish-born professor of law and U.S. judge accepted a number of presidential appointments until his retirement in 1941. The life of Judge Mack is certainly indicative of the tens of thousands of Jewish advisors and appointees that have helped the executive branch in a variety of capacities.

Among thousands of prominent Jewish presidential advisors and appointees from whom to choose, the historian is amazed at the depth of service and the diversity of service. Like Lazarus Straus's son, Oscar (1850–1926), who was appointed as ambassador to Turkey by President Grover Cleveland and appointed as a jurist to the International Court of Arbitration at The Hague by President Theodore Roosevelt, many of these individuals served in a variety of capacities. In fact, Oscar Straus became President Teddy Roosevelt's Secretary of Commerce and Labor from 1906 to 1909, the first Jewish person to hold a cabinet post in the United States. Other Jewish presidential advisors have moved on to cabinet posts. For example, Henry Morgenthau Jr. (1891–1967) advised President Franklin Roosevelt on agriculture during the early years of the Great Depression and was appointed Secretary of the Treasury in 1934. A skillful administrator, he thoroughly reorganized the Treasury Department.

Some Jewish families have a history of national service, including the Straus and Morgenthau families mentioned above. Henry Morgenthau Sr. (1856–1946), for instance, served as ambassador to Turkey from 1913 to 1916 and headed the Morgenthau Commission for President Wilson after the First World War. Robert Morris Morgenthau (b. 1919), Henry Morgenthau Jr.'s son, served as U.S. attorney for the southern district of New York from 1961 to 1970. In the Straus family, Isidor was elected to Congress to fill an unexpired term (1894–1895), taking time off from the family business to fulfill his public duty. Isidor's son, Jesse Straus (1872–1936), was appointed ambassador to France in 1933. Nathan's son, Nathan Straus Jr. (1889–1961), served as head of the U.S. Housing Authority from 1937 to 1942; and his grandson, R. Peter Straus (b. 1917), after an illustrious international service in the 1950s, was appointed by President Lyndon Johnson to be the assistant director of the U.S. foreign aid program to Africa. The son of Oscar Straus, Roger W. Straus (1893–1957), took time off from business to serve as a member of the U.S. delegation to the United Nations General Assembly in 1954; and the grandson of Oscar Straus, Oscar Straus II (b. 1914), served in the State Department in Washington from 1940 to 1945. All of these men had an active public service record that extends far beyond what has been mentioned here.

Two brothers from New York City, Eugene and Walt Rostow, have turned academic qualifications into national service during their lifetimes. Yale Law School professor and dean Eugene V. Rostow (b. 1913) was a legal advisor to Assistant Secretary of State Dean Acheson during the Second World War (1942–1944) and served as assistant executive secretary of the Economic Commission for Europe (1949–1950). In the mid-1950s, the U.S. attorney general asked him to donate his time as part of a national committee to study antitrust laws. When John F. Kennedy's administration initiated the Peace Corps, Dean Eugene Rostow was appointed to the advisory panel. Also in 1961, he began a five-year stint as a key consultant to the Undersecretary of State. In the midst of the Vietnam crisis, President Johnson appointed Eugene Rostow to the position of Undersecretary of State (1966–1969). He became a key advisor during a number of international crises. In the 1970s and 1980s, Eugene Rostow was called upon again and again by presidents. In 1981, President Ronald Reagan appointed him director of the Arms Control and Disarmament Agency, a position he held until 1983. In 1990, he was awarded the Distinguished Civilian Service Award from the U.S. Army.

Walt W. Rostow (b. 1916) also was a graduate of Yale University (B.A., 1936; Ph.D., 1940) and a Rhodes Scholar (1936–1938). In fact, he taught American history at both Oxford University and Cambridge University after the Second World War, before returning to the United States in 1950 to teach economic history at MIT in Boston. Dr. Walt Rostow held the rank of major in World War II, being assigned to the Office of Strategic Services (OSS) in London to develop and coordinate air strategies against the Nazis. After the war, he worked in various capacities for the State Department. It was while in Boston, however, in the latter 1950s that Walt Rostow became a policy analyst for Senator John F. Kennedy. When Kennedy was elected president, Walt Rostow accepted the appointment of deputy special assistant to the president for national security affairs and also became an advisor to the policy planning council of the State Department. President Johnson appointed Walt Rostow special assistant to the president from 1966 to 1969. Like his brother Eugene, he would be embroiled in the Vietnam conflict. Before leaving office, President Johnson presented Walt with the Medal of Freedom. Dr. Walt Rostow moved to Texas and became professor of political economy there. He also helped Lyndon Johnson work on his presidential papers, established the Lyndon B. Johnson Library, and, after Johnson's death, organized the Lyndon B. Johnson School for Public Affairs. Both Eugene and Walt Rostow were prolific writers and have a number of books (in addition to many articles) to their credit.

Historically, Jewish advisors come from a variety of backgrounds, but the paths of law and academics draw many of them into presidential service. Marcus Raskin (b. 1934), the Milwaukee-born son of a plumbing and heating contractor, began serving congressmen as legislative counsel soon after receiving his Doctor of Laws degree from the University of Chicago in 1957. In the early 1960s, he was appointed to a special staff of the National Security Council and was a member of the U.S. Disarmament Delegation to the Geneva Conference. Marcus Raskin also served as a presidential educational consultant for the White House during the mid–1960s. Russian-born Simon H. Rifkind (b. 1901) became a naturalized citizen in 1924, received his Bachelor of Laws degree in 1925 from Columbia University, and served Senator Robert F. Wagner as a legislative secretary from 1927 to 1933. Pursuing a private law practice during the 1930s, Rifkind was appointed by President Franklin Roosevelt to serve as a United States District judge in 1941. General Eisenhower called upon him in 1945 to advise in the American occupation zone in Europe. Resigning his federal judge position in 1950 to pursue private practice once again, Simon Rifkin was called upon repeatedly to advise presidents, be a part of fact-finding missions, and serve on presidential commissions (including a presidential railroad commission from 1961 to 1962, and the President's Commission on the Patent System, 1966–1967).

In like manner, Democrat Max M. Kampelman (b. 1920), the son of a New York City retailer, was called out of a private law practice repeatedly to serve both Democratic and Republican presidents. Appointed senior advisor to the U.S. delegation to the United Nations from 1966 to 1967, Dr. Kampelman was asked to be ambassador to the Conference on Security and Cooperation in Europe from 1980 to 1983 and ambassador to the Negotiations on Nuclear and Space Armaments from 1985 to 1989. Every year in the early 1990s he was appointed to head another delegation. On the Republican end of the spectrum, political scientist Stephen Hess (b. 1933) has served as a White House staff member under two presidents. Hess became a staff writer for President Eisenhower and was appointed a deputy assistant for urban affairs in the Nixon administration. President Richard

61

Nixon also appointed Stephen Hess to head the White House Conference on Children and Youth from 1969 to 1971. A number of other presidential appointments followed, and Stephen Hess even became editor-in-chief for the Republican national platform in 1976. A prolific author and scintillating lecturer, Stephen Hess had his own syndicated newspaper column from 1977 to 1982 and has worked closely with the John F. Kennedy School of Government at Harvard University since 1987.

Bavarian-born Henry A. Kissinger (b. 1923) and his family fled Nazi Germany when he was a teenager, ending up in Manhattan. Drafted into the U.S. Army in 1943, Henry served with the 84th Infantry Division and with the 970th Counterintelligence Corps. After Germany's surrender, he became a district administrator with the U.S. military government. Returning to the United States, Henry Kissinger used the G.I. Bill to further his education, completing his undergraduate and advanced degrees at Harvard University (B.A., 1950; Ph.D., 1954). Known as a brilliant student and fine teacher, Dr. Kissinger was hired by Harvard as a professor. In 1958 he received the Woodrow Wilson prize for the best book in the fields of government, politics, and international affairs.

Often consulted by government officials and think tanks, Henry Kissinger was appointed by President Richard Nixon as his assistant for national security affairs and soon became Nixon's Secretary of State (the first Jewish Secretary of State in American history). He received the Nobel Peace Prize in 1973 for his efforts in bringing the different parties in the Vietnam conflict together to negotiate peace, and his envoy role between belligerents after the Middle East's Yom Kippur War established the term "shuttle diplomacy" forever in the annals of diplomatic initiative. Dr. Henry A. Kissinger continued as Secretary of State during the Ford administration and was awarded the Presidential Medal of Freedom in 1977. He has been called upon for advice by every president since and has served in a number of official capacities. In 1986 Henry Kissinger was awarded the Medal of Liberty and in 1994 was honorary vice chairman of World Cup Soccer's debut in the United States. The same year another of his many books was published: *Diplomacy* (1994).

Kissinger's senior advisor, career diplomat Helmut Sonnenfeldt (b. 1926), rose quickly through the ranks as an expert on the Soviet Union after joining the State Department in 1952. By 1966, the Jewish-born son of immigrant physicians from Berlin had become the director of Soviet and Eastern European research at the State Department and, in 1969, Kissinger appointed Sonnenfeldt to the National Security Council. Keeping a low profile, Helmut Sonnenfeldt played a key role in many of Kissinger's foreign policy initiatives. In 1974 Sonnenfeldt was appointed Undersecretary of Treasury, retiring in 1977 with the rank of career minister. Since then, he has lectured and continued his advisorial role in think tanks and discussions.

Stuart B. Eizenstat (b. 1943), the son of an Atlanta wholesale shoe store proprietor, wrote speeches for President Lyndon Johnson and advised Jimmy Carter in his gubernatorial campaign in 1970. When Carter became president in 1977, Stuart Eizenstat continued as one of his close advisors. A member of Carter's inner circle, Eizenstat was appointed head of the Domestic Policy Staff, where he helped develop proposals on welfare reform, national health insurance, consumer protection, deregulation, and education. Returning to his private law practice when Carter lost a second-term presidential bid to Ronald Reagan in 1980, Stuart Eizenstat was chosen by President Clinton to represent the United States as ambassador to the European Union in Brussels, Belgium, in 1993.

Presidential Medal of Freedom recipient Robert Schwarz Strauss (born in Lockhart, Texas, in 1918) has not only been a prominent fixture on the Democratic National Committee; but also has served in key presidential advisory roles, as well as serving as a special presidential representative for trade negotiations (1977–1979), the president's personal representative for Middle East negotiations (1979–1981), and U.S. ambassador to Russia (1991–1993). Dr. Edward Levi (b. 1911) was appointed attorney general of the United States from 1975 to 1977 after serving as the president of the University of Chicago. Dr. Harold Marvin Williams (b. 1928) was dean of the Graduate School of Business and Management at UCLA throughout the 1970s, when President Carter appointed him chairman of the Securities and Exchange Commission (SEC) in 1977. A seasoned corporate executive as well as an academician, Dr. Williams tightened up accounting procedures and worked to instill more integrity in business practices.

Jewish journalists have been called upon to serve as presidential press secretaries. Bernard Kalb, for example, served as President Ronald Reagan's press secretary. His brother, Marvin, is now called upon for advice from his new position as professor of press and public policy at the John F. Kennedy School of Government at Harvard University (note chapter 4 for more details on the Kalb brothers). Jewish public opinion analysts, such as Louis Harris (b. 1921) and Daniel Yankelovich (b. 1924), have served presidential administrations on a variety of topics and have sought as pollsters (in the words of Louis Harris) to "get people with power to act upon the facts to better the lot of the human race."

Jewish economic advisors have been prominent in many presidential administrations of the twentieth century. Baltimore-born and Harvard Ph.D. (1940) Professor Abram Bergson (b. 1914), one of America's foremost experts on the Soviet economy, has been consulted by nearly every presidential administration since Franklin Roosevelt's and often has testified before Congress on foreign policy matters. Likewise, Columbia University economist Eli Ginzberg (b. 1911) has served on numerous commissions since his study on the use of military manpower for President Franklin Roosevelt and has written nearly seventy books on economic topics.

Another Columbia University graduate, Arthur F. Burns (b. 1904), advised nearly every president from Franklin Roosevelt to Ronald Reagan. During Eisenhower's administration, for example, the Jewish economist was chairman of the President's Council of Economic Advisors (1953–1956). In October 1969, President Nixon named Arthur Burns to the chairmanship of the Board of Governors of the United States Federal Reserve System. He served until 1978, at times disagreeing with the economic policies of both the Nixon and Carter administrations as Dr. Burns stressed the importance of a balanced budget and monetary stability. Continuing his involvement in government service in the 1980s, Dr. Arthur F. Burns accepted appointment as ambassador to West Germany in 1981.

Dr. Paul A. Samuelson, the Harvard-educated son of a pharmacist in Gary, Indiana, had just begun his long teaching career at MIT when he became a government consultant for the National Resources Planning Board in 1941. Advising Presidents

Roosevelt, Truman, Eisenhower, Kennedy, and Johnson, Paul Samuelson actually shaped much of the economic policy of the Kennedy administration as the key economic advisor to President Kennedy (1959–1963). Fearless, he began criticizing subsequent presidential administrations for their economic blunders. He was awarded the Nobel Prize in Economics in 1970 (one year after it was established in 1969). In 1991, the Paul A. Samuelson Professorship was founded in his honor at MIT.

What Paul Samuelson meant to the Kennedy administration, Herbert Stein meant to the Nixon administration. The Detroit-born son of a Polish Jewish immigrant who worked for the Ford Motor Company as a machinist, Herbert Stein (b. 1916) worked as an economist for a variety of government agencies and private organizations after receiving his Ph.D. from the University of Chicago (1938). In 1964, Dr. Stein was chosen to advise Senator Barry Goldwater, the Republican candidate for president. Four years later, President Richard Nixon asked Herbert Stein to direct his administration's economic program. Serving as a key member of Nixon's Council of Economic Advisors, he was made chairman of the group from 1972 until Nixon's resignation. Dr. Stein then began his long tenure as a consultant to the Congressional Budget Office (1976–1989) and to the Department of State (1983–1992), while maintaining a professorship in economics at the University of Virginia, Charlottesville (1974–1984). When Ronald Reagan became president in 1981, he recruited Herbert Stein as a member of the President's Economic Policy Advisory Board (1981–1989) and the President's Blue Ribbon Commission on Deficit Management (1985–1986).

Even before he was president, Ronald Reagan's economic thinking (and, indeed, the economic policies of other renowned world leaders, such as Margaret Thatcher) was strongly influenced by Jewish economist and University of Chicago professor (1946–1982) Dr. Milton Friedman (b. 1912). Perhaps the leading exponent of the conservative, free-enterprise philosophy of modern economics, Milton Friedman offered such a radical departure from Keynesian economics that it won him the Nobel Prize in economics in 1976. For more than thirty years, Dr. Friedman has insisted that John Maynard Keynes greatly exaggerated the efficacy of governmental taxation and spending in determining the level of national income. He also asserted that Keynes erred in minimizing the role of money in this process. In contrast, Professor Friedman emphasized that the level of economic activity is largely determined by the quantity of money in the system and that a central bank must avoid sudden changes in the money supply, concentrating instead on gradual, regular increase. So prevalent were Milton Friedman's views that his theories gave rise to the "Chicago school" of economic philosophy.

In the later 1980s and into the mid–1990s, Alan Greenspan (b. 1926) has been one of the key orchestraters of American economic policy. As chairman of the Federal Reserve Board since 1987, the former Julliard clarinetist turned economist determined during the 1990s how much interest rates should be raised as he pursued a delicate economic symphony between inflation and stagnation. As he appeared frequently before Congress as well as the press, the eyes of the world focused on his every move. Serving all Republican presidents from Nixon to Bush, Dr. Greenspan's conservative economic policy of fiscal restraint protruded even into President Clinton's Democratic bastion. Such is the contribution, determination, and dedication of Jewish advisors and appointees.

When John F. Kennedy was inaugurated as president in 1961, he appointed Abraham A. Ribicoff to his cabinet as Secretary of Health, Education, and Welfare. The appointee was much like many of the fine Jewish cabinet officials appointed by presidents from 1906 to the present. As an extra bonus, however, Abraham Ribicoff had served his nation as a legislator, before and after his cabinet appointment.

Legislators

Quite a few Jewish political leaders have served their country in the U.S. Congress. The son of a poor immigrant Connecticut factory worker, Abraham A. Ribicoff (b. 1910) worked his way through college and was awarded a scholarship to the University of Chicago Law School. Graduating in 1933, he began his own private law practice and became involved in Democratic politics. After holding state legislative office as well as a judgeship, Abraham Ribicoff was elected a U.S. congressman in 1948. He lost a Senate bid in 1952, but was elected governor of Connecticut in 1954. He held this position until 1961, when he accepted Kennedy's cabinet appointment. Less than two years later he ran successfully for the U.S. Senate. He served in the Senate seventeen years until his retirement in January 1981.

In some respects, history repeats itself. A nineteenth-century Jewish-immigrant lad from Bavaria, Michael Hahn (1830–1886), grew up to be the first Jewish governor of a state (Louisiana) and, like Ribicoff, served in Congress before and after his governorship. Hahn was a Republican, however, not a Democrat. Another Jewish immigrant, 1878 Harvard-graduate Lucius Nathan Littauer (1859–1944), served as a Republican congressman from upstate New York (1896–1907). He was a close friend of Teddy Roosevelt and a leading member of the House Appropriations Committee. Jewish-born Julius Kahn (1861–1924) was the first member of Congress to insist that campaign expenses and contributions should be made public. Kahn served as a Republican congressman from California for twenty-three years (1899–1903; 1905–1924) and was a key member of the House Military Affairs Committee. His widow, Florence Prag Kahn (1868–1948), was appointed to Julius's congressional seat at his death.

Other Jewish women started from scratch in the world of politics. Columbia University law graduate Bella Abzug (b. 1920) had an illustrious legal career before winning her congressional seat in 1970. Passionate and independent, Bella was a favorite of the media and a bane to the Nixon administration in the midst of the Watergate fiasco. In 1976 she left the House of Representatives to run for the Senate. Even though she was narrowly defeated by the indomitable Daniel Patrick Moynihan, Bella Abzug has remained a force inside the Beltway as a key presidential advisor and a cable news commentator.

Much more could be said of the careers of Ernest Gruening (senator from Alaska), Herbert Lehman (senator from New York), Howard Metzenbaum (senator from Ohio), Carl Levin (senator from Michigan), Edward Zorinsky (senator from Nebraska), Chip Hecht (senator from Nevada), Warren Rudman (senator from New Hampshire), Jacob Javits (senator from New York), Arlen Specter (senator from Pennsylvania), Richard Stone (senator from Florida); and congresspersons Adolf Sabath, Sol Bloom, Emanuel Celler, Elizabeth Holtzman, Richard Ottinger, Stephen Solarz, Gladys Noon Spellman, and Edward Koch (former congressman turned mayor of New York City). In fact, from the

1980s onward, there were approximately thirty Jewish members of the House of Representatives and approximately eight Jewish members of the Senate. Each of these statistics represents diverse lives of public service and a variety of significant contributions. The consequential public service of Jewish politicians such as Dianne Feinstein, career politician and recently elected senator from California, continues to be recorded.

Outside the Beltway, many other Jewish elected officials have made their mark on this nation's history. For instance, Henry Horner (1878–1940), who was governor of Illinois from 1932 to 1940, has quite a history. Named after his grandfather, who had emigrated from Bavaria in 1840 and was instrumental in founding the Chicago Board of Trade, Henry Horner practiced law and was elected a probate judge in Cook County (served 1914 to 1932). He gained national recognition for his "Horner Plan," which protected the estates of servicemen during the probate process without cost. In 1932 Henry Horner was elected governor of the state of Illinois by the largest popular vote ever received. An admirer of Abraham Lincoln, Governor Horner donated his extensive collection of Lincoln artifacts to the Illinois State Historical Society in 1933. Fighting corruption and supporting good government, Henry Horner would not collaborate with the Chicago Democratic machine. The citizens of Illinois respected his integrity and returned him to the statehouse in the 1936 election. Carl Sandburg perhaps summed it up best when he noted of Governor Henry Horner, "In an age flagrant with corruption, he was among those who came through clean and unspotted."

✡ ✡ ✡

Astronaut and national servant Judy Resnik traveled into space in an exhilarating fulfillment of a cherished dream, but she never accomplished a walk in space because her life was cut short by the *Challenger* accident. Another Jewish astronaut, Dr. Jeffrey A. Hoffman (b. 1945), has become an experienced "space walker" since his dramatic unscheduled space rescue attempt to fix a balky communications satellite on his very first shuttle flight in 1985. The son of a physician, Jeff Hoffman was born in Brooklyn and grew up in Scarsdale, New York. He received his doctorate in astrophysics from Harvard University (1971) and, in his mid-thirties, applied with 10,000 others to the astronaut program at NASA. Like Dr. Judith Resnik, Jeff was one of the few dozen applicants accepted. Even his wife Barbara could not believe how their lives changed with Jeff's decision to dedicate his life to this facet of government service and with the subsequent demands of the early years of shuttle training. The rigorous training program and medical isolation from his wife and two children a week before each mission still interrupts their lives periodically and reminds them of past sacrifices.

Since his first spacewalk in 1985, Jeffrey Hoffman has been a mission specialist on the Spacelab shuttle flight in 1990 and on the STS–46 mission in 1992. In December 1993, he participated in NASA's most ambitious repair mission, STS–61, the launching of the *Endeavour* space shuttle to correct the malfunctioning Hubble Space Telescope. Dangling at the end of the shuttle's robotic arm, Dr. Hoffman at one point opened one of the Hubble telescope's equipment bays and replaced a dozen fuses. He and his colleague, Story Musgrave, also replaced two of the telescope's Rate Sensor Units, each containing two gyroscopes. At another point in the mission, Jeff observed Hanukkah inside the spacecraft and, in the spirit of the holiday, spun a dreidl with fellow astronauts even as the shuttle spun in space. He is known as an intellectual *and* a spiritual man. A favorite media interviewee, the tall and articulate Hoffman has left a special legacy to America. He agreed to tape an audio journal during one of his shuttle flights. The fifty-minute tape, *Astronaut's Journal* (1991), has given unique insight into even the most rudimentary aspects of space travel (such as eating and sleeping) as well as momentous feelings and philosophical musings that surround the liftoff, visual panorama, and weightless flight.

Astronaut Jeffrey A. Hoffman fondly remembers Judith Resnik and other colleagues who perished in the *Challenger* disaster. Nevertheless, he does not regard his vocation as *extremely* dangerous. With a slight grin, this astronaut, who is engaged in government service of a celestial nature, does admit that his missions are "riskier" than flying overseas coach class in a Boeing 747.

MEDICINE AND HEALTH

THE "POWER" OF AN ENTERTAINER TO DO "GOOD" MAY BE viewed in the life of Jewish vaudeville performer, comedian, and actor Eddie Cantor (1892–1964). Eddie channeled his fame into an influence that directly affected the health of America. Born Isidor Iskowitch on the Lower East Side of New York, Eddie Cantor toured the United States on the vaudeville circuit and became so popular that he toured the theaters of Europe as well. During the Great Depression he became a noted film actor, immediately turning his new-found fame into a vehicle to support a variety of charitable causes.

Counting among his friends the polio-stricken president, Franklin Delano Roosevelt, Eddie Cantor and President Roosevelt discussed the possibility of raising money for medical research to find a cure for the dreaded debilitating disease. Franklin Roosevelt suggested that Eddie organize a campaign that would collect one dollar from one million Americans for polio research. Eddie responded that they could more easily collect a dime from ten million Americans *if* the president would allow the money to be sent to the White House. The campaign was an immediate success, and the "March of Dimes" was born. Through Eddie Cantor's efforts, and with the help of many others, research monies were raised that eventually led to a cure for poliomyelitis.

It was a Jewish microbiologist, Jonas Edward Salk (b. 1914), who developed the first vaccine effective against polio. Born in Manhattan, Jonas Salk showed early promise in the medical field, completing his undergrad-

71

uate degree at City College of New York (B.S., 1934) and obtaining a chemistry fellowship at New York University. Awarded his M.D. in 1939, he continued postdoctoral studies in bacteriology and interned at Mt. Sinai Hospital. The day after he graduated from medical school, Jonas Salk married Donna Lindsay, a young Jewish woman who was pursuing graduate studies in the New York School of Social Work. In 1942, Dr. Salk was awarded a research fellowship at the University of Michigan's School of Public Health. Continuing his research there for five years, he progressed from a research associate to an assistant professor of epidemiology. In 1947, Jonas Salk accepted the position of associate research professor of bacteriology and director of the virus research laboratory at the University of Pittsburgh.

It was at the University of Pittsburgh that Dr. Salk expanded his experiments on a form of inactivated virus vaccine that would provide immunity against polio. Poliomyelitis, or infantile paralysis, was found to be an acute viral infection caused by one of three polioviruses. A virus entered the human being through the mouth and invaded the bloodstream. In contact with the central nervous system, it attacked motor neurons and caused lesions that resulted in paralysis. Thousands of children and young adults died from the dreaded disease, and the virus attacked the arms and legs of tens of thousands of others (including those of President Franklin Roosevelt) crippling them for life. Dr. Salk found it necessary to weaken the virus with formalin, without destroying its ability to stimulate the human body to produce protective antibodies, and his trial vaccine contained all three polio virus types recognized at the time. After widespread testing of his vaccine (including early tests on his wife Donna, three sons, and himself), Salk announced to the world in 1954 that the four-step vaccine worked. Jonas Salk's great success in immunology received international recognition and, living in a country ravaged by a polio epidemic in 1952, Americans enthusiastically applauded Salk's contribution.

Another Jewish microbiologist, Dr. Albert Bruce Sabin (1906–1993), developed a live virus polio vaccine which could be taken orally and could be stored indefinitely. A World War II veteran from Patterson, New Jersey, Albert Sabin had immigrated with his family from Poland in 1921 when he was a teenager and he, like Jonas Salk, was a graduate of New York University (B.S.,

1928; M.D., 1931). During the war, Dr. Sabin had developed a vaccine for a tropical disease that had plagued U.S. soldiers in the Pacific campaign. After the war, he continued his studies on poliomyelitis as professor of research pediatrics at the University of Cincinnati College of Medicine. After mass field tests in 1957, the use of Sabin's oral polio vaccine became more widespread than Salk's earlier-developed inactivated viral vaccine.

Jonas Salk would go on in the early 1960s to found the Salk Institute of Biological Studies in La Jolla, California, in an attempt to find cures for other diseases, including multiple sclerosis and AIDS. Dr. Salk received many honors and awards for his work, including the Presidential Citation and the Congressional Medal for Distinguished Achievement. Dr. Albert Sabin continued significant medical research, including the study of how normal cells become cancerous. Dr. Sabin published numerous scientific papers and garnered many additional honors, including the U.S. Medal of Science. In 1964, the year of his death, entertainer Eddie Cantor was awarded a medal by President Lyndon B. Johnson for his services to the United States and humanity.

American Jewish Medical Antecedents

Part of the genius of Jonas Salk lay in his ability to distill vast amounts of material published on immunology since the "Golden Age of Bacteriology" emerged during the latter half of the nineteenth century. Jews around the world contributed greatly to this Golden Age. For example, Jewish Bavarian anatomist and pathologist Jacob Henle (1809–1885) is considered one of the founders of modern medicine. In his books of the early 1840s, Henle presents the cell as a new branch of medical study and presents the theory that infectious diseases were caused by specific microorganisms (a germ theory that was not to be proved until four decades later by one of his students). In 1853, a young Jewish lecturer in botany at the University of Breslau, Ferdinand Cohn (1828–1898), classified bacteria as plants rather than protozoa. The next year he published the first book on bacteria, and by 1872 had developed a system of classification for bacteria.

In like manner, the fields of medicine and health have expanded since the latter 1800s, ever multiplying the knowledge accumulated from past decades. Historically, American Jewish scientists, researchers, and practitioners have contributed to this burgeoning field of knowledge, joining their global brethren in making significant discoveries through the decades. Philadelphia-born Isaac Hays (1796–1879) was one of the pioneers in the study of astigmatism and color blindness, and he invented a scalpel for use in cataract surgery. Descended from an early colonial Jewish family that helped in the American Revolution, Isaac Hays edited several important journals, including the prestigious *American Journal of Medical Sciences*. He also became one of the founders of the American Medical Association in 1847 when he proposed a national medical association. In fact, Isaac Hays wrote the code of medical ethics which has been adopted throughout the United States.

Another distinguished Jewish ophthalmologist, Aaron Friedenwald (1836–1902), from a prominent Baltimore family, organized the Association of American Medical Colleges in 1890 while a member of the University of Maryland medical faculty. Aaron's eldest son, Harry Friedenwald (1864–1950), taught ophthalmology at the Baltimore College of Physicians and Surgeons and became a noted author of medical histories. A pioneer in gastroenterology, Henry Illoway (1848–1932), the son of famed Orthodox Rabbi Bernard Illoway, who lived in Baltimore for a time, authored a number of medical texts.

The Philadelphia Jewish family founded by Jacob da Silva Solis, when he refused Italian royalty and immigrated to the United States in 1803, contributed to American medicine and health, as well as to a number of other professions. Grandson Jacob da Silva Solis-Cohen (1838–1927) served as a surgeon in the Union Army during the Civil War, returning home to become a pioneer researcher in laryngology (many Jewish physicians as well as the Jewish heads of both the Union and Confederate medical staffs served selflessly in the Civil War). In fact, in 1867, soon after the Civil War, Jacob Solis-Cohen performed the first laryngectomy for laryngeal cancer, and founded and edited the medical journal, *Archives of Laryngology.*

Jacob's brother, Solomon (1857–1948), was a physician who became known for his nineteenth-century clinical medical research and was appointed professor of clinical medicine at Jefferson Medical College in 1904. It was in these early years at the turn of the century that Solomon Solis-Cohen successfully challenged Philadelphia philanthropists to support a research project to determine the cause of and to aid in the prevention of poliomyelitis. Solomon's daughter, Emily da Silva Solis-Cohen (1890–1966), became a social worker and author. Numbers of other descendants from this Philadelphia Jewish family have dedicated themselves to the American medical and health professions.

A Jewish immigrant from Prussia in 1855, Dr. Simon Baruch (1840–1921), is credited with being the first doctor in the world to diagnose appendicitis and to perform a successful appendectomy in 1888. Settling in South Carolina, he received his medical degree in 1862 during the Civil War and was enlisted as a surgeon in Lee's Confederate Army. Simon Baruch served at the front for the next three years until his capture by Union forces. While imprisoned at Fort McHenry, Simon wrote a manual on military surgery entitled *Two Penetrating Wounds of the Chest*. When published shortly after the war, it remained a standard medical work through World War I.

Although active in South Carolina medicine (elected president of the South Carolina Medical Association in 1874 and elected chairman of the South Carolina Health Board in 1880), Simon Baruch moved to New York to escape the turbulence of the Reconstruction Era. He accepted the chair of hydrotherapy at Columbia University's College of Physicians and Surgeons and, besides engaging in the first operation to remove a ruptured appendix, made significant contributions in treating typhoid fever, malaria, and childhood diseases. Simon also edited the *Journal of Balneology* ("balneology" is the study of the therapeutic use of various types of bathing, i.e., mineral springs, etc.), the *Dietetic and Hygienic Gazette,* and *Gailland's Medical Journal.* One of his sons was the famed Bernard Baruch (1870–1965), a financial wizard who amassed a fortune and then dedicated himself to government service (see conclusion of chapter 7).

The Care of Children

As we have seen from earlier chapters, the welfare of the American child in the latter nineteenth and earlier twentieth centuries weighed heavily on the Jewish community. Jewish social workers and agencies abounded. Jewish hospitals and welfare institutions were founded. In the midst of such concern and activity, it is little wonder that the man who would become the Father of Pediatrics in America, Dr. Abraham Jacobi (1830–1919), was a poor Jewish-German immigrant to pre–Civil War New York. In 1854 Dr. Jacobi invented the laryngoscope, but did not get a patent before another inventor patented it. Interested in children's illnesses, Abraham Jacobi began lecturing on pediatrics in 1857, including a seminal series of lectures at the College of Physicians and Surgeons in New York City. In 1859 he coauthored a textbook for midwives, which also detailed children's diseases, and he authored a book on the throat, which detailed pediatric problems.

Abraham Jacobi was one of the first medical practitioners to practice intubation of the throat (instead of performing a tracheotomy), and he insisted that milk must be boiled for infants (his work inspired the pasteurized milk depots sponsored by New York businessman Nathan Straus—see chapter 1). Dr. Jacobi organized the children's ward at Mt. Sinai Hospital (a hospital which admitted ninety percent of its patients without charge) and, through numerous publications on child care and disease, became the recognized expert in the pediatrics of his time. In fact, Abraham Jacobi founded the American Pediatric Society and, at the age of seventy, was elected president of the American Medical Association.

New York-born Henry Koplik (1858–1927), assistant professor of pediatrics at Bellevue Medical College, was the Jewish pediatrician directly involved in founding the first "milk depot" in the United States, which supplied pasteurized milk free of charge to the needy. As pediatric consultant to New York hospitals, Dr. Koplik was held in high regard, and he published important pediatric papers and books, including *Diseases of Infancy and Childhood* (1902). Henry Koplik discovered that areas of bluish-white surrounded by inflamed red appeared inside the mouths of measles patients. This diagnostic method used by physicians became known as "Koplik's Spots."

It was an Illinois Jewish pediatrician, Isaac Arthur Abt (1867–1955), who expanded knowledge in child nutrition. Born in Wilmington, Illinois, Dr. Abt was professor of pediatrics at Northwestern University (1897–1902; 1908–1955) and Rush Medical College (1902–1908). A trailblazer in the field of nutritional disturbances in infancy, Isaac Abt was the first American pediatrician to use protein milk in the treatment of diarrhea in infants. His book, *The Baby's Food,* was published in 1917, and his eight-volume encyclopedia, *Pediatrics* (1923–1936), quickly became the standard in the field. For his many outstanding contributions to the field of child care, Dr. Isaac Abt was elected the first president of the American Academy of Pediatrics when it was formed in 1931.

Numerous other Jewish physicians and medical specialists have contributed to child care knowledge, including Dr. Julius Hess in the care of the premature infant, Dr. Alexander Nadas in pediatric cardiology, Dr. Henry Schwachman in childhood cystic fibrosis, and Dr. Louis Diamond in pediatric hematology. As a nationally recognized hematologist, Dr. Diamond served in a variety of positions at Boston Children's Hospital from 1927 to 1963, becoming professor of pediatrics at Harvard University.

In 1892, a passionate Dr. Abraham Jacobi declared that between 1866 and 1890 nearly 43,000 human beings in New York City had died of diphtheria and croup, and more than 18,000 had died of scarlet fever. Anguished at only seventy hospital beds in the entire city, Dr. Jacobi cried out in his speech to the New York County Medical Society: "Seventy beds, and 2500 cases are permitted to die annually!" When one considers the large numbers of children of past decades who died in the early years of their life from preventable disease and malnutrition, the discoveries and work of the Jewish child care specialists noted in this section and the efforts of hundreds of others not mentioned become even more significant in American history.

Health and Welfare

Jewish physicians, such as Joseph Goldberger (1874–1929), have devoted themselves to the public health of the United States. Dr. Goldberger served in the U.S. Public Health Service in Washington, D.C., from 1899 until his death. Soon recognized as a public health specialist, Joseph Goldberger researched infectious diseases and specialized in the welfare of the poverty-stricken in America. Just before World War I, Dr. Goldberger discovered the cause of pellagra and introduced nicotinic acid as a preventive cure of this dreaded disease that caused gastrointestinal disturbance, skin eruptions, and mental disorders worldwide.

Polish-born Casimir Funk (1884–1967) became one of America's premier biochemists. While attempting to find the cure for beriberi, a nutritional deficiency disease that resulted in nerve disorder and swelling of the body, the Jewish researcher found a substance in rice hulls which prevented the disease. Dr. Funk called the substance "vitamine," revolutionizing the world of nutrition and becoming the man who gave America the word "vitamin." The substance Casimir Funk isolated was actually vitamin B, a complex of several vitamins, but he continued his research and hypotheses about the importance of vitamins A, C, and D, as well as the B group. This contributed to a wave of nutritional discoveries and the growth of the field of modern dietetics. Dr. Funk also did significant study on internal secretions, diabetes, synthetic chemicals, hormones, and cancer. Joseph Goldberger used Funk's findings to promote public health and, in the process, proved that the water-soluble vitamin was actually a mixture of vitamins. Others used vitamins to cure disease. Jewish researcher Alfred Hess, for instance, introduced vitamin C as a cure for scurvy.

Hungarian-born Jewish pediatrician Bela Schick (1877–1967) developed the skin test for determining susceptibility to diphtheria (known as the "Schick Test"). It is estimated that this one discovery saved tens of thousands of American lives. As a consulting pediatrician at several New York area hospitals from 1923 to 1936, including a key role at Mt. Sinai Hospital, Dr. Schick published a number of important studies, including *Diphtheria* (1931). Appointed clinical professor of pediatrics at Columbia University in 1936, he continued to contribute in his other specialized areas of scarlet fever, tuberculosis research (he discovered what became known as the "Schick sign"), infant nutrition, and childhood diseases.

Some Jewish medical practitioners used their expertise to invent more efficient medical instruments and techniques. For example, during the Great Depression New York surgeon Harry Cohen (1885–1969) invented a surgical forceps for intravesicular use in 1930, invented the clamp tourniquet in 1934, and invented the ligature guide in 1936. Edwin Cohn (1892–1953), chairman of the department of biological chemistry at Harvard University, discovered a method of fractioning blood plasma. He would receive the U.S. Medal of Merit in 1948.

Born into a San Francisco Jewish family, physiologist Joseph Erlanger (1874–1965) of the Washington University School of Medicine in St. Louis won the 1944 Nobel Prize in Medicine with his Jewish student, Wisconsin-born neurophysiologist Herbert Spencer Gasser (1888–1963), for their work on the functional differentiation of nerves and on the influence of pulse pressure on kidney secretion. Through experiments which investigated the electrical properties of nerve fibers, Erlanger and Gasser were able to show that there were different types of fibers and that the rate of conduction was determined by the thickness of the nerve fiber. Dr. Erlanger made numerous contributions to medical science in regard to the cardiovascular system and the nervous system. He also invented a graphic method for measuring blood pressure and studied the mechanism of production of sounds used in measuring blood pressure by the auscultatory method. Dr. Gasser helped to define the differences between sensory and motor nerves, while researching the contraction of muscle and the human perception of pain.

Microbiologist Selman Abraham Waksman (1888–1973) coined the term "antibiotic" while working in his lab at Rutgers University, for years of patiently attempting to isolate a new antibiotic which, when found, he named "streptomycin." Streptomycin was successful against infections that resisted penicillin and sulfa drugs. The Jewish researcher was awarded the Nobel Prize in medicine in 1952 "for his discovery of streptomycin, the first antibiotic effective against tuberculosis." Indeed, as valuable as streptomycin was in treating a wide variety of infections, its most important initial use was in the treatment of tuberculosis. Dr. Selman Waksman used his share of the royalties from streptomycin to establish an Institute of Microbiology at Rutgers University, and he retired as director of this institute in 1958. Selman's son, Byron H. Waksman (b. 1919), became an influential neuroimmunologist, experimental pathologist, educator, and medical association administrator.

Exhibiting similar tenacity, Vienna-born Jewish pathologist Paul Klemperer (1887–1964), through patient and painstaking research into the microscopic patterns of disease, originated the concept of connective tissue disease. Metriculating to the New York Postgraduate School of Medicine in 1923 and appointed pathologist at New York's Mt. Sinai Hospital in 1926, Dr. Klemperer researched lymphomas and malignant nephrosclerosis as well as the structure of the spleen. His careful investigations led to a better understanding of a number of diseases in a quest to find cures. As a naturalized American citizen, Dr. Klemperer discovered several new diseases of the blood vessels, alimentary tract, and the hematopoietic system.

Many of these medical breakthroughs were publicized by one of the most prominent medical editors of the twentieth century, Morris Fishbein (1889–1976). While interviewing Dr. Fishbein for a position with the American Medical Association in 1913, Dr. George H. Simmons, editor and general manager of the AMA, told the twenty-four-year-old Fishbein that there were "three reasons why you should not take this job: One, you are very young; two, you are Jewish; three, the job does not pay very much." A brash young Morris Fishbein replied: "One, I will grow older; two, my religion is nobody's business but my own; three, I did not ask you how much you pay; four, I will not keep the job long anyway." Ironically, he not only was hired, but Dr. Fishbein's "job" with the AMA would span four decades.

Subsequently, the Jewish-born physician from St. Louis, Missouri, built the *Journal of the American Medical Association* into the world's largest medical periodical. During Dr. Fishbein's editorship from 1924 to 1949, the *Journal* was considered by many to be the mouthpiece of American medicine and was a valuable tool of knowledge to tens of thousands of physicians, academicians, medical researchers, and scientists (he also edited a number of other professional medical journals and newsletters).

Dr. Fishbein, however, brought medical knowledge to the average reading public as well. A prolific writer, he wrote daily health columns for a variety of newspapers and magazines, and authored and edited a large number of popular books, including *Modern Home Medical Advisor* (1935), *Popular Medical Encyclopedia* (1946), *Heart Care* (1960), *Modern Home Remedies and How to Use Them* (1966), *Modern Family Health Guide* (1967), *Modern Home Medical Adviser* (1969), and *Handy Home Medical Adviser* (1972).

While Jonas Salk was gaining the education and utilizing the research methods that would lead eventually to the first vaccine for poliomyelitis, Morris Fishbein was taking a leading role in shaping the policies of American medicine through an enormous number of lectures, meetings, and writings as well as editorial responsibilities. Among his many organizational responsibilities, Dr. Morris Fishbein was an early appointee to the advisory board of the National Foundation for Infantile Paralysis. Coincidentally, in 1940, Dr. Jonas Salk would receive a National Research Council fellowship to study viral diseases that happened to be paid for by the National Foundation. Dr. Salk used the fellowship monies to help develop a vaccine against influenza during the Second World War that would prevent an epidemic among U.S. soldiers (tens of thousands of U.S. soldiers had died of influenza during the First World War). Upon arrival at the University of Pittsburgh in 1947, Dr. Jonas Salk was chosen to participate in the National Foundation's polio virus typing program. The National Foundation also supported the work of Dr. Albert Sabin. On a number of occasions during his lifetime, Dr. Fishbein came into contact with Jewish entertainer Eddie Cantor, both on their respective missions to help the National Foundation for Infantile Paralysis and the March of Dimes.

The Shape of the Future

The contributions of American Jewish physicians and medical researchers in these early years would provide the bases for things to come. In 1988, a Jewish research scientist, Gertrude B. Elion (born in New York City in 1918), received the Nobel Prize in medicine (shared with George Hitchings) for forty years of research into cell metabolism that led to the production of the first chemotherapy drugs and antiviral agents. Many of the drugs they developed are now essential in the medical treatment of leukemia, heart disease, malaria, gout, and peptic ulcers.

Ms. Elion had completed her Master of Science degree at New York University while teaching high school chemistry and physics in the New York City school system from 1940 to 1942. Although she would garner numerous honorary doctorates during her lifetime, Gertrude Elion built her distinguished career at Wellcome Research Laboratories, where she began as a biochemist in 1944, moved up to senior research chemist in 1950, and became head of experimental therapy (1966–1983). In 1983, armed with her research skills, wisdom, and forty-two-year-old M.S. degree, Gertrude Elion became research professor of pharmacology at Duke University.

Among her many other contributions, Gertrude Elion (with her colleague Hitchings) developed azathioprine in 1957, a drug which inhibited rejection of organ transplants. Later, they developed azidothymidine (AZT), which was licensed by the U.S. Food and Drug Administration for use in the treatment of AIDS. AZT prolonged life in some AIDS patients and delayed the full-scale symptoms in others by interfering with the virus's replication process.

A consultant to the U.S. Public Health Service in the early 1960s, Elion became involved in cancer research; thus in the 1980s she actively served as president of the American Association of Cancer Research, as a member of the board of scientific counselors to the National Cancer Institute, as a member of the National Cancer Advisory Board, and as a board member of the American Cancer Society.

In 1991, Gertrude Elion was awarded the National Medal of Science and was inducted into both the National Inventors Hall of Fame and the National Women's Hall of Fame. In 1992, she was inducted into the Engineering and Science Hall of Fame. Those that honored her realized that this Jewish woman had dedicated her life to productive research that provided many more options for medical practitioners to use to improve the health of American citizens and, indeed, the peoples of the world.

Cancer Research and Treatment

Dedication to treating and conquering cancer has been held as an important mission for American Jewish physicians and researchers. For example, the Bulgarian-born son of a wealthy European businessman, Isaac Djerassi (b. 1925), pioneered techniques of leukemia treatment and therapy in the 1950s that became standard in following decades. As a member of the medical staff of Children's Hospital Medical Center in Boston from 1954 to 1957, Dr. Djerassi struggled with the massive bleeding that his cancer patients were experiencing and spearheaded the transfusion of large quantities of platelets from cancer-free donors to stop such uncontrollable bleeding in the children. He was awarded the first prize for research at the Sixth International Congress of Hematology (1956) and continued to perfect his procedure as a research associate in the pathology department at Harvard University.

During the 1960s, Isaac Djerassi held the position of assistant professor of pediatrics at the University of Pennsylvania. Here he focused on the use of massive doses of the cancer-fighting drug methotrexate, carefully formulating the proper treatment time and dosages that would lead to healing in his young patients, rather than adverse side effects. Combining other drug therapy, Dr. Djerassi was able to obtain remission in his young patients. He also worked on other types of cancers, experimenting with new forms of immunotherapy as well as chemotherapy. In 1972, the Jewish physician and researcher received one of the highest awards in American medicine—the Albert Lasker Award.

Dr. Djerassi was able to experiment with new forms of immunotherapy because of new discoveries made by medical researchers. Two American Jewish researchers that helped in this information process were Howard M. Temin (b. 1934), a Philadelphia-born oncologist and geneticist, and David Baltimore (b. 1938), a New York-born biochemist. In 1970, these medical researchers quite independently discovered "reverse transcriptase," an enzyme that carries out one of the basic molecular processes in a cell. Interestingly, David Baltimore had worked on the mechanism of replication of the poliovirus in a cell while at the Salk Institute of Biological Studies in La Jolla, California. It was this research that eventually led to his 1970 discovery. Both Baltimore and Temin shared the 1975 Nobel Prize in medicine for "discoveries concerning the interaction between tumor viruses and the genetic material of the cell." David Baltimore, who had become professor of microbiology at the Massachusetts Institute of Technology (soon becoming director of MIT's Institute for Biomedical Research), was appointed president of Rockefeller University in 1990.

Previous to Baltimore's and Temin's discovery, researchers had thought that genetic information only could be passed from DNA to RNA and proteins. Their discovery, that viral RNA could pass information to DNA and *replicate,* produced a conceptual breakthrough in molecular biology that has become an important tool for studying viruses and cancer. Delaware-born Jewish physician and medical researcher Daniel Nathans (b. 1928) applied restriction enzymes to study cancer-virus DNA molecules. This opened the field of recombitant-DNA research and gave another important lead for those dedicated to cancer research. Dr. Daniel Nathans shared the 1978 Nobel Prize in medicine with two other researchers.

An important conceptual part of these discoveries was provided by the Father of Gene-Splicing, Dr. Paul Berg (see chapter 6). One of the men that shared the 1980 Nobel Prize in chemistry with Berg was Jewish molecular biologist Walter Gilbert (b. 1932). Gilbert developed a technique that employed chemical reagents to determine the exact sequence of nucleotide building blocks in nucleic acid. Named American Cancer Society Professor of Molecular Biology at Harvard University in 1972, Dr. Gilbert has turned his attention to the implications of his discoveries on the treatment of cancer patients. Walter Gilbert's gene-splicing research, for instance, has led to bacterially produced interferon, a cellular protein which acts to inhibit the growth of a virus.

It was the Jewish Italian-American biochemist, Salvador Luria (1912–1991), whose research during the Second World War proved that genetic mutations could occur in bacteriophages (viruses that infect bacteria). In 1959 Salvador Luria took a teaching position at MIT, and shared the 1969 Nobel Prize in medicine for his discoveries concerning the genetic structures of viruses and the replication mechanism they employ. His many awards and prominence in the field led to his founding and directing the Center for Cancer Research at MIT (1972–1985). Dr. Luria's discoveries, however, had significant implications for subsequent medical research concerning infectious diseases. Once again, Jewish researchers would make important contributions in the field of viral research and bacterial genetics.

Infectious Diseases

Building on past discoveries and research knowledge, Baruch S. Blumberg (b. 1925) shared the 1976 Nobel Prize in medicine for his part in "discoveries concerning new mechanisms for the origin and dissemination of infectious diseases." Specifically, Dr. Blumberg had discovered the hepatitis B antigen, isolated it, and proved that it triggers an antibody response to the hepatitis virus. Baruch Blumberg's discovery was crucial in laying the foundation for later work on hepatitis B vaccines. His discovery also provided ideas on how to screen blood donors and prevent them from passing on the virus to unsuspecting recipients.

Two other Jewish Nobel Prize winners who were active during the time of Jonas Salk, geneticist Joshua Lederberg (b. 1925) and biochemist Arthur Kornberg (b. 1918), made important strides in the study of infectious diseases. Lederberg shared the 1958 Nobel Prize in medicine for his discovery of how bacterial genes are recombined, exchanged, and inherited. Through a process he named "transduction," Joshua Lederberg displayed how viruses could transfer genetic material from one bacterium to another. In his 1956 article, "Genetic Transduction" in *American Scientist* (1956), the Yale Ph.D. emphasized to researchers that the discovery of transduction was "an enterprise which can challenge the skills and imagination of specialists in a dozen sciences." His analysis was prophetic, and Dr. Lederberg's discoveries had broad significance in regard to differentiating tumor cells.

Arthur Kornberg would share the Nobel Prize in medicine the next year for (in the words of the Nobel Prize committee) "their discoveries of the mechanisms of the biologic synthesis of ribonucleic and deoxyribonucleic acids." His significant accomplishment was in his 1956 formation of DNA molecules in vitro (literally, "in glass," artificially maintained in a test tube, etc.). The DNA he formed was biologically inactive, but it did reveal unknown enzymes that contribute to problems in cell growth. Thus, while Dr. Joshua Lederberg added information on the biological mechanisms involving nucleic acids in the life of a cell, Dr. Arthur Kornberg discovered enzymes that held the key to cell growth and transmission of genetic information. Dr. Kornberg went on to head a research team at Stanford University that a decade later (1967) would produce the first in vitro replication of infective viral DNA with full biological activity. Thus, his contribution to further research of infectious diseases was priceless.

Other researchers, such as Jewish biochemist Marshall W. Nirenberg (b. 1927), would add to cell knowledge, laying the groundwork for the solution of the genetic code. Dr. Nirenberg shared the 1968 Nobel Prize in medicine by demonstrating another key to how genes determine cell function. (In 1961 through complicated procedures, he and his colleagues made the first discovery of a code equivalence between a nucleic acid component and an amino acid.) Jewish biochemist and immunologist Gerald Maurice Edelman (b. 1929) shared the 1972 Nobel Prize in medicine for his research in the structure of antibody molecules. Dr. Edelman was able to establish the complete chemical structure of gamma globulin, an antibody molecule which has a crucial role in protecting the human body against disease. Such important discoveries helped Harvard scientist and professor, Venezuela-born Baruj Benacerraf (b. 1920) bring his lifelong quest to an apex. The Jewish physician and former head of the Department of Allergy and Infectious Diseases of the National Institute of Health in Bethesda, Maryland, received the 1980 Nobel Prize in medicine for his discovery of a group of genes instrumental in building an organic immune system. This discovery has led to more progress in helping human beings fight infectious diseases and, also, has furthered cancer research.

It is impossible to elucidate the tens of thousands of Jewish physicians and medical researchers that have dedicated their energies to solving health problems in the United States. From clinical practitioners and professors to lab directors and medical administrators, they often labor tirelessly in their medical niches—almost all without national recognition. Some discoveries, such as George Wald's discovery that vitamin A was in the retina of the eye (which led to a greater emphasis on proper nutrition for eyesight as well as general health), would lead decades later to national and international recognition (Nobel Prize, 1954). American Jewish geneticist Stanley Cohen and Italian-Jewish biochemist Rita Levi-Montalcini finally would be recognized for their seminal isolation of the protein called nerve growth factor in the early 1950s that led to so many subsequent discoveries and challenges to disease. By the time of their 1986 Nobel Prize in medicine for this feat, they had made numerous other important discoveries and contributions. Like Gertrude Elion, their belated recognition four decades later only served as a reminder of the importance of doing one's best in a lifetime of medical service.

But, for most of these American Jews in the fields of medicine and health, their historic efforts are basically rewarded by the recognition that they are making the world a better place and that they are building an edifice that may provide better health, better medical care, and a better life for billions of peoples around the globe. It is the same courage, tenacity, and spirit that led Jonas Salk to use his experimental vaccine on himself and on his family. And, medical study itself has touched the lives of many American Jews who did not pursue a career in medicine, but have been deeply touched by their experience with medicine.

Even an influential Jewish businessman, such as Armand Hammer (1898–1990), was touched early on in his life by the field of medicine. After earning his Bachelor of Science degree from Columbia University in 1919, Armand Hammer studied medicine at Columbia's medical school, earning his M.D. in 1921. Among his many philanthropic endeavors, the wealthy Hammer established a center for cancer research at the Salk Institute for Biological Studies many decades after choosing business over medicine. Jewish entertainer Eddie Cantor would have been proud that funds sufficient to build the original Salk Institute for Biological Studies and $2 million annually for ten years to maintain the Salk Institute were donated by the National Foundation for Infantile Paralysis (including funds from the March of Dimes, to which Cantor and President Franklin Roosevelt had conceived and contributed).

In fact, historically, Jewish entertainers, government officials, and business executives have been intricately linked in such humanitarian endeavors. As for designers and builders, one of the major architects of the twentieth century, Jewish-born Louis Isadore Kahn (1901–1974), designed and oversaw the construction of the Salk Institute for Biological Studies (see chapter 7).

JOURNALISM AND LITERATURE

THE PULITZER PRIZE IS A HIGHLY COVETED AWARD. BESTOWED each spring in the United States for distinguished achievements in journalism, literature, music, the arts (as well as a gold medal for meritorious public service by a newspaper), Pulitzer Prizes exude prestige and symbolize success. Famed American editor and publisher Joseph Pulitzer (1847–1911) established the award by specifying in his will that $2 million be given to Columbia University to found a school of journalism and that $500,000 be used for annual prizes for the advancement of journalism and literature. Joseph Pulitzer suggested that there should be four journalism awards and four awards for "letters" (novel, play, history, and biography). Since the first Pulitzer Prizes were awarded in 1917, the advisory board has expanded additional awards and categories. To this day, Pulitzer Prizes are administered by the Graduate School of Journalism at Columbia University founded by Joseph Pulitzer and are bestowed by Columbia's board of trustees. A wide variety of literary experts play a role, however, in the nominations and final selections.

Joseph Pulitzer would have wanted it that way, for his own work had survived critical analysis and a demanding public. Born the son of a Jewish grain merchant in Hungary, young Pulitzer had thoughts of military grandeur and left home at the age of seventeen to find a European army that would let him fight. Discouraged that the armed forces of Austria, France, and Great Britain rejected him because of poor eyesight and debatable health,

Joseph happened upon a U.S. recruiter in Germany who was enlisting Europeans to fight for the Union Army in the Civil War. Joseph Pulitzer signed up, journeyed to America, and fought in the cavalry of the Union Army.

After the war, Pulitzer worked as a laborer in St. Louis, Missouri, and became a United States citizen. He began his journalistic career as a reporter for the German-language newspaper the *Westliche Post* in 1868. He gained such a fine reputation as a journalist that he was encouraged to run for the Missouri House of Representatives. He won. Joseph Pulitzer also bought part interest in the newspaper and became managing editor. His journalistic and managerial skills catapulted the newspaper to prominence, and he sold his shares at a large profit in 1875. Serving as the Washington, D.C. correspondent for the *New York Sun* (1876–1877), Pulitzer proved his journalistic skills in English. Returning to Missouri, he purchased the *St. Louis Dispatch* and the *Evening Post,* two newspapers that were struggling. Joseph Pulitzer combined them into the *St. Louis Post-Dispatch* and turned them into reform-minded bastions of journalistic pride, investigative reporting, and complete news coverage. Circulation and advertisement increased dramatically with Pulitzer's innovative ideas and managerial skill. Within four years, Joseph Pulitzer gained great wealth.

Joseph Pulitzer had recognized the signs of the times. Following the Civil War, the rise of the Industrial Revolution in the United States, the growth and expansion of the American population, advances in communication, and increased advertising had paved the way for mass circulation newspapers. Certainly, the *St. Louis Post-Dispatch* had earned a fortune as well as the respect of the nation. (To this day the Pulitzer family owns the newspaper and it continues to be well-respected.) Nevertheless, friends groaned and rivals smirked when Joseph Pulitzer decided to move to New York City to buy the poorly managed and money-losing *New York World* in 1883. Joseph Pulitzer had initiated a new age of journalism, however, and added flourishes that have become standards in newspapers today. By 1886 the *New York World* was earning $500,000 a year and had the largest circulation in the nation.

Pulitzer had pulled off this major coup through creative ideas, such as adding a sports section and a section for women's fash-

ions. He composed better illustrations and a more commanding look for his papers. Above all, expanded news coverage,
journalistic skill, and a crusading spirit won readers. Pulitzer established a sister paper, the *New York Evening World* in 1887. The
results were the same. Unwilling to rest on his laurels, Joseph
Pulitzer continued to improve his newspapers. Pulitzer's *New
York World* even ran the first successful comic strip series (Richard
Outcault's "Down in Hogan's Alley"). Ethically, his newspapers
attacked intolerance and fought prejudice. His rivals often
referred to him as the "Jew Pulitzer," and he responded with
sensitive articles on the value of immigrants and their cultural
contributions. There is no question that Joseph Pulitzer helped
to establish the foundations and modern techniques used by
American newspapers in the twentieth century, and he is indicative of the diverse American Jewish contributions throughout
the literary world.

The Journalist's Craft

Growing numbers of Jewish men and women contributed to
the nation's expanding press coverage. Early examples may be
found in enterprising editors, such as Mordecai Manuel Noah
(1785–1851). Born in Philadelphia, Noah edited the *City Gazette*
in Charleston, South Carolina, before the War of 1812 and
edited the *National Advocate* newspaper in New York City after
the War of 1812. Mordecai Manuel Noah exhibited a pure journalistic style and flair for editing. A prolific playwright and a
passionate patriot, he also became a respected political leader,
diplomat, law enforcement officer, and justice of the Court of
Sessions during his forty-year career.

Mordecai Noah had set the stage for a cadre of devoted and
multitalented journalists of the twentieth century. Jewish journalists that had immigrated to the United States or traveled to
other countries brought a cross-cultural expertise that helped
to inform the American reader. For example, Russian-born
Eugene Lyons (b. 1898) had emigrated from Russia as a child
and received his education in New York City. After the Russian
Revolution, Lyons spent seven years as the United Press correspondent in Russia and alerted the American public to the weak-
nesses inherent in Communist totalitarianism. Kentucky-born

Isaac Marcosson (1876–1961), an expert in business and commerce, was in St. Petersburg during the Russian Revolution and recorded his experiences for the American public. Both Lyons and Marcosson wrote for national magazines as well as authoring numerous books. After the Second World War, Lyons became senior editor of *Reader's Digest.*

The "Father of Photojournalism," German-born Alfred Eisenstaedt (1898–1995), was also Jewish. He began his career in 1929 with Pacific and Atlantic Photos in Berlin. Fortunate for Eisenstaedt, the Associated Press purchased the firm in 1931. Eisenstaedt's superb documentary photographs for the Associated Press launched his reputation in the early 1930s as Europe's premier press photographer. He traveled to the hotspots in Europe and around the world. In 1935, he covered the Ethiopian War with Italy for the Associated Press, and his "Feet of an Ethiopian Soldier" photograph in 1935 won him international acclaim. When he immigrated to the United States later that year, newly founded *Life* magazine employed him. At *Life* he perfected the candid camera technique that subsequent photojournalists would copy. After World War II, he photographed hundreds of prominent individuals and covered thousands of significant events. Photojournalist Alfred Eisenstaedt had the canny ability to be in the right place at the right time and the patience to record the event on film for the American people and, indeed, the world.

Jewish-born and Harvard-educated journalist Walter Lippmann (1889–1974) has been widely acclaimed as the "renaissance man" of the American press. Certainly, he had a powerful effect on the American public, and readers marveled at his understanding of the world of politics, economics, foreign affairs, and philosophy. Co-founder of the *New Republic* journal, Lippmann joined the staff of the *New York World* in 1921 and seemed to fit in well with the crusading spirit of the newspaper. By 1929 he was the editorial page editor. In the 1930s he began to write a column on public affairs for the *New York Herald Tribune.* Soon it was syndicated in newspapers around the world. In his lifetime, Walter Lippmann was awarded two Pulitzer Prizes (1958 and 1962, for international reporting), and he authored nearly thirty books.

As for influential twentieth-century columnists, the Jewish community has contributed quite a few. Art Buchwald (b. 1925), for instance, served in the U.S. Marine Corps during World War II and, after attending the University of Southern California, became the Paris correspondent for *Variety,* a Hollywood trade paper founded in 1905 by another Jewish journalist, Sime Silverman (1872–1933). Honing his talents as a columnist, he wrote "Paris After Dark" for the *New York Herald Tribune.* Humorous and satirical columns entitled "Europe's Lighter Side" and "Art Buchwald in Paris" began appearing in U.S. newspapers in the early 1950s. When Buchwald returned to the United States in the mid–1950s, he aimed his humor at government officials and the Washington, D.C. milieu. His column became so popular that *The Los Angeles Times* syndicated it. In 1982 Art Buchwald received the Pulitzer Prize for distinguished commentary, and he has authored a variety of humorous books. Art Buchwald's recent book about his traumatic childhood is, however, serious and powerful. This best-selling memoir, *Leaving Home,* touched the hearts of tens of thousands of Americans.

New York-born Walter Winchell (1897–1972) has at times been labeled the "Father of the Modern Gossip Column." A young vaudeville actor who entered the field of journalism, his syndicated column "On Broadway" at one time commanded space in over 800 daily newspaper franchises across the United States (over 35 million readers). He began writing about political figures as well as the rich and famous, and became friends with industrial tycoons and world leaders. Dedicated fans waited breathlessly for his sensational disclosures (even stock market tips peppered his reporting), and Winchell garnered an illustrious spectrum of sources that sky-rocketed him to the top of the journalistic enterprise. Beginning in 1932, Walter Winchell broadcast his own Sunday evening radio program and gathered tens of millions of listeners.

The New York Times features a number of Jewish columnists from a spectrum of conservative to liberal ideologies. William L. Safire (b. 1929), Anthony J. Lewis (b. 1927), and A. M. Rosenthal (b. 1922) appear on the op-ed pages during each week, and each man has a distinguished journalistic career. William Safire's investigation of the financial affairs of President Jimmy Carter's special assistant and friend, Bert Lance, won a Pulitzer Prize in 1978. Anthony Lewis won the Pulitzer Prize for national reporting in 1955 for his disclosure of false charges against a U.S. Navy civilian employee (Abraham Chasanow) during the heyday of McCarthyism. The whole incident was turned into a popular film, and Lewis continued a career of attacking injustice. A. M. Rosenthal served all over the world as a *Times* correspondent before assuming duties as executive editor. In 1960 he won the Pulitzer Prize for international reporting. Passing on his editorial responsibilities to others, his columns now reflect the vintage views of a veteran journalist. And, much could be said for the columns and reporting of veteran newswoman, Flora Lewis, who has not only graced the op-ed section of *The New York Times,* but has had her own syndicated column (in *Newsday,* 1967–1972), has published articles in many major American magazines, has written several books, and has won numerous journalistic awards for foreign reporting.

The historian marvels at the number of Pulitzer Prizes awarded to Jewish reporters, far outnumbering their percentage of the population. Gentile colleagues often have nominated them and recognized them for their journalistic skill and meritorious service. David Broder (b. 1929), son of a dentist in Chicago, has used the scholarly approach to his journalism and has been acclaimed as one of the premier interpreters of the contemporary political scene. Working the beat for a number of newspapers, he received the Pulitzer Prize in 1973 for his commentary on politics in America. The same year, German-born Max Frankel (b. 1930) of *The New York Times* won the Pulitzer Prize for international reporting. He and his family had to flee the Nazis in 1938, and he became a naturalized citizen after World War II. Like Broder, he earned a master's degree and never really ended his educational pursuits.

Harvard-educated Sydney Schanberg (b. 1934), the son of a Jewish grocer in Clinton, Massachusetts, won the 1976 Pulitzer Prize for international reporting. After serving in the Army, Schanberg began his career at *The New York Times* as a copyboy in 1959. Working as a reporter in the 1960s, he was appointed the *Times'* Southeast Asia correspondent in 1973. He became known for his accurate and graphic descriptions of the turmoil in Vietnam and Cambodia after the U.S. pullout. Even when the editors at *The New York Times* determined that the situation had deteriorated to the point of being extremely dangerous and asked Sydney Schanberg to come back to the United States, he continued to stay and file stories on the atrocities under the Pol Pot regime in Cambodia. These reports earned him the commendation of the Pulitzer committee.

Meyer Berger (1898–1959) of *The New York Times* won the Pulitzer Prize for general and local reporting in 1950. An expert on the lore and life of the East Coast, a collection of his articles had appeared in print during World War II. Berger was recognized by the Pulitzer committee, however, for his coverage of a shooting spree by a mentally despondent war veteran. Thirteen people were killed. With a sensitive spirit, Meyer Berger sent the Pulitzer Prize money to the attacker's mother in an effort to help her in her period of grief. The next year Berger's *The Story of The New York Times, 1851–1951* was published. By that time, *The New York Times* had won two Pulitzer "meritorious service" awards (1918 and 1944) and had a cadre of Pulitzer winners (both Jewish and Gentile) on its staff. Like the *St. Louis Post-Dispatch,* the *Times* was one of the few newspapers in the United States to continue to be owned and operated by a family from Jewish roots during the twentieth century. It is without question considered to be the most authoritative daily newspaper in the United States and has more Pulitzer Prize winners on its staff than any other newspaper today.

Since 1922 Pulitzer Prizes have also been awarded for exemplary cartoons. In the field of journalism, many Jewish cartoonists have made their mark. For example, an all-purpose cartoonist, Reuben L. "Rube" Goldberg (1883–1970) started his career creating sports cartoons for San Francisco newspapers. In 1907 he moved to New York to work for the *Evening Mail.* For the next thirty years, Rube Goldberg's syndicated comic strips, humor panels, and editorial cartoons gained an international following. He had the canny ability to monitor the pulse of the world. Becoming a political cartoonist for the *New York Sun* in 1938, Goldberg won the Pulitzer Prize in 1947 for his satirical drawing "Peace Today." So respected was he by his fellow cartoonists that the National Cartoonists' Society named its annual award the "Reuben."

Another famed Jewish newspaper cartoonist, Chicago-born Herbert L. Block (b. 1909), won three Pulitzers (1942, 1954, and 1979) for his boldly drawn satirical political cartoons. He signed his cartoons "Herblock," and his editorial drawings have been republished in a number of collections, including *The Herblock Book* (1952) and *Straight Herblock* (1964). In 1966 Herbert L. Block was commissioned to design a postage stamp commemorating the 175th anniversary of the Bill of Rights. Herbert L. Block is considered one of the most influential editorial cartoonists in the modern period.

In the realm of investigative reporting, Jewish reporters have exhibited bravery, single-minded purpose, and skill in the midst of very difficult circumstances. With his Yale-educated and Gentile colleague Bob Woodward, Carl Bernstein (b. 1944) pieced together the Watergate scandal of the Nixon administration in the midst of intense opposition and governmental deception. The son of labor union leaders, Bernstein was born and raised in Washington, D.C., and had worked for newspapers since the age of sixteen. Although he attended several universities parttime while working full-time, Bernstein never finished college. Carl Bernstein had a passion, however, for news reporting and had gained a reputation as a street-wise, tough-nosed reporter. Longer-haired Bernstein and preppy Woodward made a strong team when they were assigned to what appeared to be a "routine break-in" in the Watergate complex. Their dedicated investigative reporting and the editorial support of the newspaper produced a 1973 Pulitzer gold medal for the *Washington Post* for public service. The editorial cartoons that backed the men up were drawn by none other than Herbert A. Block (Herblock).

Television Journalism

With the advent of television journalism, many Jewish men and women found their niche. While a whole volume could be written on these individuals and their impact, the brief mention of a few will underscore Jewish contributions in this area. For instance, Barbara Walters (b. 1931) was born into a Jewish family in Boston, Massachusetts. Her father owned a number of nightclubs, and she traveled back and forth during her schooling from New York to Miami. She received a B.A. in English from Sarah Lawrence College (1953), where she decided to pursue a career in television. For eight years she helped as a writer at the NBC affiliate, RCA-TV, and even showed some talent at public relations. In 1961 she joined the "Today Show" on NBC as a writer and occasional on-the-air feature reporter.

Although there were few opportunities in the 1960s for female television news reporters, Barbara Walters exhibited keen intellect and skillful questioning as an interviewer. The trust she elicited from those she interviewed and the success of each interview prodded NBC executives to add any interview she landed into the "Today Show." In 1971 she was given her own television show, "Not for Women Only" and, with great media attention, she switched networks in 1976 to co-anchor "The ABC Evening News" (at the unprecedented annual salary of $1 million). She continues her interview "specials" and co-hosts "20/20" with Hugh Downs. Barbara Walters has reached the summit of television journalism and is credited with turning the personal interview into an artform.

Jewish correspondent Mike Wallace is best known for his work on the news program "60 Minutes." Wallace co-anchored and co-edited the program from its inception in 1968. Born Myron Leon Wallace in 1918, "Mike" was raised in an immigrant family in a Boston suburb. A dedicated reporter for his high school newspaper, Wallace was also a crucial member of the debate team. After graduating in 1935, he attended the University of Michigan, intending to become a teacher. The college radio station, however, captured his attention, and he devoted long hours to that pursuit. Receiving a bachelor's degree in 1939, he worked the next few years for a number of Michigan radio stations as an announcer and radio "actor." Serving in the Navy during World War II, Mike Wallace returned to a fairly successful radio career and during the 1950s began his television career as a news reporter.

In 1957 "The Mike Wallace Interview" aired on ABC. His respected but, at times, inquisitorial interviews earned him a reputation as a fierce investigative journalist. Ratings increased and, in 1963, he joined CBS as a special correspondent. Soon he was hosting "Morning News with Mike Wallace," a popular CBS program. His many journalistic awards and international fame have come, however, from his long tenure with "60 Minutes." The popular Sunday evening news program has garnered high ratings and spawned a plethora of shows trying to copy its success. "60 Minutes" as a television magazine program and Mike Wallace's involvement with it has opened new avenues for television journalism.

Jewish journalists have been actively involved in sports writing and broadcasting throughout the twentieth century. Many colorful figures have enlivened sports journalism during the twentieth century. In the modern era, none matched the *chutzpa* of Howard Cosell (1920–1995). If Mike Wallace at times was termed "abrasive," Cosell was that and more. Outrageous, obnoxious, and outspoken, Howard Cosell became the sportscaster fans loved to hate. He played the part well, but sports lovers soon saw beyond the showman's facade and found in Howard Cosell a television journalist of integrity and sincerity—a man who cared about people and about the higher values inherent in sports.

Howard Cosell was born William Howard Cohen in Winston-Salem, North Carolina, to Polish immigrant parents. While still a young boy, Howard's father found work as an accountant for a chain of clothing stores. The young lad grew up in Brooklyn during the Roaring Twenties and the Great Depression. Even then he loved sports and became sports editor of the Alexander Hamilton High School newspaper. He also ran track. Howard wanted to be a reporter, but his family insisted that he go to college and on to law school. He completed his B.A. degree in English at New York University in 1940 (Phi Beta Kappa) and soon graduated from the NYU Law School as his parents had wished. He passed the law exam in 1941. After serving in the Army during the Second World War, Howard Cosell had a successful law practice, but destiny dictated that he enter broadcasting. When an ABC program manager asked him to donate his time to host a Saturday afternoon television program in which Little League players were introduced to professional stars, Cosell could not resist. The program was such a hit that ABC offered him a full-time contract in 1956.

Nothing but success followed. He worked in both radio and television for ABC and was active in a number of sports. He covered heavyweight boxing matches. He announced the first Monday night football telecasts in 1971 and continued for more than two decades. In 1977 he added Monday night baseball to his repertoire. Through every decade of his broadcasting career, he hosted a number of radio and television sports shows and produced a number of television documentaries. A civil rights advocate, Howard Cosell was the first announcer to express outrage when Muhammad Ali was deprived of his heavyweight boxing title in 1967 for the boxer's refusal on religious grounds to fight in Vietnam. Howard also denounced international racism at the 1968 Olympic Games and in 1982 actually stopped announcing boxing matches because of the serious injury that could occur from mismatched bouts. Among his numerous awards, Howard Cosell was named Broadcaster of the Year by the International Radio and Television Society in 1974 and was the first television sports journalist to be honored as Poynter Fellow at Yale University.

Perhaps the joining of the writer's craft to television journalism is viewed most distinctly in the lives of two Jewish brothers—Bernard Kalb (b. 1922) and Marvin Kalb (b. 1930)—the sons of East European immigrants who settled in New York City. Bernard graduated from the City College of New York in 1941 and served in the Army during World War II. Eight years younger, Marvin graduated from the City College of New York in 1951 and earned a master's degree at Harvard in 1953. He then went to serve in the Army for two years. By that time, Bernard had been a reporter for *The New York Times* (since 1946), and was appointed Southeast Asia correspondent in 1956. Marvin taught Russian history at Harvard the same year, then accepted a position with the U.S. State Department as press attaché in Moscow. While his brother was sending frequent articles from Southeast Asia, Marvin traveled to the area and wrote a series of articles for the *New York Times Magazine*. He also accepted a position with CBS News as their New York-based reporter and staff researcher.

The two brothers' lives converged once again at CBS News. Marvin was appointed Moscow correspondent in 1960. Bernard joined CBS News in 1962, serving much of the 1960s as bureau chief and reporter in Southeast Asia. Both men had central roles to play during the turbulent decade. Marvin Kalb was in the midst of the Cold War, enlightening Americans on everything from the building of the Berlin Wall to the Cuban Missile Crisis. Marvin also introduced Americans to the writings of dissident Russian novelist Alexander Solzhenitsyn. The excellence of his reporting won him his first Emmy Award. Southeast Asia-based Bernard Kalb was in the midst of the escalation of the Vietnam War during the 1960s. His fine reporting earned him an Overseas Press Club Award.

Superb journalistic talents and a professional style thrust the brothers into more exposure on American television. Marvin Kalb became CBS News diplomatic correspondent in Washington. Bernard Kalb began anchoring the "CBS Morning News" in 1970. Both brothers left CBS News for NBC News in 1980. They were familiar faces throughout the decade, not only during news reports, but as guests on interview programs and hosts of documentaries and specials. From CNN reports in the 1990s to PBS specials, the Kalb brothers may be viewed weekly on television. Individually, the Kalb brothers have won many awards. As the world approached the twenty-first century, the Kalb brothers displayed their journalistic skills through regular articles in magazines and newspapers, and dedicated their lives to bringing foreign and domestic events to the American reader and viewer.

Literary Skill

In the twentieth century, numbers of Jewish journalists have turned their reporter's instinct into literary creativity. Among their many journalistic endeavors, Bernard and Marvin Kalb wrote the biography *Kissinger* (1974), and they later composed a novel entitled *The Last Ambassadors* (1981) about the last days of Vietnam. Marvin Kalb wrote a number of books on his own, including *Eastern Exposure* (1958) about politics in Eastern Europe and *The Volga: A Political Journey Through Russia* (1967). Marvin also co-authored a novel with "Nightline" host Ted Koppel. Carl Bernstein (with Bob Woodward) wrote *All The President's Men* (1974), a behind-the-scenes look at the unraveling of the Watergate story. It soon became a movie, with Dustin Hoffman acting the role of Bernstein and Robert Redford playing Woodward. Bernstein and Woodward collaborated one more time on another bestseller, *The Final Days* (1976), about the final fifteen months of the Nixon presidency. The *New York Post*'s Jewish correspondent and editorial writer Joseph P. Lash (b. 1909) won the Pulitzer Prize, Francis Parkman Prize, and National Book Award for *Eleanor and Franklin* (1971), one of his many books.

Among his other works, Anthony Lewis wrote the popular *Gideon's Trumpet* in 1964, about the Supreme Court's reversal of the conviction of poverty-stricken Clarence Earl Gideon. His op-ed colleagues at *The New York Times* published books as well. The same year that *Gideon's Trumpet* was published, William Safire wrote *Plunging into Politics,* suggesting methods for running political campaigns without party bosses in control, and A. M. Rosenthal wrote *Thirty-Eight Witnesses.* In a touching and riveting account, Rosenthal's book pointed out that in 1964 thirty-eight neighbors had heard the screams of twenty-eight-year-old Catherine Genovese as she was brutally attacked in a residential area of New York City. Some may have even viewed the assault and murder as she was stabbed in three separate attacks during a forty-minute period. No one, however, came forward to help her. No one called the police during the prolonged assault. Her neighbors refused to get involved. A. M. Rosenthal's ethical challenge in *Thirty-Eight Witnesses* pierced the moral conscience of the American public.

The Father of Photojournalism, Alfred Eisenstaedt, not only lived to see his work exhibited in museums in the United States and around the world, but his photographs were collected into books with his scintillating descriptions and recollections. After nearly four decades of work, *Witness to Our Time* appeared in 1966. It was followed in 1969 by his first autobiographical work, *The Eye of Eisenstaedt,* and a number of other collections, including *Witness to Nature* (1971), *Eisenstaedt's Album* (1976). Another autobiographical work, *Eisenstaedt on Eisenstaedt,* was published in 1985.

David Halberstam (b. 1934), son of a Jewish surgeon and a Jewish schoolteacher, began his journalistic career even as he attended Harvard University during the early 1950s (he graduated in 1955). Active in reporting the growing Civil Rights movement in the South, Halberstam was a veteran newspaper journalist by the time he joined the staff of *The New York Times* in 1960. Critical of the Kennedy administration's handling of Vietnam, he shared a Pulitzer Prize in 1964 for his critical reporting of the Southeast Asia situation in 1963. His experiences and detailed research led to publication of *The Making of a Quagmire* (1965) and his best-seller, *The Best and the Brightest* (1972). By the time of the latter volume, David Halberstam was a free-lance journalist for major American magazines. His next research project concerned the media's influence on elections

101

and the political process. It resulted in another blockbuster, *The Powers That Be* (1979). A prolific writer, Halberstam even has a volume on sports entitled *The Breaks of the Game* (1981).

In similar fashion, Theodore H. White, born in the Boston family of a Jewish lawyer in 1915, turned his journalistic career into literary gold. His father had died during the Great Depression, and Theodore worked as a newsboy. He received a newspaper scholarship and with it was able to work his way through Harvard (graduating in 1938 with a degree in Chinese history and oriental languages). He became *Time* magazine's China correspondent in 1939 and coauthored his first book, *Thunder Out of China* (1946). A number of other books followed, but it was his volume *The Making of the President 1960* (1961) that gained him national fame. He chronicled the presidential elections of 1964, 1968, and 1972 in similar fashion. American readers found his analyses fresh and enlightening. Theodore H. White had begun a new genre of popular literature. Other books and articles followed in the wake of a flourishing career. In a grand finale of sorts to a series that had brought him such fame, White published *America in Search of Itself: The Making of the President 1956–1980* (1982).

In the realm of historical research, Jewish contributions are far too numerous to do justice in this short chapter. For example, Brooklyn-born Oscar Handlin won the 1952 Pulitzer Prize for his book *The Uprooted: The Epic Story of the Great Migrations that Made the American People* (1951) and went on to an illustrious literary career as well as academic career (as a Harvard history professor). The American historian Barbara Wertheim Tuchman (1912–1989) built upon her early research technique as a correspondent and her captivating style as a magazine journalist. With detailed documentation from primary written sources and with travel to the area about which she was writing, Barbara Tuchman captured the environment as well as the time period.

Tuchman was awarded two Pulitzer Prizes in her lifetime, but each of her eight books warranted rave reviews. In the general nonfiction category, she won the 1963 Pulitzer for her best-seller *The Guns of August* (1962) about the early battles of the First World War. The 1972 Pulitzer Prize for general nonfiction was awarded to her for *Stilwell and the American Experience in China, 1911–1945* (1971). It was a Book-of-the-Month Club selection.

Her *A Distant Mirror: The Calamitous 14th Century* (1978) was a blockbusting best-seller, and she was awarded a gold medal for history by the American Academy and Institute of Arts and Letters the same year. Early in 1979, Barbara Wertheim Tuchman was elected the president of the American Academy, the first woman to hold this position.

The Gentile historian continues to be amazed at the expertise and contributions of his Jewish colleagues. Some of them have laid the groundwork upon which modern historians and graduate students continue to build. Born in Buffalo, New York, Columbia University professor Richard Hofstadter (1916–1970), who had a Jewish father, questioned traditional positive views of the old rural order and saw Franklin D. Roosevelt's New Deal as a "drastic new departure" that was "different from anything that had yet happened in the United States." Hofstadter's earlier works, such as *Social Darwinism in American Thought, 1860–1915* (1944), *American Political Tradition and the Men Who Made It* (1948), *The Development and Scope of Higher Education in the United States* (1953), and *The Development of Academic Freedom in the United States* (1955), set the stage for his two Pulitzer Prize winners. Professor Hofstadter's *The Age of Reform from Bryan to FDR* (1955) was the book which won the Pulitzer for history in 1956 for its skill in linking the middle class progressive movement to psychological "status anxiety" rather than economic factors; and his 1964 Pulitzer Prize winner for general nonfiction, *Anti-Intellectualism in American Life* (1963), was a significant contribution to the field of intellectual history. Richard Hofstadter's *Paranoid Style in American Politics* (1965), which catalogued right-wing failures, built upon and expanded the earlier themes. While historians might disagree with some of Hofstadter's theses, they cannot ignore him or his important contributions.

In the 1940s when Hofstadter began making his mark at Columbia University, Atlanta-born Daniel J. Boorstin (b. 1914) joined the faculty at the University of Chicago, emphasizing in his writing the social, economic, political, and environmental factors that shaped the American experience. The son of a Russian lawyer and his wife, Jewish immigrants who moved to Tulsa, Oklahoma, when he was two years old, Daniel Boorstin graduated from Harvard University and studied at Oxford University under a Rhodes Scholarship. Author of many important works, he is best known for his historical trilogy of the United States entitled *The Americans* (*The Colonial Experience,* 1958; *The National Experience,* 1965; *The Democratic Experience,* 1973), for which he received the 1974 Pulitzer Prize for history at the age of sixty. Daniel Boorstin was appointed director of the Smithsonian Institution's National Museum of History and Technology in 1969, and in 1975 he became the twelfth librarian of Congress.

The year before Boorstin won his Pulitzer, a young Jewish scholar who taught at Cornell University, thirty-five-year-old Michael Kammen, won the Pulitzer Prize for history for his monumental fifth book, *People of Paradox: An Inquiry Concerning the Origin of American Civilization* (1972). A historian who had grown up in Washington, D.C., Michael Kammen had studied under famed Harvard University historian Bernard Bailyn (b. 1922). Professor Bailyn, the son of a Jewish family in Hartford, Connecticut, specialized in American colonial and revolutionary history. Professor Bailyn's book, *The Ideological Origins of the American Revolution* (1967), had won the 1968 Pulitzer Prize for distinguished book of the year on U.S. history. Bailyn, in turn, had done his doctoral dissertation under Oscar Handlin! (see above). Jewish historians have indeed become crucial interpreters of the American experience.

One could compose a whole volume on other Jewish scholarly works concerning education, sociology, religion, and philosophy. Consider sociologist Nathan Glazer's *Beyond the Melting Pot* (1963) and subsequent works, or Rabbi Harold S. Kushner's *When Bad Things Happen to Good People* (1981) and recent books. In the realm of education, Lawrence A. Cremin (1925–1990), a faculty member at Columbia University (from 1949) who became president of its Teacher's College (1974–1984), wrote his own significant national trilogy. His three-volume *American Education* (*The Colonial Experience,* 1970; *The National Experience,* 1980, winner of the Pulitzer Prize for history in 1981; and *The Metropolitan Experience,* 1988) has become the standard research effort in the field. The son of the Jewish founder and director of the New York Schools of Music, Dr. Lawrence Cremin won the 1962 Bancroft prize in American history for his study, *The Transformation of the School: Progressivism in American Education, 1876–1957* (1961). He also worked closely with many educational institutions, including the Children's Television Workshop, the Carnegie Foundation for the Advancement of Teaching, and the U.S. Office of Education.

In a related effort to affect modern America, playwright Arthur Miller, born into a Jewish Austro-Hungarian family in Harlem in 1915, has contributed both to the Broadway stage and to popular films for decades. Arthur distinguished himself as a playwright even while a student at the University of Michigan (he graduated with a B.A. in English in 1938). He worked his way through college laboring in an automobile factory and even became a newspaper editor. Through his plays and prolific writing, Arthur Miller built a reputation for tackling important issues in contemporary society through the backdrop of familiar settings. Within a decade, his literary work had achieved national acclaim. His 1947 play "All My Sons" won the Drama Critics Circle Award and the Antoinette Perry Award. It was produced as a popular film in 1948.

Miller's "Death of a Salesman" won both the Drama Critics award and the Pulitzer Prize for drama when it opened on Broadway in 1949. It pierced the viewer's soul in its condemnation of the moral compromises most individuals must make to achieve the American ideal of prosperity and success. "Death of a Salesman" remains one of the best plays ever written and became a popular film in 1952. The next year Arthur Miller's "The Crucible" appeared, quickly amassing awards including the Tony Award. He also wrote numerous movie screenplays, including "The Misfits" (1961), as well as novels, articles, television screenplays, and travel pieces. In May 1994, seventy-eight-year-old Arthur Miller opened on Broadway with a gripping new play, "Broken Glass." The play received good reviews, even as his first play had garnered fifty years before. The longevity and influence of Arthur Miller's work have become legend.

Many other Jewish playwrights have made their mark on American society. For example, New Orleans-born Lillian Hellman (1907–1984) also exhibited a passion for social justice. Her first play, "The Children's Hour" (1934), was adapted to film in 1936 and again in 1962. Hellman's play "The Little Foxes" (1939), which emphasized the tantalizing and yet debilitating effect of human greed, was produced as a popular film in 1941.

In the midst of the Nazi regime in Europe, Lillian Hellman's play, "Watch on the Rhine," was highly acclaimed in 1941 (film version 1943) and won the New York Drama Critics Circle Award (as did her play "Toys in the Attic" in 1960). Another popular Jewish playwright, Abe Burrows (1910–1985), turned a successful radio career as a comedy writer into such memorable Broadway collaborations as "Guys and Dolls" (1950), "Can-Can" (1953), and "How to Succeed in Business Without Really Trying" (1961, the winner of a Pulitzer Prize for drama in 1962). Born Abram Solman Borowitz, Abe Burrows was also known as a "play doctor," rewriting and editing many scripts into presentable commodities. He even directed a number of films.

Jewish poets have also made their mark since the days of Emma Lazarus. Philadelphia-born poet and Tufts University instructor in English, Maxine Kumin (b. 1925), an author of children's books, novels, and poetry collections, won the 1973 Pulitzer Prize for *Up Country: Poems for New England*. Professor Kumin was cited for her canny ability to capture the smallest details and characteristics of her subjects, bringing them to life in the mind of the reader. Another Pulitzer Prize winning poet, Stanley Kunitz (b. 1905), native son of Worcester, Massachusetts, had written feature articles and edited biographical reference books before his first volume of poetry was published in 1930 (*Intellectual Things*). He was awarded the Pulitzer Prize for poetry for his *Collected Poems* (1958); he has had a number of other important collections that have received other awards and have been highly acclaimed, including *Selected Poems 1928–1978* (1979) and *The Poems of Stanley Kunitz 1928–1978* (1980).

Professor Howard Nemerov (b. 1920), a New Yorker who taught at a number of colleges and universities, was awarded both the Pulitzer Prize and the National Book Award for his *Collected Poems* (1977). His usage of symbols and the sheer volume of his many works in literature, as well as poetry, had garnered him a considerable reputation from the mid–1950s onward. Fellow New Yorker and prominent feminist, Erica Jong (b. 1942), also established herself as a poet as well as a writer. Jong's poetry collections *Fruits and Vegetables* (1971) and *Half-Lives* (1973) combined feminist concerns with psychoanalysis. Her best-selling novel, *Fear of Flying* (1973) earned her overnight success as a novelist and a feminist. She continued to add to that reputation through successive novels, such as *How to Save Your Own Life* (1977), *Fanny* (1980), and *Serenissima: A Novel of Venice* (1987), but continued to express herself through poetry (cf. Erica Jong's poetry collections, *Loveroot,* 1975, and *Parachutes and Kisses,* 1984). The daughter of an importer (father) and a designer of ceramics (mother), Erica Jong illustrated her wit in *Time* magazine's special 1990 issue, "Women: The Road Ahead," where she is quoted in a large block as saying to women: "BEWARE OF THE MAN WHO PRAISES WOMEN'S LIBERATION; HE IS ABOUT TO QUIT HIS JOB."

Novelists

As can be seen from the above examples, Jewish novelists have provided intellectual stimulation and recreational outlets to generations of their fellow Americans. Many Americans, however, have little knowledge that some of their favorite novelists have a Jewish heritage. The American writer, Saul Bellow (b. 1915), for example, was the son of Russian Jewish parents who moved from Canada to Chicago when he was nine years old. He was born Solomon Bellows, a street-wise young man with a keen mind. He won a scholarship to the University of Chicago (1933–1935) and graduated with a Bachelor of Science degree in anthropology from Northwestern University (graduated 1937 with honors). He attempted graduate work at the University of Wisconsin, but lamented that every time he tried to do his Master's thesis "it turned out to be a story."

Indeed, the "story" has dominated Saul Bellow's life. After stints on the editorial staff of the *Encyclopedia Britannica* (1943–1946) and teaching creative writing at Princeton (1952–1953), he would return to the University of Chicago in the 1950s to teach his craft to a younger generation. By that time, he had won an extensive following of readers. His first large popular audience was captivated in 1953 with the publication of *The Adventures of Augie March*. A contemporary urban Huck Finn type of character, Augie happened to be a young Chicagoan grappling with the challenges of the big city (not unlike young Solomon Bellows). *The Adventures of Augie March* won the National Book Award in 1953 and established the reputation of Saul Bellow. It was followed by *Seize the Day* (1956), a sensitive look at loneliness and the challenge of entering the middle-age stage of life, and *Henderson the Rain King* (1959), a portrayal of a wealthy American who searches for truth among primitive African tribespeople. In each of these works, the protagonists are caught in moral and psychological dilemmas that force them to confront the truth about themselves and the true meaning of life.

Bellow's *Herzog* (1964) was an international best-seller with its heroic professor trying to bring moral values to an inhuman world, while *Mr. Sammler's Planet* (1970) was very popular in the United States. Both of these novels won the National Book Award. *Humbolt's Gift* (1975) won Bellow the Pulitzer Prize in 1976. Saul Bellow continued taking his main characters through moral dilemmas and temptations in the 1980s in an effort to teach moral values and project the absurd situations one must confront. For example, in *The Dean's December* (1981), a college dean and his wife encounter such difficulties and moral dilemmas when visiting Romania. Subsequent Bellow novels, such as *More Die of Heartbreak* (1987), *A Theft* (1989), and *The Bellarosa Connection* (1989), entranced as well as taught readers in similar fashion.

In addition to his novels and teaching, Saul Bellow took time to try his hand at writing several plays and short stories, to serve as *Newsday*'s special correspondent in the Middle East during the 1967 Six-Day War, and to combine his serialized accounts of a 1975 trip to Israel published in *The New Yorker* as the book *To Jerusalem and Back* (1976). Saul Bellow received the Nobel Prize in literature in 1976 for his numerous contributions to American literature.

From the urbane and luxurious apartments high atop the skyscrapers of New York and Los Angeles to the midwestern farmhouse nestled among snowdrifts and warmed by a roaring fire, Herman Wouk's historical novels *The Winds of War* (1971) and *War and Remembrance* (1978) have been thoughtfully read. These panoramas of the Second World War intertwine the lives of scores of Americans as they are affected by this grand sweep of history, including the horrors, the anomalies, and the victories. Herman Wouk (b. 1915) has been working such magic through the American novel ever since he was awarded the 1952 Pulitzer Prize in fiction for *The Caine Mutiny* (1951). Like *The Winds of War* on television, *The Caine Mutiny* was portrayed in film (1954 on the big screen), turning millions of other readers to his novels. *The Caine Mutiny* sold over three million copies. Through his skillfully written play-adaptation ("The Caine Mutiny Court Martial"), Wouk also turned the book into a successful Broadway play.

The Caine Mutiny portrays a paranoid World War II captain (Queeg), whose crew on a U.S. naval destroyer must struggle between concepts of law and order and necessary action. Interestingly, Herman Wouk, the son of Jewish Russian immigrants who settled in the Bronx, served with the Navy in the Pacific during the Second World War. He also worked as a radio writer for six years before he joined the Navy in 1942. Understandably, his first novel, *Aurora Dawn* (1947), dealt with the raucous world of radio advertising. It garnered for the thirty-two-year-old Herman Wouk a Book-of-the-Month Club selection. Other novels that did not deal with the Second World War continued his fame, including the best-seller *Marjorie Morningstar* (1955), a novel that was turned into a film in 1958, and the more recent political novel *Inside, Outside* (1985).

Another Jewish writer who initially turned his Second World War combat experience into a literary goldmine was the popular Norman Mailer (b. 1923), the son of a New Jersey accountant who moved the family to Brooklyn in 1927. Mailer's *The Naked and the Dead* (1948) is considered one of the finest modern war novels. Through a number of successive novels on a variety of topics, Norman Mailer turned his fictional situations into political statements. He helped to found the newspaper *Village Voice* in 1951, wrote numerous magazine articles and essays thereafter, added documentary films and television scripts to his repertoire, and delivered a plethora of nonfiction manuscripts on a variety of topics. Concerning the latter, Norman Mailer's *The Armies of the Night* (1968), a description of his participation in a 1967 antiwar "peace march" on the Pentagon in Washington, received the Pulitzer Prize in nonfiction as well as a National Book Award. His *The Executioner's Song* (1980) continued this effort to apply fictional techniques to nonfiction writing. As Mailer has stated, his overriding goal consists of "making a revolution in the consciousness of our time."

Many science fiction buffs are totally oblivious to the fact that one of their heroes, Isaac Asimov (b. 1920), grew up in Brooklyn, the son of Russian Jewish immigrants. They are, perhaps, more aware that he completed his Ph.D. in chemistry at Columbia University (1949) and spent much of his life teaching biochemistry at the Boston University Medical School. He began writing science fiction stories while completing his bachelor's degree at Columbia in the 1930s, but received thirteen rejections from magazines before his first science fiction story was accepted. Not until 1950 did Asimov publish his first science fiction novel, *Pebble in the Sky*. By the end of 1984 he had published his 300th book—a nearly unbelievable accomplishment. His creativity in the field of science fiction relates directly to his knowledge of advanced scientific experimentation and concepts. His *A Short History of Chemistry* (1965; reprinted 1975) is indicative of his ability in nonfiction works to explain difficult concepts in modern science to lay readers. Isaac Asimov's nonfiction books cover quite a gamut of human knowledge, from interpretations of Shakespeare to a few works on theology. Many of his fans today are unaware that he has done significant research in enzymology and has written the textbook *Biochemistry and Human Metabolism* (1952; second edition 1957).

Numerous other Jewish novelists have had a great effect on American society and the important world of literature. Much could be added about J. D. Salinger's *Catcher in the Rye* (1951); Bernard Malamud's *The Natural* (1952; film version 1984); Leon Uris's *Exodus* (1957; film version 1960); Philip Roth's *Goodbye Columbus* (1959) and his Zuckerman tetralogy; Elie Wiesel's *Night* (English language edition, 1960); Joseph Heller's *Catch–22* (1961; film version 1970); Susan Sontag's *The Benefactor* (1963); Cynthia Ozick's *Trust* (1966); Herbert Gold's *Fathers* (1967); and Chaim Potok's *The Chosen* (1967). These Jewish novelists went on to publish prolifically—many others could be added to this list. The historian is impressed with the literary creativity of the Jewish peoplehood and the galaxy of contributions in journalism and literature.

✿ ✿ ✿

During the centenary celebration in 1947 of Joseph Pulitzer's birth, the U.S. Post Office issued a three-cent stamp in his honor. His circled picture appeared in the right-hand corner of the stamp and in a burst of light that took up over half of the stamp the words of Joseph Pulitzer were emblazoned: "OUR REPUBLIC AND ITS PRESS WILL RISE OR FALL TOGETHER." Faintly drawn in the background of the stamp is the Statue of Liberty.

Few realized that year that among his many contributions to journalism and literature, Joseph Pulitzer used his New York newspapers to raise funds for the completion of the monument. As the huge pieces of the French-donated statue languished in a New York warehouse, Pulitzer supported through print the importance of garnering the necessary funds to build the pedestal and assemble the parts. Through his efforts and the efforts of others, the Statue of Liberty now stands proudly in New York harbor. To Joseph Pulitzer, liberty and the literary world, justice and journalism, formed the foundations of the unique American experiment.

Sports and Entertainment

THE WORLD SERIES OF 1965 WAS ON THE LINE. THE SEVENTH and final game was about to begin. Torn between pitcher Don Drysdale with three days' rest and pitcher Sandy Koufax with only two days' rest, Los Angeles Dodgers manager Walter Alston decided to choose "the greatest pitcher I ever saw." Sandy Koufax insured his coach's faith in him (and Alston's fourth world title) by firing blistering fastballs that struck out ten batters and allowed only three hits. Led by a Jewish pitcher, the Dodgers won the World Series with a score of 2–0 over the seemingly indomitable bats of the Minnesota Twins.

Sanford Koufax was born in 1935 in Brooklyn, New York. He starred on his high school basketball team, not playing baseball until his senior year. In fact, Sandy Koufax won a basketball scholarship to the University of Cincinnati, playing baseball in the off season. His pitching performance during his high school senior year, and the fact that he struck out fifty-one batters in thirty-two innings in his freshman year at Cincinnati, won him a contract with the Brooklyn Dodgers. The Brooklyn Dodgers moved west after the 1957 season, becoming the Los Angeles Dodgers. Sandy Koufax moved with them.

Without an extensive high school, college, and minor league preparation, Koufax had to develop his skill while facing major league players from 1955 to 1966. A Jewish catcher with the Dodgers from 1959 to 1962, Norm Sherry (whose brother was the all-star relief pitcher, Larry Sherry), gave him some special advice that unlocked the key to his greatness. Sandy Koufax went on to win base-

113

ball's best pitching Cy Young Award three times (1963, 1965, and 1966) and posted a record four no-hitters during his career (including one perfectly pitched game). On two occasions, he struck out eighteen batters in one game. One season he set a record by pitching 382 strikeouts and, when his career was totaled, he had an average of more than one strikeout for every inning he pitched professionally! Known as a gentleman on and off the field, Sandy Koufax led the Los Angeles Dodgers to three pennants and two World Series titles.

On March 31, 1966, a *Los Angeles Times* sportswriter questioned: "Where would the Dodgers be in a tough league if they didn't have those twenty-seven wins by Sandy Koufax?" The column had pointed to the dismal offensive play of Dodgers players and a host of team problems. Little could the writer have known that Koufax would announce his retirement in November of that year and that the Dodgers would drop into eighth place the year following his retirement. Koufax had been pitching in pain for several years from developing arthritis in his left elbow. He had chosen to retire at the age of thirty-one, rather than risk a crippling injury. The first year he was eligible to be nominated, Stanford "Sandy" Koufax was inducted into the Baseball Hall of Fame (1972) at Cooperstown, New York, the youngest inductee ever. He went on to be a successful sportscaster and businessman, living a quiet life with his family on the West Coast. Sandy Koufax had one of the most brilliant pitching careers in the 1960s and is considered one of the greatest pitchers of all time.

National Pastimes

Jewish players, coaches, and team owners have brought considerable enjoyment and entertainment to sports fans across the United States for more than a century. Their contributions of talent and courage have been multifaceted and epoch-making. The historian is amazed at the diversity of sports upon which the American Jewish peoplehood has made its mark. Nevertheless, baseball was the first sport in U.S. history that commanded a national following from the Atlantic to the Pacific. It is baseball that has been dubbed "*the* national pastime" by journalists and sports historians alike, and the familiar diamond has given American culture a wide range of heroes and legendary exploits (not to mention an additional hundred or so new words added to the English language). And, Jews have had their share of baseball fame.

Baseball

In fact, the first professional baseball player in the United States was Jewish: New Yorker Lipman E. "Lip" Pike (1845–1893). Known as the fastest player in his time with a strong arm and powerful bat, the Philadelphia Athletics decided to pay him a regular salary of twenty dollars a week in 1866 to play third base. In one game that year, Lip hit six home runs, establishing a record for that time period. In 1870 he played for the Brooklyn Atlantics when they snapped the 130-game winning streak of baseball's first professional team, the Cincinnati Red Stockings.

In 1877, after nearly two decades of playing baseball, Lip Pike became player-manager with Cincinnati in the newly formed National League. In and out of baseball during the decade of the 1880s, he played his last professional season in 1887 at the age of forty-two for the New York Metropolitans of the American Association. (A Jewish man, Louis Kramer, had helped organize this major league association in 1882 with Aaron S. Stern, the owner of the Cincinnati Reds from 1882 to 1890). Lipman E. Pike is remembered by sports historians and trivia buffs as an all-around player, and his professional lifetime batting average of .304 in 163 recorded major league games was a phenomenal accomplishment in the age in which he played.

As the national pastime approached the twentieth century, a number of prominent Jewish baseball players, coaches, and owners helped their teams to victory. For example, Billy Nash (1865–1929) began the 1890s as third baseman with a star-studded Boston team that won the pennant in the Players League in 1890 and then proceeded to do the same thing the next three years in the National League. After fifteen years playing in the major leagues, Billy Nash became the manager of the Philadelphia team. First baseman Daniel E. Stearns contributed to his Cincinnati team's pennant win in 1882 for owner Aaron Stern in the first season of the American Association. Former New York outfielder James J. Roseman tried his hand at managing

115

the St. Louis club in 1890 after a fine career. His New York team had won the American Association pennant in 1884. Jewish lawyer Andrew Freedman was president of the New York Giants from 1894 to 1902, and Judge Harry Goldman organized the American League in 1900.

A sixteen-year-old Jewish German immigrant, Barney Dreyfuss (1865–1932), was destined to change the game of baseball forever. As a laborer in a Kentucky distillery, Barney was told by a doctor that outdoor activity would meliorate his health problems. He organized a semiprofessional baseball team so that he could play on it and get the exercise and fresh air he needed. In 1888 he became secretary-treasurer and part-owner of the Louisville Cardinals, learning even more about the big league game. In 1900 he purchased the Pittsburgh Pirates and was sole owner of that team until his death in 1932. As owner of the National League pennant winner, Dreyfuss approached the American League with the suggestion that their Boston champion meet his Pittsburgh Pirates in a series of games. The Jewish owner was attempting to foster better relations between the two leagues, while enhancing interest in baseball. The negotiations were successful and, in 1903, Barney Dreyfuss became the founder of baseball's World Series.

Barney's Pirates pounded Boston's premier pitcher, Cy Young (for whom the modern award for best pitcher is named), in the first game of the first World Series. Pittsburgh had lost some of its premier pitchers before the series, however, and this eventually took its toll after the Pirates had won three of the first four games. They went down to defeat in the final game 3–0. Although his Pirates failed to win the first World Series, they would go on to win two World Series and six National League pennants under Barney's ownership. Before his death, the Pirates would finish in the first division twenty-six times in thirty-two seasons.

In 1909 Barney Dreyfuss built a triple-decked Forbes Field in Pittsburgh for his team, the first modern baseball stadium. To many it seemed a financial gamble, but a rejuvenated Pirates team demolished the American League champion Detroit Tigers to win the 1909 World Series for owner Dreyfuss. Fan loyalty and national exposure underscored Barney's foresight. The dedicated owner also personally scouted minor league prospects to keep talent on his team. And, Barney seemed to genuinely care about his players. When the Pirates lost the 1903 World Series by a thin margin, Barney Dreyfuss threw his owner's share of the receipts into the players' pot, giving his men higher earnings than the Boston players who won the series. Players that starred for the Pittsburgh Pirates under owner Dreyfuss are noticeably prominent today in Baseball's Hall of Fame. At his death in 1932, Dreyfuss's Pirates passed to his son-in-law, forty-year-old Bill Benswanger, who headed the Pirates organization until the family sold the club in 1946.

Jewish men and women were passionate baseball fans, and many Jewish immigrants viewed the mastery of the rules of the game as an entrance exam into American society. Jewish journalists explored the game, and Jewish novelists incorporated baseball into their literary scenes and backgrounds. In the 1930s a Jewish baseball hero emerged that towered in the game for two decades: Henry Benjamin "Hank" Greenberg (1911–1986). He would be the first Jewish player elected to the Baseball Hall of Fame.

Born in the Bronx, Hank Greenberg joined the Detroit Tigers in 1933 after three years of professional play. With the big man's help at bat and at first base, the Tigers won an American League pennant the following year. It had been twenty-five years since Detroit had been able to snatch that pennant. To the delight of Detroit Tiger fans, the team repeated the feat in 1935. Hank Greenberg won the 1935 American League's Most Valuable Player Award for his contribution to Detroit's phenomenal success. During the 1937 season, he had the remarkable record of 183 Runs-Batted-In (RBI). In 1938 the whole nation watched and held its breath as Hank hit a great number of home runs during the season, coming closer and closer to Babe Ruth's single-season home run record of sixty. To heighten the suspense, Hank had surpassed Babe Ruth's season pace of home runs each week of the season until the very last week. Hank Greenberg ended the season with fifty-eight home runs, two short of matching Babe Ruth's record. Appreciative fans throughout the world applauded.

Moving to the outfield in 1940, the twenty-nine-year-old Greenberg spearheaded Detroit's march to another American League pennant and, once again, won the American League's Most Valuable Player Award. Drafted the following year into the armed forces, Hank Greenberg accepted the responsibility to protect the nation and quickly joined. The American press noted that he was the first important ball player to do so. Ironically, he was mustered out a few days before the Japanese attack on Pearl Harbor. True to form, baseball hero Hank Greenberg continued the interruption of his successful major league career and joined the U.S. Army Air Corps for the duration of the Second World War. Americans applauded the six foot four inch Greenberg as a true hero.

When he was mustered out once again in 1945, many baseball experts felt that the thirty-four-year-old athlete could not return to his career. Nevertheless, Hank Greenberg rejoined the Detroit Tigers mid-season and helped them to win another American League pennant. In that partial season he contributed thirteen homers and batted-in sixty runs with a batting average of .311. Detroit Tiger home attendance swelled that season to 1,280,000. In fact, in a fairy tale ending to the final game of the season, Hank hit a grand-slam home run in the ninth inning. As if that were not enough of a climax, his batting led the Detroit Tigers to victory in the 1945 World Series (including a three-run homer in the second game of the series).

In 1946 Hank Greenberg won his third American League home run title at the age of thirty-five and, after moving to the Pittsburgh Pirates, finished his career after one season in the National League. Hank continued in baseball, becoming an executive with the Cleveland Indians and focusing his energies on making them an American League pennant contender while raising his family in the Midwest. In 1956 he was elected to the Baseball Hall of Fame. Not only had Hank Greenberg been a gentleman, patriot, and stable credit to the game of baseball; he had maintained a lifetime batting average of .313, had batted in 1,276 runs in 1,394 games (winning the American League RBI title three times), and had smashed 331 home runs.

Both major and minor league baseball has had scores of lesser-known Jewish players who entertained the fans and made great sacrifices to play the game they loved. For example, Izzy Goldstein, the son of Russian immigrants, grew up in the Bronx little more than two blocks from where Hank Greenberg was raised. In fact, after a stint in the minor leagues, Izzy pitched for the Detroit Tigers in 1932 and was known as a fine batter.

Only an arm injury sent him back to the minors and eventually into semiprofessional baseball as an outfielder. Izzy Goldstein served in the South Pacific during World War II and lived a productive life raising his family and working in the clothing retail business. His baseball years and the game itself, however, left an indelible stamp on his life. Lasting baseball fame eluded him, but he represents those Jewish players such as Bo Belinsky, Moe Berg, Ron Blomberg, Andy Cohen, Harry "Ike" Danning, Barney Dreyfuss, Mike Epstein, Harry Feldman, Joe Ginsberg, Sid Gordon, Ken Holtzman, Johnny Kling, Erskine Mayer, Charles "Buddy" Myer, Barney Pelty, Ed Reulbach, Al Rosen, "Goody" Rosen, Al Schacht, Richy Scheinblum, Dick Sharon, Bill "Chick" Starr, Steve Stone, Phil Weintraub, and hundreds of others, who definitely left their mark on the history of professional baseball.

Football

Coach Marv Levy of the Buffalo Bills professional football team had led his team to four consecutive American Football Conference (AFC) championships when they entered Atlanta's Georgia Dome to play Superbowl XXVIII on January 30, 1994. In spite of the fact that the Buffalo Bills manhandled the Dallas Cowboys in the first half of the game, Dallas's depth of players and a few quirks in the game brought the successful Jewish coach a fourth Superbowl loss. Although Coach Levy and the team felt a great disappointment and Levy admitted that it was a "bitter loss," he was already plotting the team's course for the next season. "It might upset everybody else in America," Marv Levy explained about the four back-to-back Superbowl losses and the desire of some vocal Americans for a new team to represent the AFL, "but I tell them [the other thirteen teams in the AFL] that they have sixteen weeks to line up and stop us." That tenacity characterized Coach Levy's remarkable career.

Marvin Daniel Levy was born in Chicago on August 3, 1929, and was raised in the Windy City by a supportive family. Marv joined the Army Air Corps after high school and then entered Coe College in Cedar Rapids, Iowa, intent on pursuing a career in law. He happened to be chosen to play halfback on the Coe College football team and, although he earned a Phi Beta Kappa

Key for academic excellence, Marv Levy fell in love with football and the intricacies of the game. He developed a keen interest in coaching as he spent time with the coaches of Coe College and their families.

Graduating from Coe College in 1950, Levy entered Harvard Law School. After six weeks, he knew that he did not want to be a lawyer. In a difficult decision, he told his father that he wanted to be a coach. Supportive of his son's decisions in life, his father's only advice to his son was that, if he was going to be a coach, "be a good one." Not forsaking his education, Marv Levy transferred to Harvard's history program in the graduate school of arts and science, finishing his Masters Degree in history within a year. Embarking on a career that had become his first love, he coached high school football in St. Louis for a year and then became assistant football coach at Coe College. He followed his old coach at Coe, Dick Clausen, to the University of New Mexico, where he became his able assistant football coach. Soon, Marv Levy was chosen head coach of the university's football team. Word of his coaching ability spread throughout the west, and Marv Levy was awarded Skyline Coach of the Year for two consecutive years (1958 and 1959). As the decade of the 1960s dawned, he was tapped as the head football coach at the University of California at Berkeley (1960–1963).

After a stint as head football coach at William and Mary College in Williamsburg, Virginia (1964–1968), Marv Levy entered the ranks of professional football coaching. He was assistant football coach for the Philadelphia Eagles during the 1969 season and then joined George Allen as assistant for the Los Angeles Rams. He followed Allen to the Washington Redskins football franchise in 1971. From George Allen, Levy learned the importance of attention to details in all aspects of the game, including special teams. Under Allen, Marv specialized in the kicking game, one of the first assistants to do so.

In 1973, Marv Levy received his first professional head coaching position. He traveled to Quebec to coach the Montreal Alouettes in the Canadian Football League (CFL). In five years he led the team to two league championships and furthered his reputation as a coach who understood all facets of football—offense, defense and special teams. The Kansas City Chiefs of the

National Football League were just one of the franchises that was impressed with his skill and determination. Marv Levy returned to the United States in 1978 to coach the Kansas City Chiefs for five seasons, until the 1982 football strike led to his dismissal. After a short stint in the fledgling United States Football League (USFL), Marv Levy returned to the National Football League in 1986 to take on the head coaching responsibilities for the Buffalo Bills organization. Buffalo Bills general manager Bill Polian had worked with Levy in both the CFL and USFL and knew of his multifaceted abilities.

Today, Marv Levy serves as both head coach and vice president for football operations of the Buffalo Bills organization, directly engaged in recruiting and evaluating players and positional needs. Team members and organizational personnel appreciate him for his wit and humor as well as his coaching abilities. Balanced in perspective and intellectual in approach, Marv Levy understands the potential of human beings and the emotional side of football as well as the mechanics of the game—the national pastime to which he has dedicated his life.

Other Jewish coaches, owners, and players have made their mark on professional football. For example, Sid Gillman of the Houston Oilers was named 1974 American Conference "Coach of the Year" in the NFL. He was inducted into the Professional Football Hall of Fame in 1983. In 1972 Carroll Rosenbloom (1907–1979) exchanged ownership of the Baltimore Colts for the same position with the Los Angeles Rams of the NFL. And, the legendary Al Davis of the Oakland Raiders was chosen NFL Executive of the Year in 1976, and in 1980 his team won the Super Bowl. Today, his Oakland Raiders command considerable attention in the world of sports.

Eugene Klein finally sold his San Diego Chargers in 1984, while another Jewish entrepreneur, Norman Braman, purchased the Philadelphia Eagles in 1985. Art Modell has owned the Cleveland Browns since 1961. The Jewish executive was president of the National Football League from 1967 to 1970. Robert Kraft, the Jewish president of the Rand-Whitney Group and the International Forest Products group (one of the largest privately owned paper and packaging companies in the United States), purchased Foxboro Stadium in 1988 and then purchased its main attraction, the New England Patriots football team, in

121

1993. Kraft was applauded by Patriots' fans for keeping the NFL team in Massachusetts (the previous owner wanted to move them to another state).

For over half a century, Jewish players such as Randy Grossman have impacted both college and professional football. Randy Grossman won All-America honors in 1973 as an end at Temple University and went on to win four championships as tight end with the Pittsburgh Steelers. He retired in 1982. Ron Mix, offensive tackle with the San Diego Chargers, retired in 1973 after playing thirteen productive years. In 1979 he was named to the Professional Football Hall of Fame. Ed Newman of the Miami Dolphins won All-Pro honors as offensive guard four times in the early 1980s, retiring in 1986 because of injury after twelve years of dedicated service.

All-Pro defensive end Lyle Alzado also retired from football in 1986 after fifteen years with such teams as the Denver Broncos, Cleveland Browns, and Los Angeles Raiders. New Orleans Saints guard, Brad Edelman, played in the 1988 Pro Bowl. University of North Carolina offensive tackle, Harris Barton, earned All-American honors in 1986, becoming the number one draft selection of the San Francisco 49ers. In 1987 Barton was named to the NFL's all-Rookie team. Even Jewish referees, such as Jerry Markbriet, have been honored for their officiating expertise (chosen to officiate the 1987 Superbowl). These are but a few of the Jewish players who have brought cheers from fans and chagrin to foes while they entertained the general American public with their expertise and dedication.

The history is a long one. The 1980s recorded the deaths of many Jewish pioneers of football, including Irving "Red" Pearlman who played for Cleveland in the early days of the NFL and Arnold Horween who was Chicago's player-coach in the early 1920s. Horween, in fact, had been an All-American fullback at Harvard University in 1920 and returned as head coach at Harvard after his professional career. Benny Friedman of the Michigan Wolverines rates as one of the finest passing quarterbacks in college football in the mid–1920s, revolutionizing a game that had sparsely used the potential of the forward pass. Harry Newman and Sid Luckman, outstanding Jewish quarterbacks from Michigan and Columbia respectively, repeated the feat in the 1930s.

In testimony to a long Jewish career in college football (the game that finally brought some respectability to the illegal and brutal professional contests of the nineteenth century), Moses Henry Epstein had played for Columbia University in 1870, sixty years before Luckman stepped on the Columbia gridiron. In 1871, famed Reform Rabbi Emil G. Hirsh played in the first football game that the Pennsylvania University football team played, and Jewish-born Phil King, quarterback of Princeton University, was an All-American selection all four years (1890–1893). King led Princeton to the championship in his final year. He returned to Princeton as head football coach, later becoming one of the scores of Jewish players elected to the College Football Hall of Fame.

Basketball

In 1968, the first year the Basketball Hall of Fame opened the doors of its new building on the Springfield College campus in Springfield, Massachusetts, Arnold Jacob "Red" Auerbach (b. 1917) was inducted as the "winningest coach" in the history of basketball. The Jewish-born varsity basketball player from George Washington University had by then coached such greats as Bob Cousy, John Havlicek, and Bill Russell, amassing a record of, 1,037 wins during his illustrious professional coaching career. (Red's career NBA record of 938 wins was only surpassed on January 6, 1995.)

Born in Brooklyn to Russian immigrants, Red was popular in high school, playing varsity basketball and leading the student body as president. Later playing basketball for George Washington University in Washington, D.C., he earned his bachelor's degree in physical education in 1940 and his master's degree a year later. Teaching history and health in addition to his basketball and baseball coaching at Roosevelt High School in Washington in the early 1940s, Red Auerbach enlisted in the Navy in 1943. At the end of World War II, he was chosen to coach a new professional basketball franchise, the Washington Capitols. The team won over eighty percent of their games.

In 1950 he took over the hapless Boston Celtics, a last place team that rarely won a game, and built them into the powerhouse of the National Basketball Association (NBA). Red Auerbach's teams dominated professional basketball from 1956 to 1966, winning nine divisional titles and eight straight world titles during that period. In 1965 Auerbach was named the NBA Coach of the Year, and he was chosen to coach the East teams in NBA All-Star games no less than eleven times. The next year, he turned the coaching duties over to Bill Russell and joined the front office of the Celtics organization as general manager and vice president. The next two decades were both profitable for the Celtics organization and exciting for fans across the country.

The feisty coach had created a dynasty, leaving his mark imprinted on the history of the only international sport that had been a uniquely American creation. As another Jewish basketball wizard, William "Red" Holzman, coach of the New York Knickerbockers, stated in the 1970s, "Red Auerbach had the class of the league." Holzman certainly knew expertise. He himself would lead his New York Knicks team to the championship of the National Basketball Association in 1973. He saw in Auerbach a disciplined and dedicated coach, who emphasized excellence and teamwork in successful professional play.

Another Jewish player from New York City, however, garnered the title "Mr. Basketball" decades before Red Auerbach coached the Celtics. Ironically, he was a player for the original Celtics during the 1920s, whose collegiate coaching career would span nearly four decades and would overlap the early years of Auerbach's career. He preceded Auerbach into the Hall of Fame by four years. His name was Nat Holman, and he became a legend in the game.

Born in 1896, Nat Holman had just assumed the position of physical education instructor and soccer coach at the City College of New York (CCNY) when the United States entered the First World War. He immediately enlisted in the Navy and fought for his country. Upon returning to America, Nat was appointed CCNY's head basketball coach. He loved the game so much that he began playing for the original Celtics professional team in 1921, becoming the greatest basketball player of the 1920s. When the original Celtics disbanded in 1929, Holman returned to CCNY as head basketball coach, amassing a 422–188 win-loss record. The highlight of his coaching career was when his team won both the National Collegiate Championship and the National Invitation Tournament in 1950. *Sport* magazine named him Coach of the Year. Like Red Auerbach, Coach Holman wrote a number of books on basketball strategy, but it was as a spectacular basketball player that he entered the Basketball Hall of Fame. He died in February 1995 at the age of ninety-eight.

Volumes could be written on the entertainment and excitement generated by Jewish basketball players and coaches, both men and women. From the first Jewish professional basketball player at the turn of the century, Paul "Twister" Steinberg, who later coached at Cornell University, to Nancy Lieberman from Old Dominion College, who was named outstanding women's college basketball player twice and led the American team to silver medals in the Olympic Games and gold and silver medals in the Pan-American Games in the latter 1970s, Jewish players have contributed to the game. The names and faces of Jewish players and coaches, such as Eddie Gottlieb, Max "Marty" Friedman, Adolph "Dolph" Schayers, Harry Litwack, and Maurice Podoloff are honored in the Basketball Hall of Fame. Podoloff, in fact, was the first president of the National Basketball Association.

And, tens of thousands of audiences have been awed and delighted by the antics of Jewish-born Abe Saperstein's Harlem Globetrotters. Too small to play college basketball himself, the son of emigrants from London, England, who immigrated to Chicago, Abe decided to coach the game, later forming the all-black Harlem Globetrotters (in 1927). As founder, owner, and first coach, Abe Saperstein toured the world with his team, at times substituting as a player. The comedy routine he instituted became the trademark for the team and, as a promoter, Coach Saperstein at one time had to field a number of teams to cover global engagements. Today, the Harlem Globetrotters defeat the all-white Washington Generals who travel with them in an endless display of creativity, skill, and humor.

Other Sports

Through expanded news coverage and the advent of radio and television, additional sports contests engaged the attention of specific segments of the American population. Jewish athletes have made their share of contributions to this kaleidoscope of sports history and sports entertainment. At times, they have overcome incredible odds.

For example, Jews came late to professional golf because racists barred them from country clubs and premier golf courses for much of the twentieth century. When they finally overcame that barrier, Jewish young people began to rise to prominence on the national and international golf scene. Jewish-born Amy Alcott was heralded as the top newcomer on the ladies professional tour in 1975. She captured the title of leading money winner in 1976 and 1978, and her name became intrically linked with a maturing Ladies Professional Golf Association. By 1990, Amy Alcott had won nearly thirty major tournaments and had amassed millions of dollars in career earnings. At the same time, Corey Pavin was one of the Jewish men who was quickly rising up the tournament-win and money-earned list of the Professional Golf Association. He followed in the path carved by Jewish golf enthusiasts, such as Richard Siderowf, an American who won the Canadian Amateur Tournament in 1971 and the British Amateur Tournament in 1973 and 1976.

Jewish bowlers Mark Roth and Marshall Holman delighted bowling enthusiasts in the 1970s and 1980s. Mark Roth had set a professional bowling record in amassing eight major tournament victories in 1978. With thirty-three major tournament wins by the end of 1987, Roth had become the game's all-time money winner and was inducted immediately into the Professional Bowlers Association's Hall of Fame (an honor he added to his numerous "Bowler of the Year" awards). The same year, Roth's doubles partner, Marshall Holman, was honored with the title of "Bowler of the Year" by the Bowling Writers of America. After winning major tournaments in 1985 and 1986, Holman had become bowling's third millionaire. In 1988, Jewish bowling great Barry Asher (All American selection 1972–73) was inducted into the Hall of Fame. He had come back from a national tournament drought of eight years to win the American Bowling Congress's all-events title in 1985. Jewish women, such as Sylvia Wene, have from time to time made their mark in the sport of bowling.

Volumes could be written on the Jewish contribution to American sports. In both the amateur and professional ranks, Jewish men and women have made substantial contributions historically. Jewish champions in tennis, swimming, boxing, judo, automobile racing, motorboat racing, yachting, rowing, track and field, wrestling, weightlifting, ice skating, equestrian events, horse racing, gymnastics, fencing, skiing, and a plethora of other sports competitions have shown stamina, skill, devotion, and courage.

Mark Spitz

By the time of the terrorist horrors of the 1972 Olympic Games in Munich, Germany, which claimed the lives of eleven Israeli athletes, a young Jewish swimmer had captured the hearts of millions of people around the world. Born in Modesto, California, in 1950, Mark Spitz learned to swim at the age of six. His parents provided swimming lessons and encouragement for him from the age of eight. Mark soon was breaking swimming records at a phenomenal pace. By the time he entered the 1968 Olympic Games in Mexico City, Mark had accumulated hundreds of awards and medals, including four gold medals in the 1965 Maccabiah Games in Israel. At the 1968 Olympic Games he won two gold medals in relays, and a silver and a bronze medal in individual events.

The first Jewish athlete to be awarded the Sullivan Award for outstanding amateur achievement (1971), Mark Spitz entered the twentieth Olympic Games in 1972 with a sense of destiny. He set world records in the 100-meter and 200-meter butterfly and the 100-meter and 200-meter freestyle. He also collected three more gold medals in relay events. Mark Spitz's seven gold medals in one Olympiad was unprecedented, and his nine Olympic gold medals (1968 and 1972) tied the record for total Olympic gold medals. During his career, he set thirty-two world and thirty-eight U.S. swimming records. Heralded by many as the greatest all-around swimmer in the history of sports, Mark retired from competitive swimming to pursue a career in show business.

Although he was unsuccessful in the highly competitive field of acting, his legend continued as he was inducted into the Swimming Hall of Fame. Using the discipline he had cultivated as a swimmer, Mark Spitz finished his college education and pursued a successful business career. In 1990, at the age of forty, he began a rigorous training schedule to hone his superb middle age physique into competitive strength for the 1992 Olympic Games in Barcelona. Although he fell short of his goal of representing the United States once again, Mark Spitz knew that he had given the challenge his all and that he had trained as rigorously as he could. Like acting, the Olympic comeback failed, but the man, Mark Spitz, was a better man for accepting the challenge and attacking the unknown.

127

Entertainment

Although Mark Spitz's desire to become a famous actor in the 1970s did not materialize, his attempt at American "show business" had historic foundations in the Jewish community. Jewish men and women have contributed significantly to entertainment on the "silver screen," on amateur and professional stages across the nation, and in music halls and cabarets in towns of all sizes. In turn, they have delighted audiences across the United States and throughout the world. Many Americans, however, are unaware that some of their favorite actors and actresses spring from Jewish roots.

Film and Television

The quintessential story of a twentieth-century Jewish entertainment star is exemplified in the life of George Burns. Born Nathan Birnbaum in 1896, Burns was the ninth child of hardworking immigrant parents from Eastern Europe who lived on the Lower East Side of Manhattan. His father died when he was seven years old, and young Nathan helped to support the family by singing in the neighborhood, selling newspapers, and shining shoes. By his teen years he had progressed to vaudeville as a comedian, dancer, and all-around entertainer. When he met Grace Allen in 1923, they became stand-up comedy partners and close friends. They were married in 1926, gaining a national following through radio during the Great Depression. CBS radio offered them their own program in 1932, which aired for eighteen years. In 1950, Burns and Allen moved to television, receiving top ten ratings for their comedy show until "Gracie" retired in 1958. George continued for one more year with his own show, produced several network comedy shows, and developed a popular nightclub comedy act. Gracie died in 1964.

George Burns kept on entertaining. Few could have predicted that he would return to film. He and Gracie had made more than two dozen short and feature length films from 1929 to 1939; then, at the age of eighty he replaced his friend Jack Benny in the film "The Sunshine Boys." Benny had died suddenly before shooting began, and replacement George Burns won the 1976 Academy Award for Best Supporting Actor in the hit film about two aging vaudeville entertainers. The other aged vaude-villian was played by another Jewish actor from the Lower East Side of New York, Walter Matthau (b. 1920), who would continue a brilliant film career that had roots in a distinguished Broadway acting career. An Air Force veteran from World War II, Walter Matthau had received an Oscar nomination for his performance with George Burns in "The Sunshine Boys."

It is perhaps fitting that in his early eighties the resilient and witty George Burns was cast as the star in "Oh, God!" (1977) and its sequels, "Oh God! Book Two" (1980) and "Oh God. You Devil!" (1984). Throughout the 1980s and into the mid–1990s, George Burns has delighted millions of fans worldwide with his comedy in films, television specials, records, books, and night-club routines. CBS broadcast a television special in honor of his ninetieth birthday, and the 1400 seat Mai Kai Theater in Detroit was renamed the "George Burns Theater for the Performing Arts" in 1992. Burns quipped to the audience and the reporters: "The first time I played Detroit was in 1917, and I like to play there every seventy-five years." George Burns was booked years in advance to "play" the Palladium in London on his 100th birthday (January 20, 1996). "I hope the Palladium is still there," he joked at the time. "I *know* I will be."

Like George Burns, Kirk Douglas has had an illustrious and productive career as an actor, producer, and author. Born Issur Danielovitch on December 9, 1916, to a Jewish immigrant couple from Russia, Kirk Douglas has stated that his given ethnic name would have been fine in a more recent period of American history or if he had pursued a career as a ballet dancer. As so many actors and actresses of earlier decades of the twentieth century, he was forced to change to a career name. Raised in upstate New York, Kirk has never ceased to give his parents credit for their fortitude and perseverance. "My parents were illiterate immigrants who worked hard all their lives and never had a chance to learn to read and write," he has stated. "Perhaps this is why learning was always so important to me. The public library was my favorite hangout . . . the written word inspired all my dreams." As for religious affiliation, Kirk Douglas has proudly told many an audience, "I'm of the same religion as Albert Einstein and Jesus." He received a college education at St. Lawrence University and after graduation studied at the

American Academy of Dramatic Arts in New York City, landing small acting parts on Broadway. The Second World War interrupted his career and he served in the Navy.

Returning to Broadway, Kirk Douglas was recommended to Hollywood producer Hal Wallis by Jewish actress Lauren Bacall (born in 1924 as Betty Joan Perske). Bacall had attended acting classes with Douglas and remembered his raw talent. She had obtained her own fame by playing opposite Humphrey Bogart in "To Have and Have Not" (1944). Lauren Bacall and Humphrey Bogart were married in 1945. Bacall would make her mark on the stage as well as in film, and Kirk Douglas was cast by Wallis to play opposite Barbara Stanwyck in "The Strange Love of Martha Ivers" (1946). Subsequently, Douglas landed a number of roles in Hollywood films.

In 1949, Kirk Douglas received acclaim as a prize fighter in the film "Champion." His film career solidified in the 1950s with such films as "Young Man with a Horn" (1950), "Detective Story" (1951), "Ace in the Hole" (1951), "Along the Great Divide" (1951), "The Bad and the Beautiful" (1952), "The Juggler" (1953), "Lust for Life" (1956), and "Gunfight at the O.K. Corral" (1957).

One of the first actors to start his own production company, Kirk named his company, *Bryna*, after his mother's first name. A joyful moment in his life was teaching his mother to write "Bryna" and then taking her in 1960 by limousine to see Broadway lights which read, "Bryna Presents Spartacus." His mother declared, "Ah, America . . . such a wonderful land!" Indeed, her son would garner many awards in his lifetime, including the Cecil B. DeMille Award in 1967 for his contributions to the world of entertainment; the Medal of Freedom Award in 1981 (presented to him by President Jimmy Carter during the last days of Carter's presidency); and the American Film Institute's Lifetime Achievement Award in 1991.

Today, Kirk Douglas has over eighty films to his credit, including "Paths of Glory" (1958), "Spartacus" (1960), "Heroes of Telemark" (1965), "Cast A Giant Shadow" (1966), "The Brotherhood" (1968), "Catch Me A Spy" (1971), "Once Is Not Enough" (1975), "The Fury" (1978), "The Man from Snowy River" (1982), "Tough Guys" (1986), "Greedy" (1994) and, his favorite, "Lonely Are the Brave" (1962). The father of four sons, including actor

130

Michael Douglas, Kirk has in his latter years pursued the writing of novels, including *Last Tango in Brooklyn* (1994). He refers to his writing as a "change of career." Indeed, his autobiography, *The Ragman's Son* (1988), quickly reached best-seller status. Lauren Bacall, who lent a hand to jump-start Kirk's career, published *Now* in 1994 (her second autobiographical work) and starred in "Ready to Wear" (released at the end of 1994).

Like Kirk Douglas, many Jewish actors and actresses have devoted themselves to charitable causes as well as American war efforts. Danny Kaye (born Daniel Kominski in 1913 in Brooklyn to Russian Jewish immigrant parents) was a popular nightclub entertainer and theater performer when he tried to enlist in the U.S. Army during the Second World War. Rejected because of a poor back, Danny Kaye dedicated himself to performing at Army camps and hospitals. Even as his movie career launched and prospered ["Up in Arms," (1944), "Kid from Brooklyn," (1945), "Secret Life of Walter Mitty," (1946) etc.] and his television career began [the Emmy Award winning "The Danny Kaye Show," (early 1960s), and numerous television specials], Danny Kaye performed for U.S. troops and served as ambassador at large for the United Nations International Children's Emergency Fund (UNICEF). His energetic benefit performances for children around the world, as well as fund raisers for numerous charitable causes, became models for entertainers around the world.

The Roaring Twenties and the Great Depression in America saw the birth of a great number of Jewish children, like Walter Matthau and Lauren Bacall, who would become popular television and film notables. Many of their contributions are familiar to American audiences today. Among these are Tony Randall (born Leonard Rosenberg in Tulsa, Oklahoma, in 1920); Carl Reiner (born in the Bronx in 1922, and father of another popular actor Rob Reiner); Shelly Winters (born Shirley Schrift in East St. Louis, Illinois, in 1923); Jerry Lewis (born Joseph Levich in Newark, New Jersey, in 1926); Mel Brooks (born Melvyn Kaminsky in the Williamsburg section of Brooklyn in 1926); Ed Asner (born in Kansas City, Missouri, in 1929); Joel Grey (born Joel Katz in Cleveland, Ohio); Ben Wattenberg (born in New York City in 1933 to a Jewish attorney and Jewish dietician); George Segal, Jr. (born in New York City in 1934 and raised in Great Neck, New York); Gene Wilder (born Jerome Silberman in Milwaukee, Wisconsin, in 1935); Woody Allen (born Allen Konigsberg in New York City in 1935); Dustin Hoffman (born in Los Angeles in 1937); and Elliott Gould (born Elliott Goldstein in Brooklyn in 1938). For many of these "stars", the medium of television both advertised their cinematic efforts and provided another avenue for their entertainment expertise. They joined Milton Berle (born Milton Berlinger in Harlem in 1908), the first television variety show host, in expanding the horizons of television transformation.

Jewish contributions to film and television entertainment are enduring as well as historic. The son of Russian immigrants, Larry King (changed from Larry Zeiger when he began his radio career), appears to have logged more hours than any broadcaster in history and may be the most famous broadcaster in the world today. CNN's *Larry King Live* airs to more than two hundred countries. The American public delights in the talents of other Brooklyn-born stars, such as Barbra Streisand and Richard Dreyfuss, as well as Goldie Hawn, Leonard Nimoy, William Shatner, and Debra Winger, who spring from Jewish roots. "Happy Days" reruns starring the son of a Jewish international lumber company president, Henry Winkler ("The Fonz"), still amuse viewers that have little idea that Henry is a graduate of the Yale School of Drama (Master of Fine Arts, 1970) and is not Italian. Detroit-born Gilda Radner (1946–1989) gave the nation laughter in the 1970s and 1980s, and helped promote cancer awareness in the midst of her own painful struggle with cancer. With her husband, Gene Wilder, Gilda Radner funded cancer support groups. Modern comic Jerry Seinfeld and world famous magician David Copperfield (whose mother wanted him to be a rabbi) are household names with millions of viewers in the 1990s. As detailed in chapter 7, the contributions of Steven Spielberg are legend. These entertainment specialists continue a twentieth-century American tradition that in some ways was hallmarked by the Jewish showman and escape artist, Harry Houdini (1874–1926).

Today, thousands of talented Jewish writers, directors, producers, stage hands, support workers, actors, and actresses pour out their lives on entertainment. And, Americans feel their efforts. For example, as 1994 came to a close, the hearts of young and old alike were touched by the little girl on Kris Kringle's lap in the remake of "Miracle on 34th Street." Few realized that the child with the bright eyes, sweet expression, and wisdom beyond her years was Jewish. Actress Mara Wilson, who had already captured hearts as the youngest child in the film "Mrs. Doubtfire," celebrates Hanukkah, not Christmas. As for seventy-four-year-old Walter Matthau (born Walter Matuschanskyavasky), his starring role as Einstein in the cupid tale "I.Q." was released in theaters across the nation on Christmas Day.

Musicians

Ironically, even the song "White Christmas," sung with such fervor during the holiday, was written by the Jewish composer Irving Berlin (1888–1989). In 1942 Irving Berlin won an Oscar for "White Christmas," and in 1943 he was honored by the National Association for American Composers and Conductors as "the outstanding composer of popular music." In 1945 President Harry Truman presented him the Medal of Merit for his wartime song, "This Is the Army, Mr. Jones" (1942). Irving Berlin's life, creativity, and initiative underscore the immense talent and versatility of Jewish musicians who have entertained America as well as the world.

The son of a cantor, Irving Berlin was born Israel Baline on May 11, 1888, in Russia. Berlin's family immigrated to the Lower East Side of New York City when he was four years old, and the whole family worked to help the family survive. Young Irving would sing songs in taverns and on street corners to collect a few coins and would join his brothers in selling newspapers on the street in their spare time from their work in the sweat shops of the city. At the age of nineteen, Irving landed a job as a singing waiter and began composing songs. Soon, he was hired by a music company, later becoming a partner in the company. Although he never learned to read music, Irving Berlin would compose over 1500 songs during his lifetime (music as well as lyrics) and would dominate the world of American popular music for half a century.

Irving Berlin's first big hit was "Alexander's Ragtime Band" (1911). Other hits included "All Alone," "Always," "Top Hat," "Blue Skies," and "Easter Parade." As a sergeant in World War I, Irving wrote and produced the all-soldier show "Yip Yip Yaphank" (1918). The hit song "Oh, How I Hate to Get Up in the Morning" came from that show, and "Yip Yip Yaphank" was the first of many musicals written and produced by Irving Berlin during the American world wars that earned millions of dollars for war charities. The prolific Irving Berlin went on to write Broadway musicals and motion picture scores that produced dozens of additional hits. For example, his Broadway musical, "Annie Get Your Gun" (1946), included such favorites as "Doin' What Comes Naturally," "Show Business," and "They Say It's Wonderful."

In 1954 President Dwight D. Eisenhower signed a bill authorizing a gold medal for Irving Berlin "in recognition of his services in composing many popular songs, including "God Bless America." He had written the song "God Bless America" (1917) when he served in the First World War, but did not release it until 1938. It has functioned as a popular patriotic song of the American citizenry ever since.

While Irving Berlin had no formal musical training, Jewish composer, conductor, and pianist Leonard Bernstein has been often called a "musical renaissance man." He exemplifies the meticulous musical training and accuracy of a world renowned musician, while exhibiting a unique talent for composing music of an extraordinary diversity (from symphonies and chamber music to musical comedies with jazz rhythms).

Leonard Bernstein was born in Lawrence, Massachusetts, in 1918. His life was transformed at the age of ten when his aunt gave his family her piano. He became good enough on the instrument during his teen years to give piano lessons to others and to play in a dance band. He majored in music at Harvard University (B.A., 1939), where he honed both his performance and composition skills. He also studied music with the head of the orchestral department of the Curtis Institute of Music, Fritz Reiner (who later became principal conductor of the New York Metropolitan Opera, 1948 to 1953, and Chicago Symphony Orchestra, 1953 to 1962). Dubbed as a musical "genius" by those who came into contact with him, Leonard Bernstein was appointed assistant conductor of the New York Philharmonic in 1942.

A year later, when a guest conductor of the New York Philharmonic, Bruno Walter, suddenly took ill, Leonard Bernstein filled in with a brilliant performance. In a front page article, "Young Aide Leads Philharmonic, Steps In When Bruno Walter Is Ill," *The New York Times* (November 15, 1943) reported:

A nation-wide radio audience and several thousand persons in Carnegie Hall were treated to a dramatic musical event yesterday afternoon when the 25-year-old assistant conductor of The New York Philharmonic Symphony Orchestra, Leonard Bernstein, substituted on a few hours' notice for Bruno Walter, who had become ill, and led the orchestra through its entire program. Enthusiastic applause greeted the performance of the youthful musician, who went through the ordeal with no signs of strain or nervousness.

The permanent conductor, Arthur Rodzinski, who arrived by intermission to view the latter half of Bernstein's performance, declared Leonard to be a "prodigious talent" and vowed, "we wish to give him every opportunity in the future."

That Bernstein could perform a difficult and musically diverse program so remarkably without rehearsal impressed the critics as well as Rodzinski. In a back page article, "Bernstein Shows Mastery of Score," beside a large photograph of Leonard being congratulated by members of the orchestra, New York Times' music critic Olin Downes declared that Leonard Bernstein "showed that he is one of the very few conductors of the rising generation who are indubitably to be reckoned with." Indeed, within a year, Bernstein's diverse talents were acclaimed once again when he composed the "Jeremiah Symphony" (1944), the "Fancy Free Ballet" (1944), and the score for the Broadway musical "On the Town" (1944).

From 1945 to 1947, Leonard Bernstein was the musical director for the New York City Center Orchestra. His guest appearances with American and European orchestras further solidified his reputation as one of the most talented conductors of his generation. He taught at Brandeis University (1951–1954), and he delivered academic lectures in following years (including the Charles Elliot Norton Lectures at Harvard, which were published in 1982). Leonard Bernstein also composed many more symphonies, ballets, choral works, broadway musicals, and operas. His powerful score for the popular "West Side Story" (1957) was acclaimed by lay audiences and critics alike (the lyrics were written by another highly acclaimed Jewish composer and lyricist, Stephen Sondheim, who after seven Tony Awards, three Grammy Awards, a Pulitzer Prize, and an Oscar to his credit, is still composing in his

135

mid-sixties). The success of both the stage and cinema version owed much to Bernstein's composition skills. In 1958, Leonard Bernstein was appointed musical director and conductor of the New York Philharmonic, the first American-born, American-trained musician to hold the post. When he retired from full-time conducting in 1969 to devote himself to his composition work, he was named conductor laureate for life by the New York Philharmonic. In the following decades, he became as popular for his television appearances as he did for his stage work. He even developed educational programs for television.

Twentieth-century America has thrilled to the talent and rich variety of Jewish musicians. When just an infant, violinist Isaac Stern (b. 1920) emigrated from the Ukraine to the San Francisco Bay area with his parents. His mother was a piano teacher, and young Isaac took up the violin at the age of eight. By the age of fourteen, he appeared as a soloist with the San Francisco Orchestra. His fame became worldwide after the Second World War, and he has served as a musical ambassador for the United States ever since (even in China!). He is as comfortable playing contemporary compositions (he has played for several movie soundtracks) as he is in playing concert soloist with esteemed symphonies. In the forefront of the movement to save Carnegie Hall in 1960, Isaac Stern has helped young musicians throughout the world gain access to the bastions of symphonic power. In fact, two modern famed Jewish violinists, Itzhak Perlman (b. 1945) and Pinchas Zuckerman (b. 1948), owe their "discovery" and career success to arrangements made by Isaac Stern. Perlman overcame the crippling effects of polio to win the Levintritt Competition in 1964; Zuckerman won the prestigious competition in 1967.

In contrast to Isaac Stern, the celebrated pianist Arthur Rubinstein (1887–1982) achieved international fame *before* immigrating to the United States (the Polish native had settled in Los Angeles in 1941 and became a U.S. citizen in 1946). He soon became one of the most frequently recorded classical musicians in America, and continued on a frantic international concert pace even into his eighties. Rubenstein's and Stern's manager, however, was the same man: Sol (Solomon) Hurok (1888–1974), who represented clients as diverse as Christian pianist Van Cliburn, dancer Isadora Duncan, and bandleader Benny Goodman. Hurok became famous for organizing concerts and sponsoring cultural exchange programs. For example, Sol Hurok sponsored the Bolshoi Ballet and the Moscow Art Players in their travels to the United States. Sol Hurok is representative of a number of Jewish agents and promoters who have worked to spread entertainment to the far reaches of the American continent and throughout the world.

The eighth of eleven children of a poor Chicago tailor, Benny Goodman was born Benjamin David Goodman on May 30, 1909. The clarinetist became one of the most famous band leaders of the 1930s and 1940s, garnering the title "The King of Swing." Even famous Jewish trumpeter, Harry James (born in Albany, Georgia, in 1916), spent two years with Goodman before starting his own group. The first white bandleader to make African American musicians full members of his band and to regularly integrate his ensemble performances, Benny Goodman was versatile at moving from jazz and "swing" to classical performances. He played a number of classical concerts in the 1940s and even taught at the Juilliard School of Music.

Even earlier than efforts of bandleader Benny Goodman, George Gershwin (1898–1937) was the Jewish composer responsible for preparing a largely white American concert audience for the onslaught of the African American jazz revolution. In the process, Gershwin became one of America's most popular songwriters.

Born in Brooklyn, George Gershwin wrote his first songs while playing piano at a music publishing company. His first theatrical productions were "Half Past Eight" (1918) and "La La Lucille" (1919). "La La Lucille" enjoyed quite a bit of success, but it was eclipsed by the rave reviews Gershwin received for his song, "Swanee," which Al Jolson sang in the production "Sinbad." It was George Gershwin's first hit song, and it made him one of the composition whiz kids of the theatrical world. Through his compositions for George White's "Scandals" revues in the early 1920s, Gershwin met Paul Whiteman, who commissioned him to write a jazz composition for a concert at Aeolian Hall in New York City. George Gershwin's resultant "Rhapsody in Blue" (1924) for piano and orchestra was a resounding success. It was first performed with Gershwin himself at the piano, and it solidified his fame. Jazz became respectable on the American concert stage from the mid–1920s onward, delighting hundreds of thousands of listeners.

Not only had George Gershwin become popular, but he also proved to be extremely versatile. When the conductor of the New York Symphony, Walter Johannes Damrosch (1862–1950, from the famed Jewish family of classical musicians) asked Gershwin to compose a symphonic work, Gershwin complied with the "Concerto in F" (1925). Walter Damrosch had himself played an important part in the development of American concert life, even inviting Tchaikovsky to tour America in the early 1890s. In 1927, Walter Damrosch toured the United States, taking the classical concert to some areas in which it had never appeared. Both Tchaikovsky's works and Gershwin's "Concerto in F" were part of his repertoire. Damrosch also became music advisor to the National Broadcasting Corporation (NBC) radio, exerting great influence on American music education.

George Gershwin realized that he had limited music education himself, and he determined to bolster his composition skills. He studied with Rubin Goldmark (1872–1936), the Jewish head of the department of composition of the Julliard Graduate School, and with Joseph Schillinger (1895–1943), a Jewish immigrant from Russia who developed mathematical principles for composition and taught at the New York School for Social Research. George Gershwin applied his honed composition skills into such classical-oriented works as "An American in Paris" (1928) and "Second Rhapsody" (1931). With his brother, Ira Gershwin (1896–1983), writing lyrics to his musical compositions, George Gershwin also composed popular musical shows, such as "Lady Be Good" (1924), "Strike Up the Band" (1927), "Girl Crazy" (1930), and "Of Thee I Sing" (1931). The musical show "Of Thee I Sing" was a political satire which won the Pulitzer Prize in drama in 1932.

One of George Gershwin's goals in life was to create an American opera. He achieved this magnificent feat with the production of his famed opera, *Porgy and Bess* (1935). Based on the DuBose Heyward book, *Catfish Row,* about the life of Southern blacks, and bolstered by lyrics written by his brother Ira and Heyward, *Porgy and Bess* was a powerful composition with enduring songs, such as "Summertime."

Composer George Gershwin's life was cut short before his thirty-ninth birthday, when he developed a brain tumor in the year following the success of *Porgy and Bess.* At the time, he and

Ira were working on songs for films in Hollywood. On February 28, 1973, the United States government issued an eight-cent commemorative stamp in honor of George Gershwin on the occasion of the seventy-fifth anniversary of his birth. On this first stamp in the U.S. Postal Service's American Arts series, George Gershwin was seated at the piano, a Jewish representative of the talent of the American musical world.

Jewish composers, musicians, and promoters were significant in the transformation of American jazz and "swing" to the "rock 'n' roll," "soul music," "folk music," and "doo wop" popular entertainment sounds of later decades. For example, Jewish songwriter and recording artist Carole King (born Carole Klein in Brooklyn, New York, in 1942) turned out over one hundred songs, including the 1960 rhythm-and-blues ballad, "Will You Love Me Tomorrow?" Recorded by the African American women's group, The Shirelles, the ballad reached the top of the charts at the beginning of 1961. Other hits included "Go Away, Little Girl," "Up On The Roof," and "The Locomotion." In 1971 Carole performed her own works in the album "Tapestry." "Tapestry" sold more than 13 million copies, and Carole's musical effort won four Grammy awards (Best Album, Best Song "You've Got A Friend," Best Single Record "It's Too Late," and Best Female Performer in the Pop Field).

Art Garfunkel, of the noted Simon and Garfunkel vocal and instrumental duo, was born in Forest Hills, New York. The Jewish performer had just finished his B.A. degree in art history and had begun work on his master's degree in mathematics education when his and Simon's "The Sounds of Silence" climbed to the top of the music charts. Art Garfunkel composed the music and harmonies that made future albums successful, including "Sounds of Silence" (1966), "Parsley, Sage, Rosemary and Thyme" (1966), "Bookends" (1968), and "Bridge over Troubled Water" (1970), which sold over 8 million. The song "Mrs. Robinson" from the album "Bookends" was used for Dustin Hoffman's hit film "The Graduate" (1968), soon becoming a classic. Finishing his master's degree in 1967 and beginning work on a doctorate, Art Garfunkel basked in the music awards he and Paul Simon were accumulating. Nevertheless, they separated in 1970, and Art Garfunkel went on to achieve some acclaim in a film career ("Catch–22," 1970; "Carnal Knowledge," 1971; "Bad Timing,"

1980), while Paul Simon explored other areas of music recording. Art Garfunkel did record several other solo albums; he and Paul Simon have performed together from time to time in the 1980s and 1990s. The influence of Simon and Garfunkel on modern music, however, will never be forgotten by their millions of fans worldwide.

Much more could be said about the entertainment contributions of Jewish recording artist and composer, Barry Manilow (b. 1946); or famed Jewish opera singers, Beverly Sills (born Belle Miriam Silverman in 1929) and Roberta Peters (born Roberta Peterman in 1930), or the dramatic contributions of Jewish prima ballerina, Nora Kaye (b. 1920), and Jewish choreographer, Jerome Robbins (born Jerome Rabinowitz in 1918). What about the thousands of local stories that are lost in the vast world press—such as Jewish Milwaukee businessman, Sy Lefco, whose love for jazz music never abated and whose support of young local jazz talent (such as African American vocalist Penny Goodwin) continued in the 1970s? What will be the historic entertainment contributions of Jewish pianists John Browning, Misha Dichter, Gary Graffman, Murray Perahia, or pianist turned conductor Leon Fleisher? What further contributions will be made by Jewish conductors Eve Queler, James Levine, and Michael Tilson Thomas, composer Marvin David Levy, or violinist Paul Zukofsky? A cadre of Jewish musical talent joins its Gentile counterpart in taking American entertainment to new frontiers in the twenty-first century.

*　*　*

On June 30, 1994, Kirk Douglas addressed the National Press Club in Washington, D.C., entertaining and sparring with the news professionals in a delightful address and a challenging question and answer session. He told the premier American newscasters that "coming from the world of make-believe, I depend on news reporters to bring me into the world of reality. I resent it when they don't. But now I am more and more alarmed by the fuzziness. Everywhere I feel the world of make-believe creeping into the world of reality." He challenged the men and women of the news media that in the midst of an American society that likes its reality seasoned with make-believe, they must realize the danger of such "make-believe seasoning" becoming a "tool of self deception." "Of course the media must report the news," Kirk later explained. "They must not go into show business, they must not say, 'Ah, this is a hot item, let's milk this.' They must rationally report the news."

In the midst of clarifying the difference between the news media and the entertainer, Kirk Douglas summed up the contribution of the entertainer and entertainment in American society: "The world of entertainment is so essential, because in this world of tension we need something to forget all our problems and to get wrapped up in the problems and excitement of some other people."

Realizing that American entertainment in some ways reflects American society and in some ways influences American society (as well as societies around the world), Kirk Douglas has been very concerned about a popular entertainer's responsibility. "We have an unfair advantage, and we must take our public role seriously," the entertainer concluded. "People in the public eye do have an impact on the public. The public comes to acknowledge them, and it is a *power*. And, any power is dangerous, because it can be used for good things or for bad things. That is the danger."

IDEAS AND INVENTIONS

THE YEAR WAS 1850. A YOUNG JEWISH IMMIGRANT, LEVI Strauss (1829–1902) from Bavaria, found himself in Sacramento, California, during the year-old gold rush. Gold prospectors had complained that their pants did not hold up under the stress and strain of panning and digging for the precious metal. Levi started a dry goods business and came up with an idea to help the thousands of prospectors and the local folks as well. He made sturdy blue denim trousers that were reinforced with copper rivets. Popular with the miners, the quality of the denim pants soon captured the fancy of farmers and ranch hands. By 1853, Levi Strauss had to open another store in San Francisco. The idea had developed into a full-fledged enterprise by the time of the Civil War. Today, a century and a half later, *Levis* is still a household word, popular throughout the world.

Shortly after the Civil War, twenty-two-year-old Isador Kitsee (1845–1931) emigrated from Vienna, Austria, to the United States. He traveled west to Cincinnati, Ohio, and became city chemist there. Nearly two decades later, in 1886, as he entered his forties, he moved east to Philadelphia. Known for his creativity and ingenuity, Isador Kitsee became an inventor in "The City of Brotherly Love." In fact, it is estimated that his inventions numbered approximately 2,000, and he single-handedly transformed the life of his city (and many towns and villages across the United States). For example, Isador Kitsee invented Philadelphia's first trolley streetcar and, since railroads were spreading throughout the nation carrying

143

passengers and freight in a lifeline of transportation, he invented a refrigerator car, railroad signals, and an underground telegraph. Wherever a problem developed, Isador invented a solution. As his patents relate, he made improvements in the manufacture of sulfuric acid as well as proposing better methods for extracting gold from its ores. Isador even invented a coal breaker.

In 1889 Isador Kitsee sold a wireless patent to Guglielmo Marconi, the man who is credited with inventing radio seven years later. At the dawn of the twentieth century with its promised advancements in communications and entertainment, Isador took out patents on a phonograph disc and even designed a method for making color motion pictures. In fact, in 1912 Isador Kitsee patented a device for the use of speech with motion pictures. Isador Kitsee and Levi Strauss demonstrate the ideas and inventions that proceeded from the Jewish community and enhanced the life and future of their fellow Americans. While this chapter can only scratch the surface of Jewish contributions, the historian is captivated by the breadth and depth of the effect of such inventiveness on American culture and society.

Entrepreneurs and Engineers

Many of the German immigrants who made the United States their home before the Civil War traveled to small towns in the Midwest and South. Quite a few became itinerant peddlers, finally settling in towns where they established general stores, dry good shops, and clothing outlets. From these humble beginnings, a number of large department store chains emerged. For instance, Bavarian Adam Gimbel (1817–1896) arrived in New Orleans in 1835 and peddled dry goods along the Mississippi River in the late 1830s before opening his first general store in Vincennes, Indiana, in 1842. Known as an honest and dedicated merchant, Adam refunded the purchase price of any item sold by his store if his customer was dissatisfied enough to bring it back. He enlarged his selection of goods to meet the needs of the community and provided personal service regardless of status or race. With much sacrifice and perserverance, the Gimbel Brothers department store chain was founded by Adam's seven sons, who opened stores in Milwaukee (in 1887), Philadelphia (in 1894), and finally New York City (in 1919).

Lazarus Straus (1809–1898) immigrated alone from Germany to Georgia in 1852. His wife and three sons joined him two years later. Moving his family to New York City at the end of the Civil War in 1865, he became a successful crockery importer. His sons, Isidor (1845–1912, who died in the sinking of the *Titanic*) and Nathan (1848–1931), became partners in the R. H. Macy Department Store in 1874, where they had rented the basement to display their father's glassware. By 1887, they were sole owners of Macy's. We have seen in chapter 1 the family's deep involvement in public service and charitable endeavors. What few realize, however, is the hard work and determination that led to their economic success.

Even our friend Levi Strauss, whose first name went from a California colloquialism to an international password, struggled toward success but also shared his good fortune with others. A bachelor who had followed his two brothers to New York in 1848, Levi brought his brothers into his burgeoning California enterprise. Then he made his brother-in-law, David Stern, a partner in Levi Strauss & Company. Finally, David Stern's four sons were brought on board as well. By this time Levi Strauss had assumed directorship of a bank, owned an insurance company and woolen mills, and headed the San Francisco Board of Trade. A pillar of the San Francisco community, he gave large sums of money to educational programs and to Catholic, Protestant, and Jewish orphanages. His firm became an "equal opportunity" employer long before it was fashionable or required by law.

While we will meet many other entrepreneurs in the next chapter, one readily notes the progressive concepts in these examples: refund policies, expanded personal service, and new quality products. Other ideas flourished from Jewish businesspersons. Californian David Lubin marked clear prices on each item in his store. This concept of fixed prices in his "One Price Store" helped the Polish immigrant to expand from Sacramento to San Francisco in a series of chain stores. Julius Rosenwald of Sears, Roebuck, & Company developed the mail order catalogue into an American tradition.

Enterprising success stories intertwine with inventiveness and skill. A poor Jewish peddler, Louis Borgnicht, began making children's aprons for little girls. They sold quickly. He and his energetic wife realized that there was no ready-to-wear children's clothing being manufactured. Even in the 1880s mothers made their children's clothes. The Borgnichts took a chance in the last decade of the nineteenth century and began manufacturing a line of children's clothes. A total new industry emerged, and Louis Borgnicht became known as the "King of the Children's Dress Trade." By the end of the first decade of the twentieth century, the Russian immigrant family had become one of the successful clothing manufacturers in New York City.

Much has been made of Jewish involvement in the earliest history of the automobile. Louis Blaustein (1869–1937) and his son Jacob (1892–1970), however, pioneered the distribution of gasoline in an era when automobile sales mushroomed and the gas-guzzling vehicle became a "necessity" for the American consumer. Their inventiveness and ingenuity are legend.

Russian-born Louis Blaustein immigrated to the United States in 1888. He began his journey of fame by peddling kerosene on the streets. In 1892, his son Jacob was born, and Louis landed a more steady job with the Standard Oil Company at its Baltimore facility. His keen ideas and inventiveness impressed Standard Oil officials, and he quickly moved into executive leadership. Saving his money as best he could and sensing the future development of the motorcar, Louis left Standard Oil in 1910 and founded the fledgling American Oil Company. His eighteen-year-old son, Jacob, joined his father in the enterprise. Their creative distribution system sparked a phenomenal growth as they were one of the first companies to open "drive-in" gas stations. They also developed a gas pump that told motorists exactly how many gallons of gas they were getting for their money. Experimenting and inventing improved forms of gasoline, the Blausteins sold some of the first "high-test" gasoline in the country.

The American Oil Company filling stations spread from Baltimore to surrounding states. Soon they covered the East Coast. They built petroleum refineries and opened steamship terminals. As he amassed great wealth, Louis Blaustein gave massive amounts to charity. In most cases he preferred to remain anonymous in his donations. Jacob Blaustein served as president of the company from 1933 until his father's death in 1937. He spent the latter part of his life in philanthropic endeavors and international peacemaking efforts. He served as a member of the American delegation to the tenth UN General Assembly and worked diligently for the organization of the Convention on Genocide and the Declaration of Human Rights. When Jacob Blaustein died in 1971, the inventions, the company, and the investments he and his father had developed made him one of the ten richest men in the United States. *Amoco* has become a well known word.

Inventiveness and engineering came together in the life of Emile Berliner (1851–1929). A Jewish immigrant from Germany, Berliner entered the United States in 1870, working various jobs in New York City and Washington, D.C., as a clerk, a salesman, and a laboratory assistant. He was fascinated with electricity, reading and studying about the induction principles incorporated into electric generators and transformers by Englishman Michael Faraday and American Joseph Henry in the 1830s. In 1876 Berliner refined Alexander Graham Bell's newly invented telephone, using an induction coil and loose-contact transmitter. The Bell Telephone Company immediately recognized the significance of Emile Berliner's improvements. With his inventive genius, Berliner had made the telephone a viable communication tool for long-distance use, and historians credit him with the invention of the telephone receiver. Bell Telephone purchased the invention and made Berliner chief electrical instruments inspector of the company.

Within a decade, Emile Berliner had improved Thomas Edison's phonograph by using shallow grooves on a flat disc to replace the older-style cylinders. The Victor Talking Machine Company purchased Berliner's patent and developed the modern gramophone. Berliner kept improving the medium and, with his improvements, the modern phonograph and sound recording industry was born. Unlike Edison who wanted to use the phonograph as an office dictation machine, Emile foresaw the home entertainment value of the invention. The Berliner Gramophone Company introduced the concept of royalties for singers and musicians, and instituted the recording contract. In 1897 Berliner's company produced the first shellac records, opened a recording studio and, adjacent to it, the first record shop. The Victor Talking Machine Company finally absorbed the Berliner Gramophone Company, later becoming RCA.

When aviation was in its infancy, Emile Berliner added important developments, such as the use of a revolving cylindered light

147

engine. Although he was in his sixties, he designed a variety of helicopters and tested them in flight himself. By this time, he indeed had become a part of the Roaring Twenties. His son, Henry Adler Berliner, who was born in 1895, became president of Berliner Aircraft, in Washington, D.C. Both father and son were known for their contributions in time and finances to philanthropic causes.

In fact, Emile Berliner attempted to give back to American society at all stages of his success. He founded the Society for the Prevention of Sickness in the 1890s and organized a conference in Washington in 1907 to analyze the quality of milk and to promote the pasteurization process. He devoted much of his time to children's health and nutrition, leading the fight against tuberculosis, emphasizing preventive medicine, and supporting the cause of proper hygiene.

David Sarnoff and Broadcasting

Jewish contributions to broadcasting escalated. In all actuality, Emile Berliner had developed the forerunner of the microphone and had extended the range of communications. Isador Kitsee had contributed with his wireless patent, his device for the use of speech with motion pictures, and his early research into developing color motion pictures. Russian-born David Sarnoff (1891–1971) became an important pioneer in the development of radio and television broadcasting. His life epitomizes Jewish perception and creativity in these mediums.

David Sarnoff immigrated with his family to the United States in 1900. Interested in communications and electronics, he taught himself to operate the telegraph and landed a job with the Marconi Telegraph Company of America at the age of fifteen. He happened to be on duty when the *Titanic* sent its distress signal in 1912 and was the operator that relayed it. When RCA (Radio Corporation of America) gained control of the American branch of Marconi Telegraph in 1919, Sarnoff was appointed commercial manager. In 1926 he founded NBC (National Broadcasting Company) as a subsidiary of RCA. Four years later, his skill, savvy, genius, and dedication apparent to all, David Sarnoff became president of RCA. The former office boy and telegrapher had moved to the top executive position of a communications giant.

In the realm of "ideas," it was David Sarnoff who advanced the idea that radio should (and would!) become a "household utility." As early as 1916, Sarnoff suggested that music could be brought into millions of households using a wireless receiver ("a simple Radio Box"). To prove his point, Sarnoff began to manufacture radios, and the wireless units became a major source of RCA profits in the 1920s. Through the formation of NBC, Sarnoff determined to prove the practicality of coast-to-coast broadcasting through a network that would provide entertainment, information, and education to the nation. As a nucleus for NBC, RCA purchased radio station WEAF from AT&T for one million dollars. In the midst of the Great Depression in 1931, NBC made its first profit—two million dollars. In 1933 David Sarnoff moved RCA-NBC to Rockefeller Plaza in New York City.

In 1929 David Sarnoff learned of the television experiments of Russian immigrant Vladimir Kosma Zworykin, who worked for Westinghouse. Zworykin had tried to develop an all-electronic system to reproduce visual images as opposed to the mechanical systems proposed by other inventors. Sarnoff announced RCA's commitment to television in 1935, eventually investing over $50 million in the Zworykin all-electronic system. At the 1939 World's Fair in New York City, RCA demonstrated a television system and voiced Sarnoff's commitment to making it a practical "household utility." Although the Second World War and other complications postponed television to a postwar phenomenon, David Sarnoff's ideas and persistence paid off.

David Sarnoff also battled to develop color television, an idea even his own executives vehemently opposed. The large outlays of capital to develop color television, however, were soon recouped in its phenomenal success. By the time of his death in 1971, David Sarnoff's ideas and abilities had built RCA into the world's largest electronic complex, competitive in (if not dominating) the fields of radio, television, and computers. Doing more than a $2 billion business annually by the end of the 1960s, Sarnoff's RCA employed more than 100,000 men and women in the United States and forty-three foreign countries. He also foresaw the importance of earth-orbiting satellites, and RCA became a leader in that field as well. Within four years of David Sarnoff's death, RCA orbited the first communications satellite designed for the relaying of television signals.

In the realm of communications, David Sarnoff serves as only one example. Jews have played a major role in the development of broadcasting and, as will be seen in the next chapter, have been well represented in most executive positions as well as in most technical aspects.

Adolph Zukor and Film

Hungarian-born Adolph Zukor (1873–1976) was a comparable Jewish pioneer in the movie industry. Immigrating to the United States in 1888, he worked in the fur trade in New York and Chicago, before entering the penny-arcade business with Marcus Loew in 1903. It was Adolph Zukor who had the idea that there was a need for motion pictures that were longer and of better quality. Zukor also promoted the "star" system and hired big-name actors and actresses to produce film versions of popular stage shows. Almost single-handedly transforming the motion picture industry into a modern, integrated business enterprise, Zukor combined stars and good stories with state of the art production facilities and efficient distribution centers. He also built movie theaters in the central business districts of towns and cities across the nation and convinced skeptical conservative investors that there was a great deal of money to be made in the projection of celluloid images.

Zukor seemed to realize before many others that the film industry was a mass-consumption business with awesome potential for growth. And yet, unlike most of the businessmen of the day, he saw the ability of movies to influence public opinion, to affect culture, and to provide a new art form. In 1923 Adolph Zukor urged producers to set higher standards for their craft and reminded them of the powerful responsibility they wielded. He even offered a $10,000 annual prize for the best story produced as a motion picture. By the mid–1930s, the film industry was a $2 billion business that employed well over 300,000 men and women. In 1935 a movie had the potential of being distributed to 23,000 movie theaters with a total seating capacity of over eleven million. In the depths of the Great Depression, it was estimated that an average of 115 million Americans went to the movie theaters at least once a week.

To this day, Jews have remained prominent in all phases of the movie industry, although their actual ownership of the industry has declined from the early decades of the twentieth century. Even by the mid–1930s, Jewish entrepreneurs only owned three of the eight largest studios. Adolph Zukor served as president of Paramount until 1935, and in 1948 won a special Academy Award for four decades of service to the film industry. He lived to be 103 years old and was privileged to see changes he could not have fathomed in the art form he loved and respected. And yet, the perception and foresight of Adolph Zukor transformed a creative idea into reality.

Other Jewish Inventors

A few other Jewish inventors should be mentioned. Born in Baltimore, Maryland, in 1899, Charles Adler invented a variety of light systems, including railroad and highway traffic signals. Electric traffic signals were introduced in America in 1928, and traffic control reached a new plateau. Later, he invented traffic sound detectors. Charles Adler also experimented with lighting systems for aircraft. This led to his invention of navigation lights, reflector lamps, and anticollision lights. He is also credited with inventing aircraft proximity indicators.

If Charles Adler's field was lighting, Jerome Wiesner's bastion was radar. Born in Detroit, Michigan, in 1915 and raised in the home of a dry goods merchant, Jerome Wiesner was one of the first developers of radar. During World War II, "radar" was the name given to the electronic system by which radio waves were bounced off an airplane in order to detect its presence and locate its position (acronym for "radio detection and ranging"). Wiesner joined a number of other researchers in laying the groundwork for Sir Robert Watson-Watt's successful practical application of radar.

Jewish inventors of machines are plentiful as well. Russian-born Hyman Ledeen, who emigrated with his family in 1903 at the age of seven, invented an air hoist, a steel punch, and a pump for oil wells as well as many other smaller inventions. Moses David Heyman, who was born in Newark, New Jersey, in 1896, invented a mechanical hand in 1938 as well as a number of other heavy-duty machines used in metalworking and mining. Heyman also has been credited with producing the first continuous sheets of synthetic mica. This was crucial to the war effort against Nazi Germany when imports of mica from other countries were impeded. Mica, in fact, became an indispensable element of electronic and electrical devices, including radar equipment.

151

Just before the Second World War began, Walter Juda was one of the fortunate members of the Jewish community to get out of Nazi Germany. Born in Berlin in 1916, he settled in the United States in 1939. After years of research at Harvard Medical School, he joined the division of industrial cooperation at Massachusetts Institute of Technology in 1948. Among his many inventions, Walter Juda has been recognized as an early pioneer in the desalination of water by electrodialysis. As reliable supplies of water rapidly diminish all over the globe, Juda's contribution looms larger every day. In contrast to the distillation processes of boiling brackish water to remove the water from the salt, Walter Juda's invention centered on the fact that most minerals dissolved in water dissociate into electrically charged particles (ions). He found that by means of two special membranes that allow the passage of only positive (cation) charged ions or only negative (anion) charged ions, and the application of a direct current electric field, salts could be removed from brackish water to produce water of a desired purity, fit for human consumption or for agricultural needs. Walter Juda had revolutionized the desalination process.

Finally, in the field of photography, a number of Jewish inventors have contributed. For example, Leopold Mannes (1899–1964) and Leopold Godowsky (b. 1900), musician-scientists, in 1933 invented the Kodachrome color process and in 1938 produced Ektachrome. And, Edwin Herbert Land (1909–1991) invented a one-step method of developing and printing photographs. While a student at Harvard University, young Land experimented with polarized light. By the mid–1930s, he had applied polarization to camera filters and three-dimensional motion pictures as well as to antiglare headlights and reduced-glare sunglasses. In 1937, Edwin Land founded the Polaroid Corporation. By the end of World War II, he had developed the Polaroid Land Camera, a camera that took and developed pictures in a single-step process. First marketed in 1948 using a special black and white film, Edwin Land had developed a color film version by 1963. He even experimented with a movie version in the 1970s.

Like so many of the inventors that we have viewed in this chapter, Edwin Herbert Land mastered the theoretical as well as the mechanical and technical. Land developed many theories during his scientific experiments, but one seemed to dominate his later enterprise. Edwin Land discovered a theory of color perception that stated that at least three independent image-forming mechanisms work together to indicate the color seen by the eye. His thesis guides us into a world of Jewish contributions that often boggle the mind, but that have literally fashioned our modern scientific age—a world of theorems and theories.

Theorems and Theories

The first American to be awarded a Nobel Prize in science was a Jewish physicist, Albert Abraham Michelson (1852–1931). In 1907 he was awarded the Nobel Prize in physics. Born in Germany, Michelson's family brought him to the United States at the age of two. After graduating from Annapolis in 1873, he spent two years at sea, returning to become an instructor in physics at his alma mater. While teaching at the naval academy, he began to experiment with the velocity of light. The pursuit would become a lifelong passion. Spending the years 1881 to 1882 overseas in Berlin studying and experimenting, Albert Michelson developed the *interferometer,* an instrument to measure wavelengths of light. The simple invention would revolutionize scientific study and would change the course of theoretical work in physics, astronomy, and cosmology.

Professor Michelson possessed a canny ability for devising the simplest of mechanisms to prove or disprove the most complicated of theorems. His interferometer consisted of two straight arms set at right angles to each other. Each arm had a mirror at one end. At the point in which the arms were joined a half-silvered mirror split a light beam from an outside light source in two. Each half of the split beam traveled down an arm and was reflected back by the mirrors at the end of each arm. When the two beams recombined, they "interfere" (thus, "interferometer") in such a way as to produce a characteristic pattern of fringes that depended on the difference in time required for the two beams to travel the round trip. Returning to the United States in 1883 to teach at the Case School of Applied Science in Cleveland, Ohio, Professor Michelson continued his experimentation and discovery. In 1887, with the assistance of Edward Williams Morley, he performed what scholars consider to be one of the most important experiments in the history of science.

Accepted theories of nineteenth-century physics held that space was filled with a medium at absolute rest that scientists named the "aether." Scientists believed that light traveled through the aether in waves. As the earth moved through the aether, they believed, the speed of a light ray as measured on earth would depend on its direction (much as an object going with a current of water or struggling against a current of water). Until the development of Michelson's interferometer, scientists doubted that there would ever be a way to measure the motion of a body relative to the aether. Michelson proved that measurement was possible and in the early 1880s established the standard international meter in terms of a wavelength of cadmium.

According to accepted theory, if Michelson's interferometer was rotated through ninety degrees, the roles of parallel and perpendicular arms were reversed and the fringe pattern should shift. Belief in the aether required a fringe shift of perhaps four-*tenths* of a wavelength. In the Michelson-Morley experiment of 1887 no fringe shift as large as four-*hundredths* of a wavelength was observed. Subsequent experiments by scientists from all over the world confirmed Michelson-Morley's astonishing findings. There was no medium at absolute rest in space—there was no aether! In 1905 another Jewish physicist, Albert Einstein, proposed his theory of relativity which postulated that the speed of light is always the same, regardless of the motion of the observer, and therefore travels the same speed along each arm of the interferometer. Newtonian concepts of time and space had been replaced by Einstein's relativistic physics.

Michelson continued a distinguished academic career at the University of Chicago (1892–1929). He was the first person to measure the diameter of a star (Alpha Orion), designed a number of instruments for the U.S. Navy, and wrote a number of scientific studies, including *Velocity of Light* (1902), *Light Waves and Their Uses* (1903), and *Studies in Optics* (1927).

In the field of nuclear physics, Isidor Isaac Rabi (1898–1988) sought to determine the nature of the force that holds together the protons within the nucleus of an atom. When German-Jewish physicist Otto Stern (who immigrated to the United States in 1933 to escape Nazi persecution) developed a molecular beam that helped determine the magnetic moment of a proton, Rabi developed the molecular beam magnetic-resonance method.

While a professor at Columbia University in 1937, Isidor Rabi discovered that the behavior of a molecular or atomic beam in the presence of two inhomogeneous magnetic fields will reveal the magnetic moments of atoms or atomic nuclei. This method made it possible to receive and interpret such beams. Otto Stern, who was continuing his research in molecular physics at Carnegie Institute of Technology in Pittsburgh, and had become an American citizen, was awarded the 1943 Nobel Prize in physics for his earlier discoveries. Isidor Rabi, who had become associate director of the Radiation Laboratory at MIT in 1940, was awarded the 1944 Nobel Prize in physics for his molecular beam magnetic-resonance method. The Jewish physicists had indeed complemented one another's work.

Cleveland-born Donald A. Glaser (b. 1926), a Jewish professor of physics at the University of Michigan, felt limited in his experimentation in nuclear physics by the standard cloud chamber used to record the high-speed trajectories of nuclear particles. In the early 1950s he invented a small "bubble chamber" that subsequently became an indispensable research tool in nuclear physics. This invention and the research he derived from it led to his being awarded the Nobel Prize in physics in 1960. The following year a Jewish professor at Stanford University, Robert Hofstadter (1915–1990), won the Nobel Prize in physics for designing a device that enabled the first exact measurements of the size and shape of protons and neutrons in the nucleus of an atom. He also posited from his findings the probable existence of two powerful subparticles, i.e., the rho-meson and the omega-meson. Later, both of these subparticles were detected.

Rosalyn Sussman Yalow (b. 1921) won the Nobel Prize in medicine in 1977 for another innovative technique. She applied nuclear physics to clinical medicine. While professor of medicine at Mt. Sinai Hospital in New York City, Rosalyn Yalow perfected "radioimmunoassay," a technique she had used since 1959. Radioimmunoassay permitted scientists to use radioisotopic tracers to measure the concentration of substances in blood and other fluids in humans, plants, and animals.

Born in the Bronx, Rosalyn Sussman Yalow became the second woman in history to win the Nobel Prize in medicine. (The first woman was Czech-born American scientist, Gerty Radnitz Cori, who in 1947 had shared the Nobel Prize in physiology and medicine with her husband, Carl Cori.) Ironically, while in Hunter College finishing her advanced courses in physics, Rosalyn was told that she would never make it through graduate school without earning money as a secretary. She would chuckle years later that she had taken supplementary typing and shorthand courses in her senior year to prepare for that possibility. Rosalyn never worked as a secretary. She received a teaching fellowship in the engineering school at the University of Illinois, and became the second woman in the history of that institution to receive a Ph.D. in physics.

Of those Jewish physicists around the world who have struggled to develop consistent theories to interpret the complex forces within the atom, Murray Gell-Mann (b. 1929) overcame huge obstacles as he formulated a classification system for subatomic particles in the early 1960s and, for his efforts, won the 1969 Nobel Prize in physics. The California Institute of Technology professor's classification system has won widespread support in the scientific community, and his various theories on the behavior of subatomic particles are being proven one by one in experimentation.

For example, Professor Gell-Mann hypothesized the existence of omega particles. Their existence was confirmed in 1964. In 1963, Professor Gell-Mann hypothesized the existence of quarks, subatomic particles carrying fractional electric charges. Gell-Mann believed that the quark was one of the basic building blocks of matter. The 1990 Nobel Prize in physics was awarded to three researchers (one from Stanford and two from MIT) whose work demonstrated the existence of the quark. To prove Murray Gell-Mann's theory, the trio had conducted "deep inelastic scattering" experiments by accelerating electrons to an energy of 20 billion electron-volts along a two-mile tube at the Stanford Linear Accelerator Center and smashing them into samples of liquid hydrogen or deuterium. Surprised at their findings, the trio of scientists realized that their discovery was going to change the way science looks at subatomic particles, because they provided the first experimental evidence that protons and neutrons, once believed indivisible, were made up of what Professor Murray Gell-Mann had termed "quarks"—elementary particles with fractional charges of $+2/3$ or $-1/3$.

Though such theorization and experimentation seldom command daily news headlines, scientists many times have the greatest impact on the world's future. As humankind approached the twenty-first century, ethical issues confronted the scientific community. Jewish scientists have had to analyze the impact of discoveries on a fragile world. Professor Gell-Mann noted that as the cold war was breaking up, the superpowers needed to redefine "global security" so that it included population issues, environmental issues, and sustainable development issues of the world—especially with regard to developing nations.

Paul Berg, a 1980 Nobel Prize-winning chemist, has led a movement to force the federal government to draft and enforce strict guidelines on genetic engineering. Professor Berg has been called the Father of Gene Splicing and was the first person to use the new science of genetic engineering to construct a recombinant DNA molecule. His Nobel Prize in chemistry (which he shared with two other scientists) cited the importance of his "fundamental studies of the biochemistry of nucleic acids, with particular regard to recombinant DNA." While the Stanford professor realized that his discovery could lead to disease prevention and cures never before imagined, he also worried about accidental or deliberate abuse of genetic engineering. As early as 1975, Professor Berg convened a meeting of one hundred scientists from around the world to study the safety and propriety of genetic engineering research. His efforts continued as discoveries mounted and a new age approached. Jewish theorists and inventors are often in the forefront of struggling with the ethics of their craft.

Prime Movers

Academician Seymour Martin Lipset (b. 1922) has made his mark as a world-renowned sociologist, political scientist, and expert on public opinion. While teaching at Columbia University, the University of Toronto, the University of California at Berkeley, Harvard University and, finally, at Stanford University, Professor Lipset published approximately forty books on a variety of topics. His ideas have had an important effect on the social sciences and have permeated other fields of study as well. One of the concepts he has emphasized concerns the role of ideas as *prime movers* of history. He has argued, for example, that one of the key motivating "ideas" in American history is

157

achievement. Perhaps the same should be said of individuals who propose such ideas. Certainly, Professor Seymour Lipset's analyses have qualified him as a "prime mover" in the postwar era. In this chapter and others, one views hundreds of Jewish men and women who similarly qualify as prime movers in history. In conclusion to this chapter on ideas and inventions, let's view a few other Jewish postwar prime movers and their ideological impact.

Jewish psychoanalyst Erik H. Erikson (1902–1994) has been a prime mover through his lifetime work of bridging the gap between theories of personal human development and the broader environmental, social, and familial influences which surround the individual. Professor Erikson has stimulated much interest in developmental psychology, because he has dealt in his studies with the whole life span of a human being. Although his work has been criticized by some, Erikson's contention that human development occurs in eight "psychosocial stages" has been quoted with affection more often than it has been demeaned. And, as a major inflence on the behavioral and social sciences, his research cannot be ignored. When African American Professor Alvin Poussaint is questioned about the black concept of self, he invariably discusses Erik Erikson. When Professor Elizabeth Douvan talks about the role of women in America, she refers to Erikson's stage of autonomy. Famed Harvard professor and psychiatrist, Dr. Robert Coles, gives credit to Erik Erikson for helping him to chart his work over three decades, documenting the thoughts and lives of children from all segments of society. (Professor emeritus at Harvard until his death in 1994, Erikson taught there from 1934 to 1935, and from 1960 to 1970.)

Importantly, it was Erik Erikson who initiated and popularized the term "identity crisis." For example, in his studies of adolescents, he documented the interaction of a teenager's inner feelings with the peer culture, school culture, and family/society values that surround a young man or young woman. Nevertheless, Professor Erikson balances his studies with impacts and crises on the development of human identity and character from childhood to old age (among his many works along these lines are *Childhood and Society,* 1950; *Identity: Youth and Crisis,* 1968; *Adulthood,* 1978). He clearly focused the responsibility each generation has to succeeding generations (*Insight and*

Responsibility, 1964). In the realm of psychoanalytic history, Erik Erikson has run the gamut from Martin Luther (*Young Man Luther*, 1958) to Mahatma Gandhi (*Gandhi's Truth*, 1970) to the Sixties Revolution (*On the Origins of Militant Nonviolence*, 1969, which won the Pulitzer Prize and the National Book Award).

In the field of economics, two Jewish Nobel Prize winners exemplify a number of prime movers (including Milton Friedman, see chapter 2) in this discipline who have affected the nation and the world. Simon S. Kuznets (1901–1985) received the Nobel Prize in economic science in 1971 for his statistical research concerning national income and economic growth. Kuznets developed the concept of "gross national product," words that proliferate our media and textbooks today. This method for measuring the nation's economic growth has inspired similar applications around the world. Simon Kuznets also popularized quantitative economic history and, through his books and articles, encouraged new studies about the economic growth of nations.

Lawrence R. Klein (b. 1920), the son of clerical workers in an Omaha, Nebraska wholesale grocery, developed the system of "econometrics," a complex system of mathematical and statistical models that analyzes the effects of economic policies and forecasts economic trends. The University of Pennsylvania professor computerized his large-scale model and applied it to both short-term and long-term forecasts of the nation's economy (although he is critical of politicians who put re-election concerns ahead of what is best economically for the nation in the long-term). In 1980 Professor Lawrence Klein was awarded the Nobel Prize in economics for his work in econometric forecasting.

Certainly, Professor Lipset's assertion that ideas are prime movers in history has been borne out through the lives, research, and ideas of the representative individuals above. And, the ideas are so diverse. Elmer Louis Winter (b. 1912) was as concerned about jobs as any economist. His idea was to cofound Manpower in 1948, the first temporary employment service in the world. This corporation provided a new avenue in the workforce that has been emulated by hundreds of other temporary services. As for forecasting trends, Louis Harris (b. 1921) developed interviewing techniques and statistical methods that attempted to understand the *reasons* behind public actions. He became one of the most influential pollsters in America, and a number of government leaders have used his polling results to ascertain public attitudes.

As for government service and a Nobel Peace Prize (1973), former Secretary of State Henry A. Kissinger (b. 1923) developed the idea of "shuttle diplomacy" by actually living the part. It has become a standard diplomatic practice of successive presidential administrations in international affairs, especially in the midst of international crises (as Kissinger first employed it in the Middle East). The concept "shuttle diplomacy" has become a well-used term in the American vocabulary. By the 1990s, shuttle diplomacy was being employed by other nations of the world.

Jewish Women

The historian is overwhelmed with the contributions of American Jews as prime movers in modern history, and many have been viewed in earlier chapters. Perhaps it is fitting, however, to underscore the influence of Jewish women as prime movers in postwar America. As one views the primary sources that surround the lives of entrepreneurs and engineers, inventors and theorists, one is touched by the sincere credit they give to their mothers, the anchors of the Jewish peoplehood. In a basically male-dominated society, Jewish women have made their mark through their children as well as through their discoveries and their careers. Many Jewish women have been partners and supporters of their husbands' discoveries, ambitions, and ideas. There is no denying this fact—the husbands and sons insist that it is a fact. One also notes in this chapter and others the contributions of individual Jewish women.

And yet, in the postwar world, Jewish women carried on a battle that had been waged for centuries. They wanted equal rights and equal respect. They wanted to be credited for their accomplishments and to have access to educational opportunities and positions of authority accorded to men. Even in the 1950s when American culture was dominated by the concept of women as wives and mothers, one-third of all women worked for wages and female employment topped 23 million. Betty Friedan (b. 1921) labeled the dominant domestic ideology concerning women of that time "the feminine mystique," publishing a book by that title in 1963. From a Jewish family in Peoria, Illinois, and a sixteen-year veteran homemaker herself (raising three children), Betty Friedan has been portrayed by historians ever since as the catalyst of the modern Women's Liberation Movement and has been recognized as the predominant spokeswoman of the feminist movement in America. In *The Feminine Mystique*, she insisted that it was time to question the idea that women belonged only at home because they were (in the eyes of America) nurturing, timid creatures entirely different from competitive, savvy, and capable men. Her "idea" of questioning the status quo eventually transformed male-female relationships in the United States. Betty Friedan's latest book, *The Fountain of Age* (1994), challenges stereotypes concerning older Americans.

Research studies show that Jewish women identified more with feminist goals than many other groups of women did. Jewish women found themselves in the forefront of the emerging modern women's movement, and the United States was ripe for change. Between 1950 and 1974, college enrollment for women increased 456 percent, nearly doubling the increase for men during the same period. By 1960, nearly thirty-eight percent of women over the age of fifteen worked, constituting one-third of the total American work force. The Equal Pay Act was passed in 1963, making it illegal to pay women less than men for doing the same job, and the Civil Rights Act of 1964 included Title VII, which prohibited discrimination on the basis of sex.

Ideologically, Jewish women viewed discrimination against women as "injustice," and they skillfully fought for social justice and equality with determination and sacrifice. By the time Susan Weidman Schneider wrote *Jewish and Female: Choices and Changes in Our Lives Today* (1984), many hopes and dreams of the 1960s movement had been realized. Susan Weidman Schneider gave credit to her involvement in the women's movement to the support offered by her immediate and extended Jewish family, including her husband and children. She particularly singled out her mother, Zora Zagrabelna Weidman, who gave her physical stamina and "dogged determination" as well as teaching her "tolerance that has been immeasurably helpful." From her father she received "loving confidence" in her abilities and plans as a woman.

Many struggles continue for the contemporary women's movement, and Jewish women are also in the forefront of questioning the goals and the price of some of the gains achieved. These female prime movers are not fearful to monitor and critically examine the spectrum of prevailing feminist ideologies. And yet, because of the ideological contribution of Jewish women as well as their inventiveness under trying circumstances, American history and culture have changed for the better.

BUSINESS AND DESIGN

BY THE TIME LOUIS ISADORE KAHN (1901–1974) DESIGNED and oversaw the construction of the Salk Institute, he had established himself as one of the major architects of the twentieth century. When one views the original buildings of the Salk Institute for Biological Studies in La Jolla, California, one senses the mystical presence of its architect. Louis Kahn believed that every institution expresses a way of life. The Jewish architect felt that the structure of the Salk Institute should create an intellectual atmosphere that would link science and art, exuding a sense of permanence that would honor the noble effort and integrity of the medical researchers that inhabited the facilities. Two parallel research laboratories, each 65 feet by 245 feet, flank a plaza overlooking the Pacific Ocean. The bold and clearly defined shaping of reinforced concrete structures with eleven-foot ceilings for the laboratories creates a sense of openness, an impressive monument. Facing the plaza are a series of study towers for the scientists, connected by bridges to the laboratories and angular in profile to catch the ocean breezes. Visiting scientists were to be housed in the "Meeting House," with circular rooms with full openings toward the light surrounded by square screening devices to cut glare and facilitate ventilation (and with square rooms that had similar circular screening devices). In words laced with a couple of his favorite phrases, Louis Kahn had harnessed "the realm of spaces" in order to capture "a way of life."

Born in Estonia, Louis had immigrated to Philadelphia with his parents at the age of four. The City of

Brotherly Love would be both his inspiration and his base of operations for the rest of his life. Gifted in painting and music, Louis was guided toward architecture by his high school art teacher. He studied architecture at the University of Pennsylvania, earning his degree in 1924. Although he made a respectable living as an architect and became noted as a city planner, Louis Kahn's first building to achieve international reputation was the Yale University Art Gallery in New Haven, Connecticut, which he designed and oversaw construction, from 1952 to 1955. Kahn had been invited to Yale as a visiting critic in 1947. He so enamored faculty, administration, and students, that he was hired as a full-time professor of architecture. In designing the extension to the Yale Art Gallery, Louis Kahn created the first modern building at Yale University. Critics were impressed with the harmony and order Kahn created as he integrated air conditioning, electrical service, elevator, and stairs into a symmetrical artistic loft space of galleries, offices, and work areas on four floors. He revived the use of the column as a means of defining space and harbored mechanical services by applying forty-foot free spaces supported by columns at twenty-foot intervals.

After ten years at Yale University, Louis Kahn returned to the University of Pennsylvania. He would spend the rest of his life as a professor there, honing his personal architectural style (which was seen as a challenge to the international style of modern architecture) and solidifying his reputation at home and abroad. Among his many projects that made a personal statement, he designed the Richards Medical Research Building at the University of Pennsylvania, with its striking Medical Towers (1958–1960). It is here that he further enunciated his architectural concept of "served" and "servant" space, differentiating between the primary spaces and those secondary ones reserved for service lines and mechanical equipment.

Kahn refined these concepts, not only at the Salk Institute (1959–1965), but also in the library at Phillips Exeter Academy in Exeter, New Hampshire (1967–1972), and in the Kimbell Art Museum in Fort Worth, Texas (1966–1972). The Exeter Library exhibits a symmetrical composition of brick, concrete, wood, and glass, that often reminds one of a classical motif. At the time of his death at the age of seventy-three, Louis Kahn was designing and working on the Mellon Center for British Art at Yale University (1969–1974), government buildings in Dacca in Bangladesh, and the Institute of Management in Ahmadabad in India. In the decades that have passed since his death, a number of architectural experts have expressed the view that Louis Isador Kahn was the last of the great modern architects. Certainly, philosophy of design and monumental artistry came together in the work of this famed Jewish architect who made his home in Philadelphia. In his choice of style, however, Louis Kahn faced some of the same conflicting global forces that American artists and architects had faced for centuries.

Early Influences at Home and Abroad

The conflicting forces that faced the American artist from the colonial period on also affected American designers in the European colonies on the Atlantic Coast and in the western outposts. Historically, American designers have been conscious of their European cultural roots and the continuing innovations that European designers were cultivating. On the other hand, American designers had to adapt their European cultural heritage to their unique situation in America. By the mid–1800s, the United States had a number of conflicting design traditions that created a dynamic synthesis. Jewish architects were in the midst of this progression, contributing to a growing America and the rise of new artforms.

For example, soon after the Revolutionary War, American architects began to be influenced by their contemporaries in Britain to introduce a rival Gothic design into the American scene. This "Gothic Revival" grew slowly, but it seemed to fit with an increasingly egalitarian American society and a romantic movement that would flower in Jacksonian Democracy. Considering the history of Gothic architecture, it is little wonder that American architects applied the design to churches and to college buildings.

An important architect in the mid-century revival of Gothic architecture was a Jewish immigrant from Prague, Leopold Eidlitz (1823–1908). At the age of twenty, Eidlitz had come to America to seek his fortune, and he soon entered an architectural partnership with Otto Blesch. Leopold Eidlitz was a versatile archi-

165

tect, designing a number of synagogues and churches. In his designs, Eidlitz had a unique ability to utilize "empathy," the projection of one's own personality into an object. He and Blesch designed and erected Shaaray Tefila synagogue in New York City (1847); the Christ Church Cathedral in St. Louis, which was completed shortly after the Civil War (1867); and Temple Emanu-El in New York City (1868). While Shaaray Tefila was in a Romanesque style that broke with the former classical style used in America, both Christ Church Cathedral and Temple Emanu-El were Gothic adaptations. Eidlitz even adapted a castle design P. T. Barnum had brought back from England, and made the edifice feasible. As a team, Eidlitz and Blesch designed many banks, churches, and homes, as well as the Capitol building in Albany, New York. That contemporaries would call Eidlitz's design for Christ Church Cathedral in St. Louis "the churchiest church in America" underscored the innovative and adaptive talent of Jewish designers. Thousands of Christians found a contemplative and worshipful atmosphere in the sanctuary of that church.

Likewise, when Americans provided the world with the "skyscraper," a Jewish designer was in the midst of the revolution. To have a tall commercial structure of numerous stories, the elevator had to be invented. Once it was perfected, the ideal American city in which to test it out was Chicago. Although Philadelphia and New York would exhibit multistory buildings during the 1850s, Chicago's Great Fire of 1871 left a multitude of commercial structures in the central area that needed to be replaced. Chicago was an important testing ground for architectural innovation, and the skyscraper design was perfected by a group of architects known as "The Chicago school of architecture."

Dankmar Adler (1844–1900) was an important member of the Chicago School. A German-born American and son of a rabbi, Adler had immigrated to Detroit in 1854, working for a variety of architectural firms before the Civil War. At the end of the Civil War, he moved to Chicago, forming his own architectural and building firm, D. Adler. Like Eidlitz, he proved to be extremely versatile. Dankmar Adler's mastery of acoustics, for instance, is evident in his architectural plans for the Central Music Hall in Chicago (completed 1879).

It was the thirty-five-year-old Chicago Jewish architect, Dankmar Adler, who took a twenty-three-year-old Catholic from

Boston, Louis H. Sullivan, under his wing in 1879. They formed a strong friendship. In 1881 Sullivan asked Adler, "How would you like to take me into partnership?" "All right," Adler responded to the young man's delight, "draw up a contract for five years, beginning the first of May. First year you one third, after that, even." Soon, the firm of Adler & Sullivan was born. In the partnership, Dankmar Adler was the engineering designer and administrator, while Louis Sullivan was the planner and artist for the buildings their firm constructed. Adler & Sullivan, Architects became a formidable force in the history of design. In the next fourteen years, Adler and Sullivan designed over one hundred structures. In his *The Autobiography of an Idea* (1924), Louis H. Sullivan recounts that his partnership with the bright and witty Dankmar Adler had boosted Sullivan's reputation and had projected him into another level of the architectural world. In the Jewish designer, Sullivan found "a man whose reputation was solidly secured in utter honesty, fine intelligence and a fund of that sort of wisdom which attracts and holds."

One of the last masonry structures designed by Adler and Sullivan was Chicago's Auditorium Building, an impressively powerful building, built 1887 to 1889. The Auditorium Building housed a hotel, a business block, and an auditorium. The auditorium had one of the finest acoustic chambers ever built. With the development of manufactured rolled steel, Adler & Sullivan then moved to the economical high-rise structure. The skyscraper was born. The Wainright Building in St. Louis (completed in 1890) and the Guaranty Building in Buffalo (completed in 1894) illustrate the smooth and soaring verticality designed by Adler & Sullivan, Architects, exemplify their tenet of "form follows function," and underscore the progress of the Chicago School of architecture. In the early 1890s, Adler & Sullivan, Architects, were honored with the contract for designing the transportation building at the world-famous Chicago Columbian Exposition of 1893. Interestingly, a young non-Jewish teenage draftsman who trained with and worked for Adler & Sullivan, Architects (from 1887 to 1893), would become a well-known legend in the world of architecture, even at that time designing innovative Chicago homes: Frank Lloyd Wright.

Jewish architects would be influenced by developing American traditions as they interacted with artistry from abroad. In

167

their own milieu, each of these Jewish designers contributed to an expanding America, some exhibiting a versatility that in retrospect seems phenomenal. As an infant, Morris Lapidus (b. 1902) was brought to the United States by his Russian Jewish parents. He would grow into a respected architect, designing houses, hospitals, office buildings, and shopping centers. He found his greatest creative genius, however, in designing luxury hotels. Morris Lapidus' luxury creations dot the United States and the West Indies. When Martina Duttmann considered this retired designer's life and work in her 1992 biography, *Morris Lapidus,* her book subtitle characterized him as "The Architect of the American Dream." With similar versatility, Jewish MIT graduate Arnold Brunner (1857–1925) designed university buildings and stadiums, hospitals, bridges, synagogues, residences, and public edifices.

Ely Jacques Kahn (1884–1972) showed his versatility in designing and building houses, department stores, office complexes, hospitals, and country clubs as well as skyscrapers and factories. A firm believer that each architectural problem demanded a fresh solution, Kahn lectured frequently on the innovation of design. Gaining prominence between the world wars, Ely Kahn wrote *Design in Art and Industry* (1935), which maintained that architectural beauty was not found in ornamentation, but in proportions and material. His life spanned significant changes and challenges confronting the architect in a rapidly expanding American consumer society.

Two American Jewish architects born in Vienna, Austria, at the end of the nineteenth century, Rudolf M. Schindler (1887–1953) and Richard Josef Neutra (1892–1970), teamed up in Southern California in the mid-1920s. The buildings Neutra and Schindler designed and built were some of the earliest examples of the international style on American soil. Rudolf M. Schindler immigrated in 1913, settling in Chicago. He went to work for Frank Lloyd Wright in 1916. In the early 1920s, Schindler moved to Los Angeles to supervise the construction of a home and decided to set up his own architectural firm in Southern California. Among other projects, he designed the Lovell House on Newport Beach (completed 1926), which appears to be a combination of Wright's American style and the European international style.

Schindler's acquaintance and correspondent over the years, the Jewish architect Richard Josef Neutra, immigrated in 1923. He traveled to Chicago, meeting an American hero of his, Louis Sullivan, a few months before Sullivan's death. He met another American architectural hero, Frank Lloyd Wright, at Sullivan's funeral, and soon was helping out in Wright's drafting room. Early in 1925, Richard and his wife Dione moved to Los Angeles, for the first few years renting an apartment in Rudolf Schindler and his wife Pauline's West Los Angeles home. Richard worked on a number of projects with Rudolf, free-lancing for other designers to supplement his income. In 1926, both men formed a partnership, and Richard Neutra began work on the Lovell Health House in Los Angeles.

The Lovell Health House was completed in 1929 to national and international acclaim (the same year Richard Neutra received his U.S. citizenship). So creative was the design that Neutra had to organize and supervise the contractors throughout the construction. Richard designed each of the many balconies of the Lovell Health House to suspend from the roof frame above large glass and concrete planes that appeared to cascade down the steep cliff on which it was built. At the lowest level a swimming pool was also suspended within the steel frame. It was an architectural and engineering phenomenon, with breathtaking views of the Pacific Ocean, the mountains of Santa Monica, and the lights of Los Angeles. "That I succeeded in such short order with the steel-skeletoned Health House, which was, as a whole, in its philosophy and in many features, so highly unorthodox, seems almost incredible now," Richard Neutra wrote in November of 1929 to a lifelong friend, American Quaker social worker, Mrs. Francis Toplitz. "How could I have proceeded from such obscurity and a starvation diet to something like a career?"

Jewish Design for a Consumer Society

German-born Albert Kahn (1869–1942; no apparent relation to Louis Kahn or Ely Kahn) came to the United States as a Jewish teenager in 1881 and received his architectural training in Detroit, Michigan. Working on a number of projects at the turn of the century, Kahn designed the General Motors Building in

Detroit (completed 1901), and was locally prominent when fledgling automobile producer, Henry Ford, revolutionized manufacturing by combining all aspects of production into a centralized location. Henry Ford hired Albert Kahn to put his ideas into architectural form and, during the early decades of the twentieth century, Kahn set the standard for industrial design. His design for Ford's Highland Park Plant (1908–1910) produced the first truly autonomous industrial plant in the world. Albert Kahn's later design for Henry Ford's River Rouge Plant at Dearborn, Michigan, was a brilliant composition of a single-story structure that permitted Ford's assembly line to proceed in a continuous flow from raw material to finished product.

Albert Kahn also designed assembly plants for other automobile producers, garnering an international reputation. Even Russia's Stalin had heard of him, and Kahn's firm was commissioned by the Russian government to design a series of factories in the Volga region. Soon, Kahn's staff was engaged to do more industrial planning for the Russian government, finally designing hundreds of factories that were built in Russian territory in the 1930s. Interestingly, with his keen oversight, Albert Kahn had subdivided tasks in his architectural office as early as 1905, developing a type of production flow not unlike an assembly line. Nevertheless, Kahn's final construction plans were extremely well planned; and there was an artistic continuity of line and material, for instance, in the metal and glass construction found in Kahn's design for the Ohio Steel Foundry Roll Shop in Lima, Ohio (1939). Albert Kahn's keen artistic sense may be viewed in beautiful buildings somewhat unrelated to his sprawling mass production industrial complexes. One excellent example would be the multistory Fisher Building in Detroit (built in 1928).

Vienna-born Jewish architect Victor Gruen (1903–1980) was trained in Europe under leading architects. In 1933, Gruen immigrated to the United States and progressively established himself as a capable designer. His first major building was the Lederer Store in New York City (completed in 1939). In 1950, he incorporated a group of designers and engineers into Victor Gruen Associates. Actually in the forefront of urban revitalization with creative and practical designs that united architecture and commercial enterprise, this Jewish designer revamped the central business districts of Fort Worth, Texas (1959), Cincinnati, Ohio (1963), and Fresno, California (1965). His beautiful designs were flush with pedestrian malls, landscaped streets, and vaulted bridged walkways that spanned city streets. Not satisfied with central city commerce, Victor Gruen developed the first suburban shopping centers in the United States. Once again, a Jewish contribution became an American tradition in an expanding consumer society.

With the advent of reinforced concrete, Harvard-educated Bertrand Goldberg (b. 1913) believed that rectangular edifices may no longer be viable in light of the possibility of more aesthetic circular designs. Discarding the rectilinear concepts of Victorian engineers, Goldberg sought to bring a living quality to city structures. The Jewish architect experimented with urban circular designs, developing Marina City overlooking the Chicago River (1963), with two impressive cylindric sixty-story residential towers (c. 900 apartments) that dominate Chicago's skyline. A dramatic architectural statement on three acres of land in the heart of Chicago's Loop, this "city within a city" includes a sixteen-story office building, a large theater and auditorium, restaurants, stores, gymnasium, skating rink, swimming pool, parking, and a marina for small boats.

During the same period Marina City was being designed, Chicago-born architect, Max Abramovitz (b. 1908), brought his historic experimentation to a new level when he designed a vast saucer dome auditorium at the University of Illinois at Urbana (1964) that could accommodate more than 18,000 people. A former deputy director of the Planning Office of the United Nations (1947–1952), the Jewish architect's firm of Harrison and Abramovitz was commissioned to build the United Nations Secretariat in New York City (1950). Specializing in office buildings with sides of shimmering glass, the firm of Harrison and Abramovitz was responsible for such creations as the Alcoa Building (1953) in Pittsburgh, with its covering of prefabricated aluminum panels that pioneered the use of metal skins on buildings, and the Socony Mobil Building (1956) in New York City, that refined the technique even further. In 1962, an impressive glass-walled exterior supported by a grid of thin, tapered columns, crowned Abramovitz's design for the new Philharmonic Hall in New York City (now called the Avery Fisher Hall at Lincoln Cen-

171

ter). Max Abramovitz also designed Protestant, Catholic, and Jewish chapels for Brandeis University (1954) and placed them around a glistening pool. He sought in this design to affirm the respect and harmony between the three faiths on the Brandeis University campus, while honoring the differences between the adherents of each faith.

Some Jewish designers taught and wrote. New York-born Percival Goodman (1904–1989), an expert on city planning and an accomplished graphic artist, became professor of architecture at Columbia University's School of Architecture and Design in 1946 and held that position until he was named professor emeritus in 1972. With his brother Paul, Percival coauthored *Communitas* (1947; rev. ed., 1960), a book which discusses how human beings interact with their environment and how the environment may be used for good or bad. Among his other publications, Percival Goodman published *The Double E* (1977), in which he explains his futuristic urban plan that would balance environment and ecology in the midst of increasing population and declining resources. Rudolf J. Wittkower (1901–1971), a former professor at Cologne University and the University of London, immigrated to the United States in 1954 and was appointed chairman of the department of art history and archaeology at Columbia University. Combining architecture and art, Dr. Wittkower wrote a number of books, including *Architectural Principles in the Age of Humanism* (1949) and *Art and Architecture in Italy, 1600–1750* (1958; revised 1965). Emphasizing to his students and colleagues that Renaissance architecture contained a universally applicable system of proportion, Rudolf Wittkower encouraged the international style in architecture.

Like Louis Isadore Kahn, other Jewish architects challenged the international style of modern architecture. MIT graduate Gordon Bunshaft (1909–1990), a Jewish architect who specialized in large-scale corporate and public buildings, used the glass and aluminum motif, complete with the smooth-skinned rectangular design (for example, his Lever Building in New York City, completed in 1952). And yet, in the early 1960s, the Buffalo-born Bunshaft began to experiment, adding neoclassical components such as massive stone-clad walls and textured marble as well as geometrical and lighting illusions that give an ethereal appearance (for example, Bunshaft's highly controversial design for the Beinecke Rare Book and Manuscript Library at Yale, completed in 1964; his Lyndon Baines Johnson Memorial Library at the University of Texas, Austin, completed in 1971; or his Hirshhorn Museum and Sculpture Garden in Washington, D.C., completed in 1974). In 1988 Gordon Bunshaft was corecipient of the Pritzker Architecture Prize, the most prestigious international award given to an architect whose work is a "significant contribution to humanity and the environment."

Some have suggested that architect Gordon Bunshaft was a precursor of an as yet unfixed architectural "postmodern" movement, a self-described "architecture of the postindustrial society." Whatever the case, as one considers the historic annals of design, the individuality, diversity, and depth of contributions by American Jewish architects are admirable. And, today, thousands of Jewish designers look toward the future. As Bertrand Goldberg stated in the mid–1980s from his Chicago office on North State Street: "New technology and engineering now give us unique power to shape buildings to our needs. To shape the world's communities might now be an architect's philosophy. For the first time we can build whatever we can think; WHAT SHALL WE THINK TO BUILD FOR MAN?"

American Jewish Entrepreneurs

If there is any merit whatsoever to President Calvin Coolidge's historic adage that "the business of America is business," the positive contributions of Jewish businesspersons to a successful economic infrastructure in the United States is limitless. In previous chapters we have seen numerous Jewish innovators and inventors who have energetically worked their ideas and creations into thriving corporations. The personal histories in chapter 6 of Adam Gimbel, Lazarus Straus, Louis Borgnicht, and Levi Strauss in the clothing and retail business, for example, have uncovered an enormous Jewish contribution. We have seen how the inventiveness of Louis Blaustein transformed the oil industry while, with a similar creativity, David Sarnoff transformed the broadcasting industry. And, almost single-handedly, Jewish entrepreneur Adolf Zukor transformed the motion picture industry.

In this book we have also viewed prosperous Jewish businesspersons who have contributed large amounts of money, time, and goods to their communities and philanthropic enterprises. From New York merchant Haym Salomon's efforts on behalf of the American Revolution to Vermont paper mill-owner Isaac Gilman's contributions to local communities, the history of American Jewish business is at once inspiring and challenging. The wide-ranging efforts of a Jacob H. Schiff as America entered the twentieth century or a Walter H. Annenberg as America enters the twenty-first century are formidable. For the historian, these examples encapsulate the significant contributions of American Jewish entrepreneurs.

Growing with the Nation

In 1792, Jewish-born Ephraim Hart (1747–1825) was one of the twenty-two founders of the New York Stock Exchange. A successful stockbroker and real estate broker, Hart had eluded the British in their capture of New York in 1776, moved to Philadelphia during the duration of the American Revolution, and returned to New York in 1787. While a number of Jewish merchant-shippers (such as beloved patriot Aaron Lopez of Newport, Rhode Island) lost their mercantile businesses during the American Revolution, Ephraim Hart was able to regather his business momentum through finance and real estate. In fact, Hart was elected to the New York senate in 1810. Although Jewish financiers would never be the most prominent members on the stock exchanges in England and the United States, they would play a role in the economic expansion of a young America.

Perhaps the oldest Jewish corporation in the United States was a metals business that was later incorporated as Hendricks Brothers by Uriah Hendricks (1802–1869) and his two brothers. Founded in 1764 by Uriah's grandfather (after whom he was named), the metals business prospered after the American Revolution under the guidance of Uriah's father, Harmon Hendricks, a graduate of Columbia University. Harmon added a copper-rolling mill to the business in 1812 (one of the first copper-rolling mills in America) and built metal parts for American warships during the War of 1812. Harmon Hendricks also supported the American cause during the War of 1812 by buying $40,000 worth of war bonds as soon as the government issued them in 1813.

Uriah learned much from his father, taking charge after Harmon's death in 1838. When Uriah died four years after the Civil War, his four sons took over Hendricks Brothers.

Some of the many peddlers of this period soon developed into retailers. A few became rich and famous. To the names of early Jewish retailers Adam Gimbel and Levi Strauss, one should add the names of Joseph Seligman, Abraham Kuhn, and Meyer Guggenheim. These men would also become great success stories in American business history, and their extended families would multiply their fortunes. All of these Jewish men immigrated to America in the nineteenth century, and their hard work and discipline would cultivate their success.

Bavarian-born Joseph Seligman (1819–1880), for instance, immigrated to the United States in 1837 at the age of seventeen. After hiking over one hundred miles to Mauch Chunk, Pennsylvania, the university-educated teenager worked diligently as a clerk and cashier. After one year, Joseph had made enough money to send for two of his brothers, William and James. Pooling their resources, the Seligman brothers peddled goods from farm to farm in Pennsylvania, saving many a farm family a grueling trip to the nearest town. Within a few years, they had made enough money to rent a building in Lancaster, Pennsylvania, as their headquarters and a warehouse for their goods. In 1841, Joseph sent for another brother, fourteen-year-old Jesse, and by fall they had relocated in Alabama. Not long thereafter, the boys learned of their mother's death and their father's woolen business failure in Bavaria. Joseph assured his father's creditors that they would be paid, and he sent for the rest of the family.

In 1846 the Seligmans located their headquarters in New York City and opened J. Seligman & Brothers, Merchants in downtown Manhattan. By this time they had opened a number of dry goods stores in the South, and had become prosperous wholesale clothiers. A St. Louis Branch, W. Seligman & Company, was the next to open. When gold was discovered in California, Joseph branched out to the West. This bold move nearly created a Seligman monopoly on California clothing for a while. Newfound California gold was traded for clothes, and gold shipments were sent regularly to Seligman headquarters in New York. Soon, the Seligmans were trading in gold bullion, becoming important financiers. The banking principles that this Jewish family had learned in the retail trade catapulted them into the New York financial community.

In 1864, they formed J. & W. Seligman & Company in New York. The firm now had major branches in London, Paris, Frankfort, New Orleans, and San Francisco. By the end of the Civil War, Joseph Seligman and his wife had nine children. With Joseph's brothers and sisters, their spouses and their children, the prosperous American Seligman family now numbered over 100!

In like manner, Abraham Kuhn (1819–1892) had started out as a peddler and had opened his own dry-goods store in Cincinnati, Ohio. Opening a small factory in Cincinnati as well, where he manufactured pants, Abraham made enough money to move his brothers and sisters to America. His partner was another German-born immigrant, Solomon Loeb (1828–1913), who opened a branch for their firm in New York (around the corner from Joseph Seligman's headquarters). Kuhn, Loeb & Company prospered as many members of the Kuhn family and Loeb family worked for the company in Cincinnati. In a historic journey similar to the Seligmans, however, the company of Kuhn and Loeb moved from the retail business into a financial establishment. When Abraham Kuhn returned to Germany, Solomon Loeb shared the financial firm with his astute son-in-law, Jacob H. Schiff.

Immigrating to Philadelphia in 1848, twenty-year-old Swiss-born Meyer Guggenheim (1828–1905) had peddled goods in the mining towns of northeastern Pennsylvania that surrounded Philadelphia. Discovering that a manufacturer made much more money than a peddler, Meyer took the product for which he had received the most complaints (a stove polish that burned and stained hands) and had a chemist develop a new formula. He then had his family make vats of the new formula for stove polish at home, while he peddled it to his now satisfied customers. Meyer soon added dye and lye to his manufactured household products. He later sold this household products company for $150,000, investing his profits in diverse financial opportunities.

One of those "opportunities" consisted of numerous shares in the Leadville mines in Colorado in the latter 1870s. This led the firm of M. Guggenheim's Sons to purchase and build copper, lead, and silver mines and smelters across the western United

States and in other countries. Worth half a billion dollars, Meyer's seven sons would continue the family business under the rubric, Guggenheim Brothers. Their corporate empire stretched from Alaska to Africa and was at its peak, perhaps, only second monetarily to the empire created by a member of the Baptist church, John D. Rockefeller.

As one readily notes, there is a difference between these Jewish corporate families that moved from clothing and retail to finance and the Jewish families that we have covered in earlier chapters that stayed in the clothing and retail business. Both groups, however, made significant contributions to a growing America. Most of the Jewish families that became heavily involved in finance functioned as investment bankers rather than commercial bankers. The insatiable demand for capital in the economically expanding American corporate world of the latter nineteenth century and early twentieth century drew the hardworking and solvent Jewish business enterprises (which had accumulating monetary reserves) into a natural relationship with the American financial community. It is not an overstatement to emphasize that such Jewish "banking houses" strengthened the process of capital formation in the United States at a critical juncture of American economic history and solidified the westward expansion. They also raised large sums for the American government at critical junctures of American history. Nevertheless, Jewish financiers have never "controlled" the banking enterprise in the United States, and their total assets were small when compared to the American banking system as a whole.

Manufacturing, Construction, and Retail in the Twentieth Century

During the twentieth century, the Jewish community in general made social and economic progress in America through the path of business. In spite of all of the contributions that the Jewish community made in other areas (science, medicine, academics, literature, sports, entertainment, government, etc.), by the 1970s at least one-third of the Jewish men and women employed in the United States were working in the wholesale and retail trade. Taking into consideration the sizable talents that Jewish men and women brought to America in other fields

177

of endeavor, it is little wonder that, in the field of business, important and diverse Jewish contributions would surface in the modern period.

Boston-born Charles Haskell Revson (1906–1975) was a sales manager for a nail polish firm when he began his own company in 1923. Innovative and resourceful, Charles introduced true-color nail enamels and matching lipstick for women. By the 1970s his Revlon was the world's largest cosmetics manufacturer, with nearly thirty companies worldwide and markets in approximately one hundred countries around the globe. With his considerable wealth from Revlon, this Jewish entrepreneur established the Charles H. Revson Foundation. Interestingly, Eli N. Evans (b. 1936), the business executive who was chosen as president of the Revson Foundation in 1977, was the son of a Jewish retail operator in Durham, North Carolina, whose store had the only integrated lunch counter in the town in the 1950s.

Max Stern (1898–1982) founded Hartz Mountain Products Corporation in 1930. A Jewish emigrant from Germany in 1926, Stern was able to creatively guide the corporation into one of the largest pet food suppliers in the United States. Sol Linowitz (b. 1913), the son of a Jewish fruit importer in Trenton, New Jersey, had earned his doctorate in law from Cornell University (1938) and had completed service in the Navy (1946), when he co-founded the Haloid Company. Sol Linowitz helped build this small manufacturer of photographic equipment into a multinational corporation that has since become a household name in America: Xerox. In like manner, two Jewish businessmen born in Paterson, New Jersey, Frank R. Lautenberg (b. 1924) and Henry Taub (b. 1927), in 1953 founded Automatic Data Processing, which grew to be the largest data processing firm in the world. Stern, Lautenberg, and Taub gained reputations for philanthropic endeavor. Frank Lautenberg was elected a U.S. senator from New Jersey in 1982 and served into the 1990s.

Examples of hard-working Jewish corporate executives abound. Gerald Swope (1872–1957), the son of a Jewish manufacturer in St. Louis, joined the Western Electric corporation after graduating as an electrical engineer from MIT in 1895. Moving up the corporate ladder in an expanding electrical industry that soon became the heartbeat of America, Swope volunteered for duty in the First World War and was highly decorated. After the war he was appointed president of international General Electric, and from 1922 to 1939 served as both president and chairman of the board. General Electric grew as a prosperous and prestigious company under Gerald Swope's guidance. During the Great Depression, Gerald offered his "Swope Plan" (published in 1931), which called for a stabilized industry that would hold itself accountable to prevent unemployment. After his own "retirement," he donated his services as chairman of the New York City Housing Authority.

One of the nation's oldest corporations, Du Pont, named Minneapolis-born Irving Shapiro (b. 1916) chairman of the board of directors and chief executive officer in 1974. The son of Lithuanian Jewish immigrants who operated a small dry cleaning business, Irving graduated from the University of Minnesota Law School in 1941. After a successful career working for the U.S. Justice Department from 1943 to 1951, he joined the legal division of E. I. du Pont de Nemours & Company. The Du Pont family grew to love and trust this competent young man. Under his able leadership, the firm tightened its management, introduced new and improved products, and became more profitable. Soon, the son of poor Jewish immigrants had become a consultant to American presidents and a spokesman for private enterprise.

When Nicholas J. Pritzker arrived in the United States from Kiev in the latter nineteenth century, the Jewish immigrant may have had some hopeful dreams about the future, but he probably neither imagined the effect his descendants would have on the city he chose nor comprehended their future influence on the nation he claimed. Nicholas became a pharmacist in Chicago, but studied law in his spare time. By 1902, he was able to open his own law office. Through family involvement in the twentieth century, this small firm became the formidable Pritzker & Pritzker, known publicly for its charitable giving probably more than it is known for its business acumen. With little fanfare, Pritzker & Pritzker built up an industrial and commercial empire that included industries as diverse as auto parts distribution and publishing.

By the 1960s, the Pritzker's private legal firm had to concern itself exclusively with the financial empire that had been built. Most famous, of course, was the Pritzker's Hyatt International Corporation, which specialized in luxury hotels. In addition to what has been mentioned, at one time or another the Pritzker empire has expanded into other diverse businesses, including air travel, real estate, steel, lumber, coal-mining equipment, truck equipment, construction equipment, cruise lines, and musical instruments. Not only would Nicholas Pritzker have been amazed to see his name on the Pritzker Architecture Award and the University of Chicago Medical School, but also that his little law firm evolved into a business enterprise worth well over one billion dollars.

In the oil industry, Denver's Marvin Davis (b. 1925) became one of industry's most prominent oil explorers and drillers in the modern period. The New Jersey-born son of a Jewish garment manufacturer, Marvin not only made Davis Oil Company and its worldwide "wildcatting" exploits famous in the mile-high city, but extended the profits from his company into a number of real estate and business enterprises (including co-ownership of 20th Century Fox from 1981 to 1985). Another self-made Jewish businessman, Leon Hess (b. 1914), built the Hess Oil & Chemical Corporation into a massive refiner and petroleum supplier. The New Jersey-born son of an immigrant fuel truck driver, Leon Hess served as a petroleum supply officer for General Patton's troops in World War II. He returned to expand the family fuel oil business into new markets, opening oil storage depots and, in 1969, acquiring the Amerada Petroleum Corporation, a leading crude oil producer. Leon Hess also became involved in a number of other enterprises, including a life insurance company and the New York Jets football team.

What Marvin Davis has meant to Denver, Pittsburgh-born Max Fisher (b. 1908) has meant to Detroit. The son of an immigrant peddler, Max Fisher was raised in Salem, Ohio, where his father had become part-owner in a small oil company. Max's family relocated to Detroit, Michigan, while he was at Ohio State University on a football scholarship (B.S., 1930). The young graduate pioneered new oil-refining techniques that rocketed the family firm into the largest independent oil company in the Midwest. His astute business dealings helped to develop a significant oil industry in Michigan. Max Fisher became an important community figure, and his Aurora Gasoline Company eventually became the Marathon Oil Company. A confirmed Republican, Fisher has been a prominent political force on both the state and national levels. In like manner, Rudy Boschwitz (b. 1930), founder of Plywood Minnesota in the early 1960s (one of the first do-it-yourself building materials and hardware stores), was a confirmed Republican. By the time he was elected a senator from Minnesota in 1978, Plywood Minnesota had over sixty retail store franchises throughout the Midwest. Rudy Boschwitz served in the Senate into the 1990s.

On the Democratic Party side, Bernard Rapoport (b. 1917), born in San Antonio, Texas, to a former peddler, would become a self-made millionaire. Rapoport would found the American Income Life Insurance Company, which evolved from handling private policies to an insurance carrier for labor unions. Holding the highest respect for labor and its unions, Bernard Rapoport often risked financial collapse in an effort to provide adequate insurance coverage to unions who were considered "risky." He gained respect in Texas, even as he was assigned prominent roles on the Democratic National Finance Committee. Another Democratic supporter, successful businessman Richard Ravitch (b. 1933) of the famed HRH Construction Corporation of New York City, has donated his time to numerous city and state agencies. In 1979, Ravitch became the unpaid chairman of New York City's Metropolitan Transportation Authority (MTA), successfully upgrading a system of transit that was dilapidated and in financial trouble.

In fact, Jewish entrepreneurs abound in the construction and real estate business (in a direct correlation between business and design). The Ravitch's HRH Construction Company specialized in middle income housing developments, as well as building a number of luxury apartment and office complexes. Likewise, Brooklyn-born Samuel J. Lefrak (b. 1918) organized the Lefrak Organization, a construction firm which specialized in modestly priced housing developments in the greater New York area. Both of these New York City companies were early innovators in the trade. Throughout the United States, similar Jewish entrepreneurs work in like fashion today in both larger cities (such as Los Angeles, Washington, D.C., Boston, Chicago, San Francisco, Miami, Houston, Cleveland, Detroit, etc.) and smaller urban areas. Often becoming important community philanthropists, these Jewish men and women seem to have a sense of the pulse of their particular locales and soon become leading, productive citizens. This should not be surprising to the

181

historian. In the area of immigration and immigrant contributions, real estate historically has been an ideal field for people who lacked large capital, but were willing to work long hours and were willing to take risks to improve themselves, their families, and their communities.

One must also keep in mind that, historically, the little towns and villages that dot the United States from the East Coast to the West have been the homes of most of the American Jewish businesspersons. During the twentieth century, a large percentage of Jewish retail businesses have been small, family-owned operations. These businesses, from jewelry stores to clothing stores to scrap-metal "junkyards," have been central fixtures in tens of thousands of communities. In the midst of competition from wholesale operatives, mass-marketing specialists, mass-mailing campaigns, and megastores (and with their children off to other areas to seek their niche in America's professional smorgasbord), such Jewish family-operated shops continue to close as the twenty-first century emerges.

Nevertheless, some larger Jewish businesses in the clothing and retail trade have adapted to the consumer society and advertising technology to such an extent that they themselves have become considerable business enterprises. For example, Leslie H. Wexner's The Limited fashion chain became one of the fastest growing specialty apparel retailers in the early 1970s by focusing on the fifteen- to thirty-year-old female market. Born in Dayton, Ohio, in 1937, and graduating from Ohio State University in 1959, Leslie Wexner founded the retail chain in 1963 in Columbus, Ohio, and continues to direct its 2500 stores as both president and chairman of the board. Wexner also obtained directorships in Banc One Corporation and Sotheby's Holdings. Today, the immediate Wexner family is worth more than one billion dollars. Another successful retail company executive based in Columbus, Saul Schottenstein (b. 1924), has directed his Schottenstein Stores to large profits since he founded the corporation in 1972. These midwestern Jewish businessmen have realized the geographical fact that three-fourths of the population of the United States is located within a 500-mile radius of Columbus, Ohio.

This Columbus phenomenon is a historic cycle that emulates many of the Jewish business cycles that surround cities throughout the United States. Before the Civil War, German-Jewish Simon Lazarus immigrated to Columbus, Ohio, and opened a store. His sons, Fred Lazarus and Ralph Lazarus, founded F. and R. Lazarus and Company, and carried the clothing retail business into the twentieth century. Fred's sons expanded the family business into a full-line department store during the Roaring Twenties. The Lazarus family established Federated Department Stores in 1929, a holding company that combined other prestigious firms, including Abraham and Straus. In the latter 1950s, Fred Lazarus Jr., president of Federated Department Stores of Cincinnati, fondly remembered his grandfather's small retail clothing store. "Among my earliest and happiest memories is that shop," he recounted, "As a child I thought the merchant's constant study of people, their needs, tastes, and buying habits was the most fascinating career a man could choose. I still think so."

By the 1960s, Federated Department Stores had become the country's largest department store chain. In June of 1967, Federated reacted to national trends and opened a discount store division. Although its headquarters was Cincinnati-based, the nation's largest department store chain opened its 116,000 square-foot prototype store in May 1968 in suburban Columbus, Ohio. In 1968 Federated Department Stores recorded a record $1,813,771,463 in sales. With such a prestigious "senior citizen" downtown chain store in the merchandising fray, discounting had become respectable. The history of hundreds of other Jewish-founded and Jewish-built retail and discount merchandising firms could be similarly recounted (from Harvard MBA Stanley Marcus's Dallas-based quality Neiman-Marcus department stores to the Feldberg family's Natick, Massachusetts expansion from "The New England Trading Company" hosiery and underwear business to their ready-to-wear Bell Shops to their Zayre Corporation).

In some cases, major Jewish retail, manufacturing, and construction firms have been sold or consolidated. Others have been the victims of new innovations, new corporations, and new financial factors. Still others are created and passed on. The jobs these Jewish entrepreneurs provided, the goods they produced, and the charitable endeavors they supported have had in the past (and continue to have) a major effect on the growth and prosperity of our nation. Many have had a direct effect on their local communities. For some of the older inhabitants of Newark, New Jersey, for instance, a store named "Bamberger's" brings back memories of advertising slogans, good prices, and quality merchandise. For others, they fondly remember the Jewish founder, Louis Bamberger (1855–1944), who, among his many gifts to hospitals, education, and charities, gave his own employees a cooperative interest in the firm; established a pension program for them long before it was fashionable; and marked his own retirement by distributing cash gifts and annuities to faithful workers.

Publishing and Communications

In the competitive business of book publishing, Jewish entrepreneurs have made significant contributions as well. For example, New York-born Alfred A. Knopf (1892–1984) and his new bride Blanche (1894–1966) began publishing in 1915. Their books quickly earned a reputation for excellence in design, materials, and editing. In the subsequent five decades Alfred A. Knopf, Publishers, produced over five thousand titles, a significant number written by preeminent authors of the twentieth century. Alfred A. Knopf, Publishers merged with Random House in 1960. Joel Elias Spingarn (1875–1939), after his return from service in World War I, helped to found Harcourt, Brace & Company in 1919. Joel and his brother Arthur (1878–1971) were very active in the Civil Rights movement and the NAACP during their lifetimes.

Similarly, Roger Williams Straus Jr. (b. 1917), whose father was chairman of the board of the American Smelting and Refining Company and whose mother was from the Guggenheim family, was one of the founders of the prestigious New York publishing house of Farrar, Straus, and Giroux in 1945. Known as a maverick who would not sacrifice his standards to marketing trends, Roger Straus has served as president of Farrar, Straus, and Giroux since 1987. Jewish entrepreneurs have been involved in many other book publishing firms, including Stein and Day, Viking Press, and Simon & Schuster. Arthur Allen Cohen (b. 1928), son of a New York City clothing manufacturer, coupled brilliant writing and editorial skills with business acumen. Before founding Ex Libris Publishing Company in 1974, Arthur Cohen had cofounded and then sold his partnerships in Noonday Press and Meridian Books. He also worked for the publishing houses of Holt, Rinehart, and Winston; E. P. Dutton; and Viking Press.

184

Thoroughly innovative, Jewish men and women have made their mark on publishing firms, as has been expounded in chapter 4. Another example out of many would be Jason Epstein (b. 1928), the son of a textiles businessman. Born in Cambridge, Massachusetts, and graduating from Columbia University (B.A. 1949, M.A. 1950), Jason started the first line of quality paperbacks at Doubleday & Company, moving on to Random House in 1958 (he eventually rose to editorial director and vice president in a long prosperous career). In addition to his Random House duties, in 1963 Jason Epstein cofounded *The New York Review of Books,* which soon became a prestigious journal of critical review and commentary in the publishing world. In the 1970s, he added educational television to his portfolio, becoming an important consultant to the Children's Television Workshop. Among his many honors, Jason Epstein received the Lifetime Achievement Award during the National Book Awards presentation in 1988, and he was given the Curtis Benjamin Award in 1993. In addition to diverse talents such as Jason Epstein, many Jewish photographers, such as Alfred Eisenstaedt of *Life* magazine, Annie Leibovitz for *Rolling Stone, Vanity Fair,* and the like, and Irving Penn of *Vogue,* have contributed to publishing enterprises, while establishing a lucrative financial career for themselves.

Other Jewish writers and businesspersons have established magazines and journals. Brandeis University graduate Letty Cottin Pogrebin (b. 1939) worked in publishing before becoming a founding editor of *Ms.* magazine (editor 1971–1987). Yale University Law School graduate Rhoda Hendrick Karpatkin (b. 1930), as president of the International Organization of Consumers Union (1984–1991) and executive director of their publications, initiated *Penny Power,* a national consumer magazine for children. Rhoda also spearheaded the daily radio program, "A Report to Consumers," and a national newspaper column, "From Consumer Reports." Under Rhoda Hendrick Karpatkin's business acumen and editorial expertise, *Consumer Reports* magazine grew in circulation to approximately three million copies each printing.

In the field of prominent magazines and newspapers, Austrian-born Henry A. Grunwald (b. 1922) worked his way from a night copyboy position in 1944 at *Time* to the top entrepreneurial position of editor-in-chief. At one time or another, Walter H. Annenberg (b. 1908) owned *TV Guide, Seventeen,* the *Daily*

185

Racing Form, the *Philadelphia Inquirer* and the *Philadelphia Daily News* (as well as radio and television stations); and the Pritzker family owned *McCall's* magazine. The Sulzberger family, which springs from Jewish roots, owns *The New York Times.* The Pulitzer family has owned the *St. Louis Post-Dispatch,* as well as a number of other newspapers and television stations. Real estate developer and publisher, Mortimer Zuckerman (b. 1937) owns *U.S. News and World Report* and *The Atlantic Monthly,* as well as having copublished the *New York Daily News.* California-born Eugene Meyer (1875–1959), who had turned his prosperous Jewish banking firm into a promoter of business enterprise and government service in the first four decades of the twentieth century, purchased the bankrupt *Washington Post* in 1933. His Washington Post Company owned and made a financial success out of *Newsweek* magazine and the *Washington Post* newspaper (as well as several radio stations). Robert B. Silvers (b. 1929), a founding Jewish editor of *The New York Review of Books* with Jason Epstein, guided *The New York Review of Books* to phenomenal growth, quality, financial success, and international influence, through long hours of devotion. The 1990s found him still guiding the enterprise.

New Jewish entrepreneurs in magazine publishing are constantly coming and going in hopeful expectation of combining their love of learning with a product the public will buy. For instance, Milton Esterow (b. 1928), the son of a New York City grocer, had become quite a versatile cultural and film writer when he purchased *ARTnews* in 1972. He turned the old journal into one of the prominent and award-winning magazines in its field. In 1975, Esterow added the biweekly *The Art newsletter,* which covered the international scene. His *Antiques World* (made public at the end of 1978) garnered a devoted readership as well.

The Newhouse family has owned the largest communications conglomerate in the world. Family members at one time owned and operated the prominent American periodicals *Vanity Fair, Vogue, Glamour, Brides, Self, The New Yorker, Mademoiselle, Parade* (the Sunday newspaper supplement), *House and Garden,* and *Gentleman's Quarterly* (as well as magazines in Britain, West Germany, France, and Italy). They have owned dozens of newspapers, a number of radio and television stations, cable systems, and Random House publishers. The formula for such business success was instituted by Samuel Irving Newhouse Sr. (1895–1979), who as a seventeen-year-old office boy was told by his law office employer to take charge of a small newspaper. As he would do throughout his life, Samuel increased advertising, sharply cut operating costs, increased circulation, and, above all, allowed successful local editors independence in crucial decision-making. He was a business entrepreneur first and foremost. He often stated that "only a newspaper which is a sound business operation can be a truly free, independent editorial enterprise, able to do the best possible job for the community." Thus, unwilling to mold the nation's opinion to a certain bent, his newspapers covered the philosophical spectrum, from Republican to Democratic views (although he was a registered Democrat).

Becoming a billionaire, Samuel I. Newhouse was known in the business world as "S.I." and, in an unobtrusive manner with a soft voice, operated his communications empire out of a battered brown briefcase with no central office. By 1960, among his other philanthropic endeavors through his foundation, Samuel Irving Newhouse donated millions of dollars to Syracuse University to fund the S. I. Newhouse School of Public Communications. He intended this communications center to be the world's largest research institute for the study of mass media. At the time of his death in 1979 at the age of eighty-four, Samuel Irving Newhouse Sr., technically controlled his vast corporate empire, because he owned the voting stock in Advance Publishing (the Newhouse print-media holdings) and Newhouse Broadcasting Corporation (the Newhouse electronic-media holdings). All nonvoting stock was held by Samuel and Newhouse family members. The communications empire had come a long way since Judge Hyman Lazarus told his teenage clerk, "Sammy, go down and take care of that money-losing *Bayonne Times* until we get rid of it."

In the field of mass media, we have seen the influence of Jewish innovator David Sarnoff on the radio and television industry as well as Jewish pioneer Adolph Zukor on the motion picture industry. Network broadcasting owes a great debt to Jewish businesspersons throughout the twentieth century. In fact, Jewish entrepreneurs had much to do with the founding and expansion of the major broadcasting networks. As we have seen, David Sarnoff (1891–1971) founded the National Broadcasting Company (NBC) and had a great influence on its parent company,

Radio Corporation of America (RCA), as general manager and vice president (1921–1929) and president and chairman of the board (1930–1969). The Federal Communications Commission ruled in 1941 that RCA had to sell one of its dual networks (the Red or the Blue). After a bitter court fight that was finally settled by the Supreme Court, RCA sold its weaker "Blue" network in 1943. This network soon became the American Broadcasting Company (ABC). In 1951, Jewish movie theater magnate Leonard Goldenson of United Paramount Theatres purchased ABC and led it into commercial programming in the mid–1950s that appealed to youthful audiences (such as "Disneyland" and "The Mickey Mouse Club"). Profits began to pour into the ABC network even as they had poured into NBC.

The third major network had similar modest beginnings and similar large success. In September 1928, shortly before his twenty-seventh birthday, William Paley (1901–1990), the son of a Jewish cigar company owner, purchased a small company called United Independent Broadcasters. Paley turned that money-losing company into the mighty profit-making empire called the Columbia Broadcasting System (CBS). "Over the past fifty years, radio and television have become an integral part of our daily lives, representing a great development in modern America," William S. Paley concluded in his autobiography, *As It Happened: A Memoir* (1979). "I have been fortunate to have been able to take part in its development right from the very beginning. In all, CBS and I have enjoyed a remarkably good and stimulating life together."

In like manner, many Jewish entrepreneurs could say the same for their involvement in the film industry in the twentieth century—an involvement that has also entertained billions of men, women, and children. For example, Russian-born immigrant, Louis B. Mayer (1885–1957), was in the ship and industrial plant salvage business before he began showing silent movies in Haverhill, Massachusetts, in 1907. He soon had purchased all of the theaters in the town. Moving to Hollywood, California, in 1918, the Jewish businessman founded Louis B. Mayer Pictures Corporation. In 1924 Louis Mayer joined with Samuel Goldwyn to form the famed Metro-Goldwyn-Mayer (MGM). Samuel Goldwyn had been born Samuel Goldfish to a Jewish couple in Poland in 1882. At the age of thirteen, Samuel immigrated to the United States and began working in a glove factory. By the age of thirty, he owned a successful glove business and, shortly thereafter, had entered the motion picture industry with Cecil B. de Mille and Jesse Lasky. In 1915, Samuel had formed Goldwyn Pictures Corporation with the Selwyn brothers (taking the "wyn" from their family name and ever after becoming Samuel Gold*wyn*). Samuel began making movies independently in 1923 (a year before he joined with Louis Mayer). Mayer and Goldwyn made a formidable combination, with their business acumen for understanding the public tastes and garnering the talent to serve those tastes.

Other Jewish pioneers made important contributions to movies, such as Harry Cohn (1891–1956), president and executive producer of Columbia Pictures Corporation, or Louis B. Selznick (1872–1933), a jeweler in Pittsburgh, who founded Select Pictures with his sons in the early 1900s and turned it into a multi-million dollar family business. Although the Selznicks lost their fortune and their company in the 1929 Wall Street Crash, Louis's sons (Myron, 1898–1944, and David, 1902–1965) went on to important careers in the film industry. They illustrate the large array of Jewish professionals that have served as a supportive cast to some of the illustrious Jewish directors that have entertained the public and contributed to the motion picture business in the past few decades—names as familiar as William Friedkin ("The French Connection" and "The Exorcist"), Stanley Kubrick ("2001: A Space Odyssey" and "Clockwork Orange"), Arthur Penn ("Bonnie and Clyde" and "Little Big Man"), Martin Ritt ("Conrack" and "Norma Rae"), and Joan Micklin Silver ("Hester Street" and "Head Over Heels").

Cincinnati-born Steven Spielberg (b. 1947) has combined a keen sense of artistic detail with business acumen in his rise to fame and fortune. The son of a Jewish electrical engineer, Steven enjoyed the cinema at an early age and, as an amateur movie maker, won a film contest at the age of thirteen for his forty-minute war movie, "Escape to Nowhere." By that time, he had lived in New Jersey and Arizona. When his family relocated to California, Steven finished high school there and then applied to some of the prominent West Coast film schools. They rejected him. Undaunted, the young Spielberg majored in English at California State University at Long Beach (B.A., 1969), making five

189

films while in college. To satisfy his craving to learn more about production, he slipped onto studio lots to watch the action. He was hired as a television director at Universal Pictures at the age of twenty, and his short film, "Amblin'" (1970), garnered him a seven-year directing contract with Universal Studios. Steven Spielberg directed television episodes for "Colombo" and "Marcus Welby" as well as the television movies "Night Gallery," "Duel," "Savage," and "Something Evil" from 1969 to 1972.

After moderate success directing the film "Sugarland Express" (1974), Steven Spielberg gained an international reputation through his blockbuster "Jaws" (1975). He opted not to direct the sequel to this film, but instead directed the science fiction classic "Close Encounters of the Third Kind" (1977). In 1978, Steven produced the film "I Wanna Hold Your Hand"; then this was followed by his directing and/or producing a cavalcade of movies, including "1941" (1979); "Raiders of the Lost Ark" (1981); "E.T.: The Extra-Terrestrial" (1982); "Twilight Zone: The Movie" (1983); "Indiana Jones and the Temple of Doom" (1984); "The Color Purple" (1985); "The Money Pit" (1986); "Empire of the Sun" (1987); "Who Framed Roger Rabbit" (1988); "Indiana Jones and the Last Crusade" (1989); "Always" (1989); and "Cape Fear" (1992), as well as serving as the coexecutive producer of the mega-hit "Back to the Future" three-part film series (1985, 1989, 1990).

This phenomenal output, that included a string of box-office hits, did not garner him even one Academy Award for Best Director (although those who worked on his films received many Academy Awards overall, and the Directors Guild of America had given him the Outstanding Directorial Achievement Award for feature films in 1985). In March 1994, an overwhelmed Steven Spielberg walked to the podium to receive the Best Director Award for "Schindler's List," a film about the Holocaust that many said was a great risk and would not be profitable. Steven Spielberg risked failure and directed it because he felt strongly that the story needed to be told and he wanted to do it for his peoplehood. Spielberg's "Schindler's List" not only was an instant box-office smash around the world when it was released in the fall of 1993, but also gave the forty-six-year-old filmmaker the "Oscar" that had eluded him throughout his successful career.

Many had been shocked when, year after year, others were chosen for Best Director over Steven Spielberg. When Clint East-

wood opened the envelope for the winning nominee, he interrupted the usual "The Oscar goes to . . ." with the interjection,
". . . this is a big surprise. . . ." Spielberg confessed to the Academy audience (who had given him a vibrant standing ovation)
that he had never even held an Oscar before. Later in the
evening, when "Schindler's List" was named Best Picture of
1993, a stunned Steven Spielberg spoke softly: "Ah . . .
Wow . . . This is the best drink of water after the longest drought
in my life." Regaining some composure, he implored all the
educators to not allow the Holocaust to remain a footnote in
history. "Please listen to the words and the echoes and the
ghosts," he pleaded, "and please teach this in your schools."

In October of 1994, director Steven Spielberg, music entrepreneur David Geffen, and recent chairman of Walt Disney Studios
(1984–1994), Jeffrey Katzenberg, formed their own movie company that would produce animated films, television programs,
and interactive entertainment. "We want to back our own movies,
be the owners of our own dreams," Spielberg told reporters. Nevertheless, in the midst of one of the biggest business mergers of the
year, Steven Spielberg declared: "Everybody sees the romance in
what we're trying to do, not just the business savvy." Everyone
did admit that the merger was a Jewish "dream team" in business
as well as creativity. New York-born David Geffen (b. 1944) had
worked his way from the mailroom of the William Morris Agency
to the presidency of a number of recording companies (including
his own Geffen Records since 1980). In 1975 Geffen had been chosen as vice chairman of Warner Brothers Pictures, and in 1978
became a member of the Yale University music faculty. Jeffrey
Katzenberg (b. 1950) was top on the hiring list of a number of U.S.
corporations, because of his proven track record of leadership,
business acumen, and creativity. Spielberg, Geffen, and Katzenberg were aware that only one moderately successful major studio had started from scratch since Walt Disney Productions was
formed during the Roaring Twenties.

Other ingenius Jewish talents, such as David Wolper (b. 1928),
one of the century's greatest producers of documentary films,
and Ben Wattenberg (b. 1933), writer-narrator of important Public Television programs, continued their educational programming in the 1990s. And, Jewish film entrepreneurs abound.
Spielberg, Geffen, and Katzenberg, for example, talked their new

corporate proposal over with Lew Wasserman (b. 1913), the eighty-one-year-old chairman and chief executive of MCA and Universal Studios, who has had an illustrious history and continues to hold considerable power in the film industry. In areas of publishing and communications, it would take volumes to describe in any significant detail *all* of the Jewish entrepreneurs involved in the rise, development, and continuance of these important areas of American business.

✡ ✡ ✡

Throughout American history, Jewish businesspersons have given not only to charitable causes and philanthropic enterprises, but also have given important months and years of their lives to government service. For instance, as senior partner of Klutznick Enterprises, real estate entrepreneur Philip M. Klutznick (b. 1907) created a business empire headquartered in Chicago. The son of a Kansas storeowner, Klutznick worked his way through the University of Kansas and Creighton University Law School during the 1920s. He began practicing law in 1930. Philip Klutznick's successful local service as a community housing planner in Omaha, Nebraska, during the Great Depression led to his appointment as Federal Housing Commissioner by President Franklin Delano Roosevelt in 1944. In a variety of official capacities, Philip Klutznick also faithfully served Presidents Truman, Eisenhower, Kennedy, Johnson, Ford, and Carter (even as he continued his local and national philanthropic endeavors, and his business enterprise). He even held the post of Secretary of Commerce late in his career (1980–1981), receiving the Ralph Bunche Award in 1981. Philip M. Klutznick was named to the Chicago Business Hall of Fame in 1985.

An older acquaintance of Klutznick's, Bernard Baruch (1870–1965), gave up business enterprise altogether to serve the nation. The son of physician and professor Simon Baruch (see chapter 3), Bernard finished college in 1889 and joined the Wall Street firm of Arthur A. Houseman. Astute in financial matters and careful in his research of the basics of commodities, Bernard was made a partner of the firm and a member of the New York Stock Exchange within seven years of his college graduation. Incredibly, Bernard Baruch amassed a fortune of over $3 million by 1902 (at a time when the average wage was approximately $500 a year).

Bernard Baruch then dedicated his life to government service and was consulted by every president from Woodrow Wilson to John F. Kennedy. During the First World War, he was appointed chairman in charge of raw materials for the War Industries Board and, at the end of the war, served on the Supreme Economic Council at the Versailles Peace Conference. During the Second World War, he chaired the committee to solve the nation's rubber shortage as well as advising War Mobilization Director James F. Byrnes. After the war, he was appointed to represent the United States on the United Nations Atomic Energy Commission. His drafts of policy plans and economic alternatives were carefully considered in the postwar world. He was on call at all hours to offices and meetings across the nation. In fact, throughout his lifetime, government officials of all branches could be seen conferring with Bernard Baruch on a park bench situated in Lafayette Square opposite the White House.

A DYNAMIC PEOPLEHOOD

AS JEWISH ASTRONAUT JEFF HOFFMAN CIRCLES THE GLOBE in the human quest for a new frontier, Jewish comet watcher David H. Levy (b. 1948) lives and breathes the sky. Brought to international attention with his codiscovery of Comet Shoemaker-Levy 9 that collided with the planet Jupiter in July of 1994, David continues to scan the universe from his home twenty miles southeast of Tucson, Arizona. When he travels, this patient and talented researcher packs his telescopes, taking every opportunity to search for anomalies on a dark clear night with a star-studded view. Respected by astronomers throughout the world, David Levy is as apt to spend time surrounded by children in an elementary school gym as he is to lecture at a scholarly astronomical conference. "I don't think an astronomer can do anything more significant than teach about the stars and the beauty of the night sky to youngsters," he often advises, adding, "It doesn't matter *how* as long as you *do* it. Take the children out and say, 'See those points of light? They are going to be your friends.'"

Certainly "the stars" have become David Levy's friends. Born in Montreal, Canada, into a talented and educated family, David remembers a second-grade gift, *The Big Book of Stars,* which sparked his interest in astronomy. In the sixth grade, he gave a speech on the formation of comets and, as he approached his teen years, he was given a small telescope by a relative. He began to observe the moon in detail, making meticulous notations on some three hundred craters and twenty-six mountain ranges. Training himself to concentrate on the smallest of details, he moved on to a five-year quest to familiarize himself with over one hundred star clusters, galaxies, and nebulae. Even to this day, this gives David Levy a special ability to analyze the universe and to sort out any comet impersonators.

David's father was a prominent lawyer, and his mother was a prominent geneticist with a doctorate. In such a literate family, the articulate and sensitive young man decided to pursue the field of language and literature, receiving his B.A. in English and his M.A. in English Literature in the 1970s. A prolific writer, he has since published quite a few books, dedicating one of his biographies (*Clyde Tombaugh: Discoverer of Pluto*, 1991) to "Mom and Dad—I always remember when they first told me how Pluto was found." For many years, David has contributed a monthly column to *Sky & Telescope* magazine, and he has written numerous articles. In 1979, David Levy moved to Arizona in a calculated effort to take advantage of the clear dark nights and to contribute to the American world of astronomy.

Electing to remain an "amateur" astronomer, David has had more time to scan the stars than a professional astronomer. In a dedicated and disciplined effort, he decided long ago to become a comet watcher. By his own thorough calculations, it actually took him 917 hours of searching over a nineteen-year period to discover his very first comet. On November 13, 1984, David Levy ended a date early to take advantage of a clear, moonless night. Setting up his sixteen-inch reflecting telescope, "Miranda," in his homemade outdoor observatory (a remodeled garden shed with a sliding roof), he scanned the starlit sky and spotted a fuzzy spot. As he had dutifully done thousands of times before, David Levy sketched the spot. He found, however, that it was not recorded on any of the astronomy charts. By the time he looked back at it, the spot had moved. At first, believing that he had made a mistake in charting, the thirty-six-year-old amateur astronomer rechecked his data. Then it dawned on him—he had discovered an uncharted comet. After certification by the Central Bureau for Astronomical Telegrams in Cambridge, Massachusetts, the feather of light became Comet Levy. Since that time, David Levy has obtained the rank of fifth in the world in discovering new comets, giving his name to over two dozen comets.

In 1989 David joined astrogeologist Eugene Shoemaker and his wife Carolyn in their effort to survey asteroids and comets. With limited funding, the Shoemakers had contracted to use an eighteen-inch camera-telescope at Palomar Mountain in California. In fact, by meticulously scanning the film from untold nights of sky photography, the matronly Carolyn Shoemaker has become the world record holder for detecting approximately forty new comets. Working closely with the Shoemakers, the affable and remarkable David Levy soon became like a son to them. His enthusiastic love of discovery also benefited Eugene and Carolyn Shoemaker in ways they never could have imagined.

On the night of March 22, 1993, David and the Shoemakers were quite discouraged by a prolonged period of cloudy nights at the Palomar Observatory. In the midst of less than ideal viewing conditions and the increasing financial strain of their project, they discovered that some of their expensive four dollar a frame film had been damaged around the edges by exposed light. Reluctant to squander more film on less than ideal conditions, the Shoemakers contemplated disbanding the filming for the evening. David, however, wanted to keep filming using the damaged film. Yielding to their enthusiastic colleague, the Shoemakers took some eight-minute frames before the clouds blocked the evening sky. It was on this film that Carolyn Shoemaker three nights later found what looked like a squashed comet. Soon, this string of pearls was confirmed as Shoemaker-Levy 9, twenty-one pieces of a comet that were on a collision course with Jupiter.

Today, the world community is more aware of comets and their potential destructive force to the earth and its environs. The need to patiently discover and chart the course of the galaxy's comets is more necessary than ever before as humankind reaches for the stars. Contingency plans on how to dispose of or move a comet on a collision course with the earth are being discussed, formulated, and weighed in the governmental bastions on earth. The patient commitment of a David H. Levy can only enhance that ongoing project. And, David's exploits serve to underscore one more time that the historic contributions from the Jewish people of America are as intriguing as they are interminable. Such dedicated efforts and self-sacrifice have been viewed in every chapter of this book as they touch on every field of endeavor and have impacted every facet of life in the United States. A dynamic Jewish peoplehood enhances the American present even as the Jewish people have enriched the past.

Relevant Statistics

The historian is impressed with where sheer discipline and devotion, as well as the love of reading, research, writing, and reasoning, has taken the American Jewish community during the twentieth century. Numbering close to 6 million (more than forty percent of world Jewry) and comprising only a small percentage of the total U.S. population (approximately 2.5 percent), American Jews are more than two times as likely as any other religious or ethnic group to be found in *Who's Who in America*. Jewish representation among successful entrepreneurs remains high (perhaps twenty percent). Most of this is achieved through privately created enterprises rather than through established corporations where prejudice or a stifling atmosphere may abide. The Jewish people are on the cutting edge of business and daily are adding creative dimensions to commerce and industry. It is estimated that over twenty percent of the books published in the United States in any given year are purchased by Jewish women, men, and children.

When a merit-based system became the criteria for academia, Jewish academicians flourished. Nevertheless, it took time for this development to affect the statistics of an insular American university system. Even in 1940, only two percent of the college professors in the United States were Jewish. This approximated their community percentage of the population. Within three decades, however, ten percent of America's professors were Jewish. By 1970, nearly forty percent of the faculty at elite law schools were Jewish (at Harvard University one-half of the law faculty were Jewish!). By the mid–1970s, statistics indicated that twenty-five percent of the faculty of the Ivy League were Jewish and, when age becomes a factor, Jewish professors constitute an even higher percentage of Ivy League professors under the age of forty. These high percentages also are maintained when one considers the faculty of the nation's elite medical schools. Comparatively, Jewish men and women comprise approximately one-fifth of the doctors and the lawyers in the United States in the 1990s.

Today, nearly half of the Jewish professors teach at top-ranked educational institutions, and they constitute approximately twenty percent of those teaching at elite universities. In addition, Jewish men and women comprise over ten percent of all college professors in the United States, and every study indicates that they are far more likely to publish articles in scholarly journals than their nonJewish counterparts. Such Jewish academic contributions are far-ranging. In the field of economics, for example, Jewish scholars have been awarded nearly half of the Nobel Memorial Prizes that Americans have won in economics. In fact, over one-third of all Nobel Prizes awarded to Americans since 1970 have gone to Jewish men and women.

Since the Second World War, approximately one-third of the American Nobel laureates in science have been Jewish, rising to prominence at the very same time that science began to explode within the cutting edge of human knowledge. Often these Jewish men and women have congregated in the most intellectually demanding areas of academic pursuit, a high percentage involved in theoretical discovery or abstract reasoning. Historically, the Jewish community has put high priority on the ancient "helping professions" (teaching, medicine, law, etc.). Today, Jewish men and women are highly represented in these areas, carrying on a tradition that spans millennia.

One hesitates to quote such figures or emphasize such success, because racists and bigots have misused such hard-earned accolades to defame the Jewish community in America. Nevertheless, the Jewish community (or any community) must not be penalized for being a successful community. Indeed, the *average* income of Jewish men and women today is statistically higher than that of most other religious or ethnic groupings. This is a testimony to their initiative and education. The student of American history should never forget that many Jewish academicians, physicians, lawyers, and entrepreneurs in the twentieth century had grandfathers and great-grandfathers who pushed peddlers' carts through cities and rural areas or skimped and scraped in small businesses to send their children through college and graduate school. Historically, a Jewish man was just as apt to be in the junkyard and salvage business as in the medical profession. The American Jewish community has never been a stranger to hard work and menial tasks.

In addition, the Jewish community far surpasses other American ethnic or religious groups in its financial contributions to charitable causes and other philanthropic endeavors. Judaism teaches that charity is a concept of justice that is to be actively pursued. The Hebrew word for "charity" (*tzedakah*), in fact, literally means "righteousness." In historic Jewish philosophy, one gives not for reward, but rather because giving is the *right thing to do*. For whatever reasons, both religious and nonreligious Jewish men and women in America seem to hold to this principle, and the American economic historian cannot help but to be fascinated by the twentieth-century philanthropic patterns of this most remarkable of communities. And, although there may be upwards of 500,000 Jewish individuals under the poverty line in America today, the Jewish community's initiative to take care of the poor has helped its own peoplehood to survive the historic rigors of depression and recession as well.

Lost in endless statistics and numerical percentages are the David Levys of America—Jewish men, women, and young people who make daily contributions that are rarely acknowledged beyond their small communities of endeavor, but are immeasurable in their long-term effects. Furthermore, some within this dynamic peoplehood have dedicated their lives to fostering better relations with much larger communities of differing faiths. They have made themselves vulnerable in an effort to reach out in understanding and honesty. Since the vast majority of Americans claim the Christian faith as their religious heritage, it is fitting in conclusion to single out a few examples of American Jews who have devoted a good portion of their lives toward enhancing meaningful interaction and positive relationships between Jews and Christians in America.

Jewish-Christian Relations

Throughout American history, individual Jews and Christians have formed personal friendships and working relationships that have overcome centuries of inaccurate assumptions and dangerous prejudices. Their accomplishments in interfaith communications have spread slowly but progressively to family members and local communities. Today, thousands of Jews and Christians in America work in surrounding locales and within state organizations to foster better relationships between their vibrant communities. In light of the ongoing spread of misinformation and rumor from radical and racist groups that would divide and destroy the United States from within, the need for the dedicated work of respect, honesty, and justice in Jewish-Christian relations never diminishes. New generations need to be educated, and older generations must be challenged with balanced perspectives. Irrational prejudice is a learned behavior, and it must be "unlearned." Fortunately, throughout this great nation, men and women, teenagers and college students, have accepted the challenge to promote understanding between the Jewish and Christian peoplehoods.

On the national level, dialogue between Jews and Christians became better organized after the Second World War, an immediacy hastened by the unimaginable horrors of the Nazi Holocaust. Protestant denominations and Roman Catholic districts added committee frameworks for Christian-Jewish dialogue. Jewish groups active in the United States, such as the Anti-Defamation League of B'nai B'rith (ADL) and the American Jewish Committee (AJC), created special departments in their organizational framework to advance interfaith activities and create a deeper understanding between Jews and Christians. Progress within America's pluralistic society has been slow but ongoing, engendering international ramifications. In 1961, for instance, the International Consultative Committee of Organizations for Christian-Jewish Cooperation was formed. This early umbrella organization was a precursor of more recent efforts to expand the American process of Jewish-Christian cooperation and understanding to global dimensions.

Jewish organizations have provided a framework to enhance interfaith relations between religious and academic leaders throughout the nation. Rabbi Marc H. Tanenbaum, national director for interreligious affairs of the American Jewish Committee, was heavily involved in Jewish-Christian dialogue in the 1950s, 1960s, and 1970s. He became one of the nation's most influential and respected religious personalities. His competent staff leaders, Judith H. Banki and A. James Rudin, who personally managed the details of the scores of Jewish-Christian meetings and convocations sponsored by the AJC in the 1970s and who became confidants of thousands of Christian leaders in the process, have taken over this mission since Rabbi Tanenbaum's retirement (and subsequent death). In fact, Jim Rudin now exercises the position of national director for inter-religious affairs and lectures nationwide. The son of a Pittsburgh dentist, Director Rudin was ordained a rabbi in 1960 and served as an Air Force chaplain from 1960 to 1962. Active in the Civil Rights movement in the mid–1960s, Rabbi Rudin coordinated AJC's national relief effort to Biafra when he first joined the AJC staff in 1968. Now, his schedule is filled with appointments to coordinate learning opportunities and quality interaction between Christians and Jews.

In the 1950s local Jewish leaders, such as Minneapolis's executive director of the Jewish Human Relations Council, Samuel Scheiner, furthered understanding between Christians and Jews with long hours of dedicated effort. Director Scheiner's growing friendship with Christian leader G. Douglas Young, for example, influenced Dr. Young to pursue a lifelong task to further Christian-Jewish understanding. Every decade the number of local Jewish representatives involved in the task of Jewish-Christian relations has grown. The need is so great that those who have dedicated themselves to such pursuits often have driven themselves to the point of exhaustion. Nevertheless, major achievements and lasting accomplishments often begin at the local level, by individuals who reach out in ever growing circles to create change in their neighborhoods and among their acquaintances. These Jews and Christians have taken the time to get to know one another, building day-to-day friendships that are fruitful and enduring.

Little known in academic circles, but with access to large charismatic and pentecostal churches with thousands of members, Rabbi Yechiel Eckstein crisscrosses the nation, entertaining and enlightening Protestants that would never consider going to a scholarly conference. A former national codirector of the Interfaith Affairs Division of the ADL in the 1970s, Rabbi Yechiel Eckstein decided to concentrate his efforts on better relations with the 60 million strong evangelical Christian community after he organized a successful unpublicized conference between Evangelicals and Jews in 1978. He began his own enterprise to fill a vacuum of knowledge and understanding between these groups, founding the Chicago-based Holyland Fellowship of Christians and Jews in 1982. A fourth-generation rabbi and one of the few Orthodox rabbis involved in Jewish-Christian relations, his "Ask the Rabbi" radio program has cemented better relationships with diverse Christian groups for more than a decade. Rabbi Eckstein is also a frequent guest on radio and television programs across the nation and is frequently quoted in newspapers during his lectures throughout the United States. One of his books, *What Christians Should Know About Jews and Judaism* (1984), continues to be circulated in churches and used on university and seminary campuses. When asked how long he believes he can continue his hectic pace in the quest of positive Jewish-Christian relations, the forty-year-old rabbi contends that he is in "for the long, long haul."

Among religious scholars, conferences and dialogues have served to clarify and illuminate. For example, Rabbi Alfred Wolf, director of the Skirball Institute on American Values in Los Angeles, has sponsored major interseminary programs in association with Monsignor Royale Vadakin of the Archdiocese of Los Angeles. Rabbi Max Shapiro, founder of the Center for Jewish-Christian Learning, University of St. Thomas, has been active in dialogue in the Midwest. Rabbi Leon Klenicki and Dr. Joseph Lichten of the ADL worked closely with Catholic leadership for decades, and Rabbi Balfour Brickner and Ms. Annette Daum of the Union of American Hebrew Congregations set the stage for Jewish-Christian cooperation that was continued by Rabbi Gary Bretton-Granatoor. Rabbi and Professor Eugene Borowitz was the first Jewish scholar to join the Catholic Liturgical Association, and must be added to the list of hundreds of other Jewish scholars (such as Samuel Sandmel, Ellis Rivkin, Joshua Haberman, Rael Jean Isaac, Michael Cook, and Michael Wyschogrod) who have published in the field in the twentieth century. Academic conferences have been held at the University of Notre Dame since the late 1970s, followed up by direct bishop-rabbi dialogues. Meetings with representatives of the Eastern Orthodox churches have escalated in recent years.

Sometimes, these individual efforts blossom into multifaceted organizations of national and international reputation. Such has been the case of Irvin J. Borowsky. With fervent energy and devotion, Mr. Borowsky has spent the past thirteen years building effective bridges between Christians and Jews. The son of emigrants escaping anti-Semitic outbreaks at the turn of the century, Irvin Borowsky pursued a successful thirty-year career as an innovative publisher, philanthropist, and activist in community affairs. A native of Philadelphia, he realized in the early 1980s that he knew little about Christianity. Determined to understand more fully why anti-Jewish attitudes pervaded otherwise decent Christian enclaves and why a few Christians overcame societal prejudices (such as the Christian neighbor who assisted his father and mother in their escape to America), he consulted and studied with eminent Christian theologians and historians from a variety of backgrounds.

Mr. Borowsky soon learned that while the Bible was basically a Jewish book, passages had been misinterpreted to separate Jesus from his Jewish heritage and the early followers of Jesus from their dedicated Judaism. Founding the American Interfaith Institute, he brought eminent Christian and Jewish scholars together to target the need and rationale for the removal of anti-Judaism from Christian theology and to suggest accurate and responsible translations of all passages of the Bible. After years of work and analysis, Bible publishers have responded favorably to his scholarly endeavors.

Indefatigable in his mission, Mr. Borowsky has addressed well over 50,000 Christian theologians, scholars, and church leaders, including the international Society of Biblical Literature and the Translation Committee of the United Bible Society. He has assembled a large spectrum of Christian and Jewish advisors for the American Interfaith Institute's publications which are circulated free to 20,000 theologians and professors.

Mr. Borowsky has organized scores of interfaith symposia and conferences which have produced a number of ground-breaking books. Expanding to a global network, he founded the World Alliance of Interfaith Organizations in 1993, which recently accepted its 100th member on the 13th anniversary of the founding of the American Interfaith Institute. In 1995 Mr. Borowsky established a museum/educational center in the heart of Philadelphia's national shrines to celebrate religious, racial and cultural diversity as a cornerstone for combating prejudice.

The initiatives of the American Interfaith Institute have been solely funded by Mr. Borowsky and a loyal group of supporters. "It is vital that everyone be educated to the fact that all of the founders of Christianity lived and died as Jews," Irvin Borowsky has written, "as did Jesus, John the Baptist, Peter and Matthew."

✡ ✡ ✡

Our brief journey through the history of American Jewish contributions has revealed a dynamic peoplehood that contributes daily to the culture, life, and livelihood of the United States. We have found that our Jewish friends, neighbors, and colleagues differ as widely in personality, practice, expertise, and background as does any other peoplehood; but we have grown to appreciate their numerous historic contributions and sacrifices for our nation. At times, the immensity and intensity of those contributions nearly overwhelm the knowledgeable student of history.

Coming full circle through contributions of national import and civic responsibility, scientific impact and medical breakthroughs, entertainment and commerce, military service and philanthropy, our study has pointed to artistic and creative influences that at some time have personally touched every citizen of the United States. On the basic human level, one might surprisingly find the positive influence of the Jewish peoplehood on America and the helpful assistance that has been so cheerfully given radiating through the give-and-take columns of two twin sisters, Esther Pauline Friedman and Pauline Esther Friedman. Born to a Sioux City, Iowa, Jewish couple on the very day that honors the historic independence of our nation (July 4, 1918), Esther and Pauline have become personally immersed in the decisions and difficulties which form the heartbeat of the local communities across America. Since the mid–1950s these Jewish twins faithfully have given witty and sensible personal advice in response to at least 5,000 letters they *each* receive *every* week. Appearing in approximately 1,000 newspapers every day, Esther and Pauline never claim to be infallible, but try to answer difficult questions as forthrightly and as accurately as possible. They have been called the "arbiters" of American popular behavior. We simply know them as "Ann Landers" (Esther Pauline) and "Dear Abby" (Pauline Esther).

INDEX

207

216